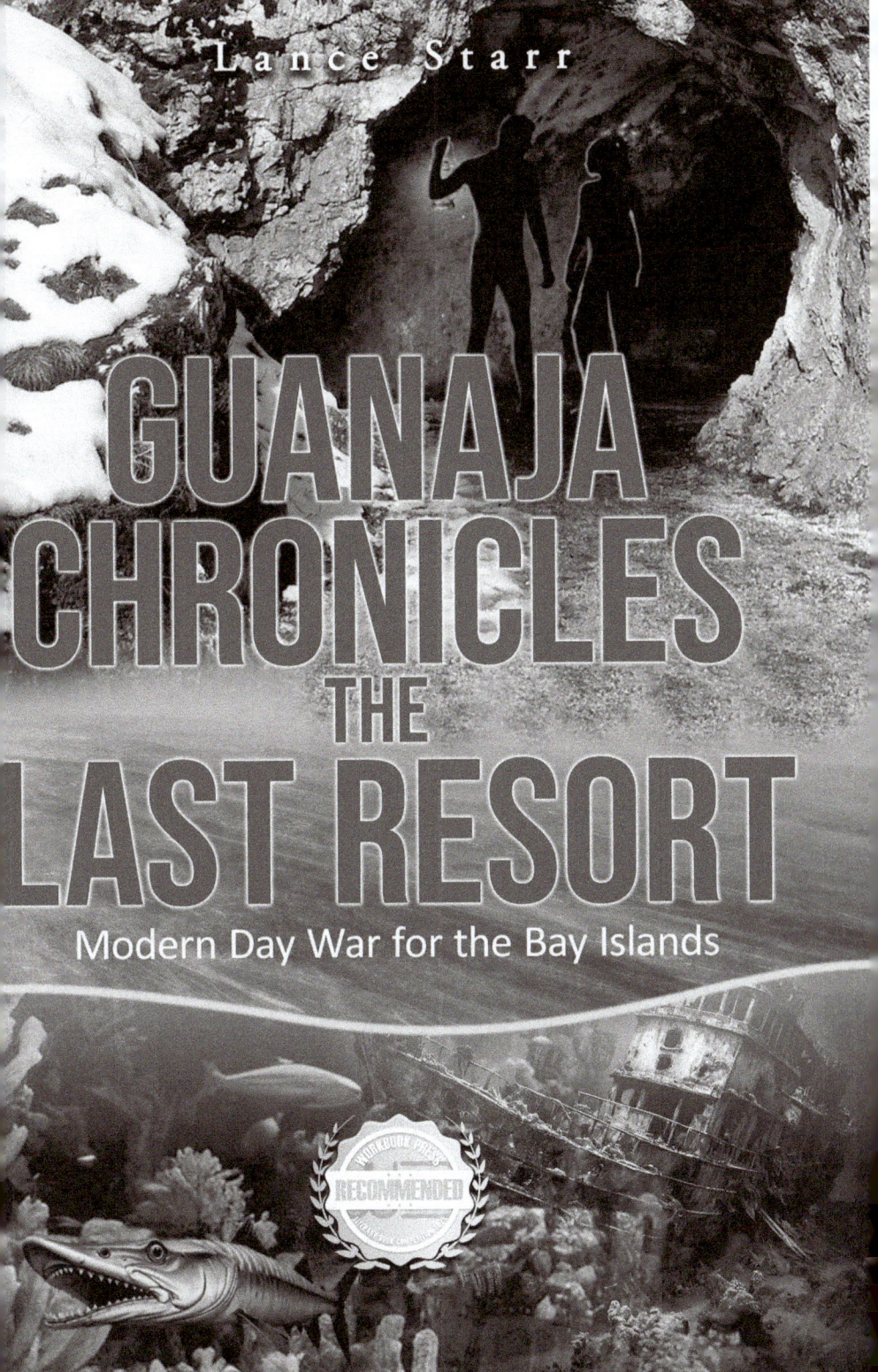

Lance Starr

GUANAJA CHRONICLES
THE
LAST RESORT

Modern Day War for the Bay Islands

WORKBOOK PRESS
RECOMMENDED

Copyright © 2025 by Lance Starr

This publication contains the opinions and ideas of its author. It is intended to provide helpful and informative material on the subjects addressed in the publication. The author and publisher specifically disclaim all responsibility for any liability, loss or risk, personal or otherwise, which is incurred as a consequence, directly or indirectly, of the use and application of any of the contents of this book.

WORKBOOK PRESS LLC
187 E Warm Springs Rd,
Suite B285 Las Vegas NV 89119 USA

Website: https://workbookpress.com/
Hotline: 1-888-818-4856
Email: admin@workbookpress.com

Ordering Information:
Quantity sales. Special discounts are available on quantity purchases by corporations, associations, and others. For details, contact the publisher at the address above.

ISBN-13:   978-1-965732-48-9 Paperback Version

REV. DATE: 11/28/2024

Lance Starr

GUANAJA'S FIERCE FERVOR TO REMAIN

Modern Day War for the Bay Islands

PROLOGUE

Hostage Hotel: Emergence Of Rage

We received a worried call from Captain Brearly. Five people from the Artificial Island were barricaded in the newer Cartel hotel in Orilla. Three women and two guys. Two mature women tourists and a nineteen-year-old girl were trapped.

Vanna and I hopped on our Starr resort security boat and headed over to Brearly's island on-board office. He was fuming and in distress. He was responsible and if the worst happened, he would be looking for a much less lucrative job. Someone hiding in a towel closet was calling on a cell phone.

I wasn't comfortable becoming the de-facto cop of the Bay Islands. Vanna and I had discussed it in our after-love bubble. We were hoping Brearly, with strong backup resources, would shoulder it. Unfortunately, this wasn't his kind of warfare. His tactics had already put people in the town hospital. The people had no other alternatives, and I couldn't get him to read "tactics of the Blue Coats in the Revolutionary War". Vanna and I went, hoping to be tactical advisors.

The situation was ten in the hotel. Five from the island. Five of the hotel staff pushed dressers and couches against the doors. One staff member had a double-barrel shotgun. Eight cartel thugs outside swearing and threatening, fully armed. U.S. White Supremacists seconded by the drug cartel brandishing American assault weapons.

Brearly reached to call his Black Private SWAT helicopters. Vanna and I stopped him. "If these guys hear rotors, they'll shoot their way in. They know that SWAT will be their end. You'll lose people, yours and others. The thugs will be drinking hard tonight. They'll be planning to go in tomorrow, salivating about the nineteen-year-old girl. We have time and can head this off tonight. Give us three hours and we'll end it." Vanna and I were back in the fight. Our tactics are not foolproof, but more efficient, and field-tested.

Lance deploys, "Octavio, where are you, over?"

"Birdcage, I'm empty, west of your Guanaja, resort lights in the distance. Where are you? Over"

"We're on the Artificial Island with the Captain, the problem is on Orilla. I need you and your cruiser tonight, not urgently. Come to Orilla and anchor by the gravel airport by 2 a.m. Keep the sodium lights off unless I say differently. We have some artificial island clients in the new hotel under siege by some Bay Island Drug gang, seconded by Midwest American White Supremacists. Out."

Lance briefs, "Captain Brearly, we're going to slip in behind them and take them down while they're drunk. Do you have another diver in your security crew?"

"Lance, I'm sorry. I've only trained sports divers, nothing like the professionals you need. Are you sure you don't want chopper support?"

"Ok, Brearly, put a chopper under my control, or yours, following my orders. That is non-negotiable; no staggered involvement by the U.S. drone base. For the moment, have them aloft, down-wind west of Orilla out of hearing. Be aware, I have dear life-long friends working to avoid choppers on scene until after the action goes down. I don't want anybody stopping, moving, or starting carefully orchestrated movements. Nobody is going to get killed in my group from reeling government rules of engagement or hunches of an incompetent self-aggrandizing commander-in-chief.

Brearly, "OK, Lance, we are in your waters, my career is hanging on your abilities."

Lance re-directs, "Roberto, where are you?"

"Birdcage, I'm floating amongst my shrimp encouraging them to reproduce. You are calling me for something more complicated than shrimp-seduction. Over?"

"We have a siege on the new hotel on Orilla. There are no cartel police there, ever. Nor would they help unless bribed. You know this better than I. We can head this off but have to do it tonight. We need another diver. How far away are you? Over."

"If absolutely necessary, I'm on the southwest peninsula of Roaban, in my shrimp farm. Over."

"Roberto, several of these captives are from the Artificial Island, some women, and one young one. I tried to get a diver from there but they have none. They want to have their rental SWAT do a frontal deluge. I convinced them they'll lose tourists. The captain, Brearly, 'Black Bird', confirms via his drone who the thugs are and they are outside drinking heavily. What White Supremacists are doing supporting brown thugs shows how badly their NRA leaders have corrupted their treasury. If we can get in there tonight, we'll save tourist lives. Tourists are the priority."

"Roberto, Vanna and I are here. Vanna is probably worth two of us; we need another diver to even the odds. We're going back to the resort to get armament. If you have a metal jacket and can deal with it and a black wetsuit, wear it. We can't use grenades unless they are tossed outside of the building. Bring a couple. Maybe we can use them campfire-side. We'll bring two RPGs. Close-in use may be dangerous to tourists facing ransom or death. Bring your sound suppressed rifles and pistols. We'll meet at the airport at 2 am. Maximum surprise critical!"

Roberto answers, "I'll come. Of course. Have you considered Bucky. He could run down the road from the town and over the bogs without floundering. I can pick him up and drop him at the airport with something of the clothes any of those terrorists are wearing. He'll smell and track them in 15 minutes. We need to get there first to hold him. Rather than a frontal attack from the water which the thugs surely expect, he can plow the path open from the land side and we'll clean up. Over"

Lance, "Ok, bring Bucky. Octavio will be at the airport. I think we need to hold him back for clean-up. He's heavily armed and speed of lightning on the water. He can get there in a minute and a half if necessary. We're heading back to the resort. Over"

"Be there at two. Roberto, out."

Vanna and I dressed in black rubber with cork black eyes; her blonde hair up and hidden. We loaded the armaments in our security boat changing the engine to electric.

"Black Bird, we're heading out. Any new drone information?"

Brearly, "Bird cage, the manager of the hotel called, in tears. He escaped out the back and now feels he was a coward. He confirms five friendlies and five staff plus himself. We now know the guests are in the conference room on the west side of reception, ground floor. The front door, water side, is barred. The staff were brave, but there are many windows right into reception. Bogies are well-armed. Over"

"Birdcage back, tell the owner to send a staff member via the basement to the airport. He'll have to wade through muck. We'll arm him and he can gain some advantage for us from the basement. The drunks may well be unaware of that. We'll give him a sound suppressed pistol. He should wait till he hears our rifles or a grenade before attacking. His cover is not more important than his life. Tell him to duck first and run if seen."

"Black Bird, can you get a description of the room arrangement down-stairs and main floor? Nobody here has ever been there."

"I'll be right back birdcage. Over."

We all arrived at the airport at 2 a.m. There are few flights to this place even during heavy season. Unspoiled reefs exist that I take the advanced groups to visit. We avoid walking up on the island due to lack of sanitary conditions.

Octavio was last in, running low rpms to stay quiet. Vanna had made a rough sketch based on the hotel manager's description. We forwarded them to Brearly and poured over them to make an attack plan.

We couldn't bring the electric motor closer than a half kilometer. We'd have to swim, quietly, the remainder. We put arms in a black inner tube to keep them accessible and dry. The swim was no challenge to any of us after all the dives we led. Roberto had his bullet proof half-vest under good control as did Vanna and I. No lead weights needed tonight.

Closer to the target, there were bogs full of garbage we had to avoid. The shore was ragged, sometimes three feet deep, sometimes over our heads. On the smelling, crusty shore, Bucky was forced, because of the muck, to jump from bog to bog for every movement forward. He arrived earlier than anticipated and had to hide in the cat-tails until I whistled.

Surely a disgusting place for a beach. For a hotel, as well. More the question why the cartel wanted to mess with it. Probably some bad blood between the owner and the Don J. Mondo, mafia chief; role model for recent U.S. leadership. Maybe the maximum stay was fifteen days.

I clicked twice on my mic to get a response the staff boy was back and in a safe location. Two clicks back confirmed. Bucky was chomping at the proverbial bit. I couldn't send him in advance if we should use hand grenades.

"Take your fins off, keep your booties on. Quietly. There isn't much drunken movement. If we lose surprise, we lose tourist lives. Do you count 8 around the fire? "

Vanna, quiet whisper, "No, hold off, we have only seven. Don't move. Wait."

In two minutes one of the criminals came around the west side of the building zipping his pants up. He'd been dangerously close to the conference room windows. There was quiet, controlling sobs.

"Lance directed, "Let him sit down, wait two beats and Roberto, throw the grenade in. Getting them, all here will guarantee safety for the tourists. Now!"

The grenade cracked. Two thugs survived or were wounded.

I whistled Bucky.

One thug ducked around where the other had peed. Vanna took one step to the side and double-tap, before he could access the conference room window. The other dived through the reception window trying to get to his feet and fire through the conference room door. He raised his U.S. assault weapon, and Bucky took him by the neck. I didn't hear the 'pfft' of the staff boy's suppressed pistol, the thug's ear erupted. Bucky recoiled back out the window.

Suddenly it was quiet. Sniffles and soft cries from inside Roberto quickly checked the receivers of the grenade. No movement. Guns removed, no life.

"Octavio, with mask on, come in stat."

He got there, revived, in only a minute.

Lance continued, "Roberto, go in and keep the tourists in that room. Don't let them see us. Put on a mask. Limit voice. If they get drunk and try to describe us, I want them to be wrong."

"Vanna, Octavio, go back and get our security boat. I don't want blood on your new cruiser."

"Lance?" The manager sidled in and I put him soundly back with the tourists. I asked the name of the staff boy who'd saved the group at the end. He stepped out; name was Jesus. With a few words, I enthused about how brave he'd been and saved lives. I asked him to look for Railroad Juan next he was in Cuenca. He returned the pistol. I sent him back with the tourists. I waited with my mask to carry away the grisly remains.

"Black bird, this is Birdcage. It's over, your people are not injured. Send a helicopter to pick them up? Nobody needs to know our names."

Brearly in relief, "Dam it, yes, on the way, Birdcage. Out!"

. . . .

IN SHORT, over the millennia, South and Central America were constantly clashing cultures. Simon Bolivar appeared on the scene and for a few years brought peace. Since his time, things have plunged adding Pirate Drug Cartels and Coyotes guiding drugs and individuals from countries with failed governments. Next door the big U.S. government siphoning money from Cartels and mixing the drugs seriously with "Lobbying" complicated the attacks. Although this narrative is fiction, elements of it exist and burst onto the world via Trump immigration cages and mountains of bribery and corruption. The hope of having another "Simon Bolivar is sadly dim. Lance Starr and Vanna Richards try to leave a hopeful mark.

MODERN DAY WAR
FOR THE BAY ISLANDS

Lance's Caribbean Central Scuba Operation
The Starr Resort. Guanaja

Book One: CONCEPT AND CREATION

CHAPTER 1

Fifteen Years Earlier-Midwest University Graduation

My early life was in the water. From swimming exhaustingly around an old rusted raft chasing friends, to ski tricks, rescue; scuba diving, I developed as an Alpha Male. That provided draw in staffing, diving and hosting generally well-to-do guests in the Bay Islands.

Scuba training had to go on hold. I was in a land-locked University eventually gaining an MS in Developmental and Marine Engineering in fresh water. I gained a room-mate, Greg, who was the imaginative designer, the one who could see most any object and find an improvement. To imagine building from scratch took him mentally away. We couldn't rouse him, though he was sitting right there. He responded like an eidetic reader remembering everything.

Greg and I shared the normal bed-on-opposite walls dorm room. Tight for trysting and too small for a party. Across the hall lived Roberto Fernandez, a Honduran with a well-to-do father. Fernandez was warm and cooperative with the largest room in that dorm. He would conveniently be out of suite if Greg or I were 'entertaining'. Co-ED was not an issue in Grad School. Roberto was in for a Masters in Marine Engineering/ Minor in Sea Mammal Health.

Greg married sooner than he had ever projected. She was besides beautiful, a Materials Engineer in her own right. We, the threesome, with d' Artagnan across the hall were the classic team.

When Greg innovated a new Mercedes dashboard, all available preset digital communication and control technologies within arms-reach, I built it. Knowing the red-neck administration tendencies, Cheryl agreed as eye candy. We visited the Mercedes offices in the mid-west. They said they would give us a call. We immediately patented it. Not going to fall for that trap. We were busy as we waited. Greg's mind would never stop. I had a dream about making a life around the sea: a scuba, water skiing and parasailing resort. That's what I did. Greg and Cheryl weren't aficionados of the salt. They shared in the one-million-dollar sale of the patent from Mercedes. My share avoided debt to my parents and smaller investors in financing the Starr Scuba Resort. It extended the size of the resort to be.

In the same time frame, my spring break took me south, not to Florida. The Bay Islands of Honduras were beginning to develop, I thought. The fellow graduate student across the corridor providing fun for us, Honduran, talked up the Salva Vida beer. Well connected. He joined me and I watched him buy a shrimp farm and a "Swim with the Dolphins" show he would develop after next year's graduation. Visiting him on the Big Island, Roaban, he recalled my dreaming in our cups at the Steel Rail bar at school. I didn't have to tell him what I was looking for.

Knowing I was coming, Roberto had looked around for a location for my water resort. It could be on the hilly north side of the Island of Guanaja. We visited. We went to the lawyer he trusted. I used the patent money to avoid any large mortgage. With yearly profits, growth continued. Two years later there was a dock, five cabanas throughout the trees on the side hill, a kitchen-bar restaurant with stools and five booths. A friend from the Banana Company and Roberto with a local builder helped me construct it. The banana guy took no pay and now stays any and every time he wishes, complements.

Mercedes was very interested in Greg's knack for invention. He was very interested in who would fabricate his new ideas. That's me. Together we were brought to Germany. Greg's portion of the million dollar patent is hidden in an IRA. Greg and Cheryl located in Munich, vconstruction and finance center. We were initially worried for what Cheryl would do. A month later we visited the military expats bar in Kaiserslautern. Two weeks later she was designing and removing military buildings in several regions of West Central Germany.

For the first two years at the resort, nobody got a vacation. We couldn't walk away. Roberto hired a day-to-day manager and found a large boat with a ramp for scuba divers. The diving business began to bloom. As time went by, the team of Greg and I blossomed with me re-designing and constructing what he imagined. I constantly created metal parts using rented ancient on-shore equipment. A hot spot was one island away. Frequently via Zoom and What's-App online specs could be accessed. Other specific engineering software was in my grasp locally or on-line. Essential shop machines came on banana boats from Gulfport, LA.

I went to Guanaja and constructed satellite access and bought a bigger generator to serve the entire site. There was one other resort on the south side of the island focused on relaxation and small glass-bottomed boat snorkeling. I was the professional scuba guy, marketing intense dives. The other resort was the drinking one, mostly in the nude. "Nude Beaches.com". Of course, I met the owner and visited her occasionally. She had a main squeeze, but hers was a body worth walking through the jungle to view. Potentially complicated, I didn't offer access to the big generator.

Occasionally a woman would come through to my resort with a dive crew, often a diver herself. A brief encounter or two developed. She went off, both of us happy.

I was succeeding working long distance, projecting in the long run I would need to be in Germany two-three months each year. This depended on Greg who was still insatiable. With Roberto's judgement and choices, the resort was well-manned, while I was away. He was marketing shrimp and "dolphin rides" at the same time, His site was only a half hour by fast boat from my resort.

There were several local men available to run the ramp boats and cook and tend bar. Dive clubs included women members and we didn't have one. We also needed to extend our marketing specifically to Europe from where we had had three walk-in groups. Our website and brochures were attracting U.S. divers. I headed to Spain to seek a potential

European Partner. Speaking decent Spanish, it was a logical first step for me.

CHAPTER TWO

First Partnership Interview and Vetting

My second semester at university, I joined the theater group. I learned and experienced acting, directing, set construction, lighting and make-up.

I went to several Zarzuela theater performances in Madrid where I had received letters of interest in the resort position. I had some additional Spanish learned at the Official School of Languages in the Moncloa suburb; enough to volunteer to join backstage of a major Zarzuela group. I chose the group of which Denya Galicia was the one paid performer. I was a complete unknown. Getting close to her to do any vetting would take patience.

At first glance, she was fit. More than that, I would need to judge her style in relationship building. Fitting into a dive operation required many elements of empathy. After the disaster of the U.S., I wasn't going to hire a husk empty of empathy as a self-proclaimed snake to work in my troop. As an ex, he was still dangerous to the country I had once been proud of. As we moved toward opening night, backstage people attended every performance and rehearsed every placement. We listened to the lovely arias over and over. Eventually we watched the choreographer enter the animation, often very suggestive, of exotics included in the dances.

CHAPTER THREE

Candidate 1: Denya Galicia, Zarzuela Icon

Denya Galicia is the lead singer and dancer in the Zarzuela troop in Madrid located several blocks east of the Plaza Del Sol. She has volume in her low alto ranges and alluring tone in her highest coloratura. She is the love interest in Zarzuela dance scenes. Other memorable features of her strong, feminine form make her the continuous lead. These strengths would transfer smoothly to resort activities.

Sitting on an actor's waiting bench behind the curtain stage left, I saw the leading woman, the first voice, and the one who was a magnetic attraction to me. She did songs only in Spanish for the shows. Back stage and at parties, she did them in English, German and French. Her languages were ideal for foreign divers. I temporarily forgot the resort interview mission.

I swooned through the first show of five each week. Her costume was transparent. There couldn't exist a more stunning form on a woman. From her toned booty to her high thrusting breasts, I was mesmerized. She danced alone and with strong feminine men. If there were a costume, it blurred in the lights as she was whirled and lowered sensuously keeping only her tiny skirt in view.

Between wild prop changes I sat on call on the two-person bench. I was alone there and Denya came to sit, tense with anticipation. I didn't interrupt her concentration. I was their stage left every show, every exit of Denya and every entrance. There was every stage effect to embolden her essence.

On her first entrance, she moved down-stage right to sing the main theme. After the thrill of her full voice range, the audience as one was on its feet in intense applause. A stage hand up on the catwalk opened a basket. Tiny bits of reflective colors showered her. They landed and stuck to her fleecy cape, her hair and filmy arms. The magic. The cast as well as the audience bathed in it. Her passion brought tears to eyes.

Eventually she saw me there often enough to content herself that I was one of the groups. She spoke to me occasionally and listened to my "Spanish" answers and comments. I improved my Spanish language pronto. I needed more vocabulary to sense her fit for the resort.

She smiled. I held my breath. Eventually she came to the scene construction shop. I heard she was the only member of the group that was paid a living wage. The fact that she was in the construction shop frequently sealed the troop's respect. I confirmed her balance and strength for handling heavy scuba tanks. The fact that she lived, walked and breathed enriched my life. She would be an excellent candidate for Lances resort if ever she would want it.

By the time we started the fourth show, I had occasional short shallow chats. Always on the bench, I was extremely careful to check her visage before saying anything that might interrupt her character. If the view was clear, I took the opportunity to get in a little snippet about me. I hadn't gotten a formal introduction. I got a number of worthwhile smiles.

The break happened on the second night of the fourth show. She rushed into stage-left in haste, face red, tension and pain radiating from her eyes. Costumes had ignored the unbalanced flower array on the left shoulder, faulty pin, and the clip on the back of her bra was digging in. Drops of blood.

"Lance, is there a costume woman here? I'm in pain and can't reset my dress. Sorry, of course there's no woman here. Lance, can you help. I'm sure you've seen a breast before."

"Miss Galicia, I can arrange your breast faster than you can accept a marriage proposal. She gave a start of surprise and presented me first the shoulder which I quickly reset adding comfort. She turned her back directly to me and I studied the bra strap clip. It was buried in her skin; would make a major scar if I didn't remove it vertically. To do that I had to remove one side of the bra. I told her.

"I don't want a scar. I'm on again in two minutes."

I raised the cup from the side of the puncture, removed the tension by slipping it up over the nipple, and eased the strap. I could bend the clip with my fingers. I did, reached around in front again, reset the nipple, and moved my fingers along under the strap to be certain there were no other snags. I told her she was good to go. In Spanish, of course. She turned and a flash confirmed a kiss on the cheek.

Later in the show she came my way for her last entrance. She wasn't due quickly. She had time to flash an embarrassed smile and thank me.

"Miss Galicia, you're welcome to my help anytime. Since for the moment we have broken the ice so to speak, may I be forward as to ask you to join me for a cup of coffee, or tea, or whiskey or whatever you like. I'd like to get to know the real you better and frankly would like to have you know me better, and my Caribbean resort. I know I haven't been formally presented to you. Maybe you would help with that?"

"Lance, ignoring for the moment whatever you think 'formal presentation' involves, please drop the Miss Galicia and call me Denya. This is Tuesday and maybe we can work something out. Wait for me at the stage door at the end of show and we'll discuss." I was proud that everything was hanging beautifully and no more pain nor damage.

Waiting heart in mouth, I wished lots of people good night. Fifteen minutes passed and I stepped back inside onto stage. Not a sound. A few lights were still on. I doused them. In the shadows, I called her name twice. Nothing. I went to her dressing room. Locked.

I went back outside the door. Jilted! I had a disappointing night. The show was on again Thursday. I had props located and ready stage left.

She came around the back curtain, saw me, and said, "Oh Dios Mio, Lance!"

I turned away.

She came over and gently took my shoulder back to meet my eyes. "Lance, please listen. I did forget, my brother was in a bicycle accident. I was called during the last scene, finished it and raced home to see what I needed to do. His lower arm was badly swollen. Definitely broken.

A neighbor helped me get him in the car. My mom came along. I rushed, saving a 250 Euro ambulance fee which would strain my parent's finances. I went back to my apartment exhausted and slept. Now I see you. I remember our talk and our plan to meet. I am so sorry. Lance if you can forgive me, please give me your cell number. Can you forgive me? I'm sincerely interested in knowing you too."

Her resort job consideration refreshed.

"I'll survive. I'm glad your brother will be ok. The role of default mother can be stressing. When will you be available again?" I had to move this vetting along.

CHAPTER FOUR

Chinchon

"**B**esides the Zarzuela, I teach voice and piano lessons to stretch the salary beyond performing. I do reserve Sunday afternoons for social life. Few men dates are interested in Sunday evening Work-a-Holics. (In the resort, she might get less free time.) I can sometimes get away on Wednesday afternoons. Tonight is Wednesday. I have to finish up with the broken arm and transition back home. Could you be patient and meet me on Sunday?"

"What time will work?"

"I have a lesson at ten in the morning and a voice student at noon. I need a nap. Would a pick-up at 3:00 p.m. be, ok?"

"How about a date to Cinchon? Its cooler there than here. Dress with a few layers in case the sun graces us. Bye."

Visions of molded breasts, firm caress and a glorious back danced in my dreams for four nights. I rehearsed conversations, reducing idiomatic phrases, and inserted Spanish words that said it better than English.

She carried a sweater which I hoped she would never need. Come on sunshine!

I asked, "Have you been to Chinchon?"

She answered, "Yes, with my parents about ten years old. Too young to drink. I know they have anise factories along with beautiful mountain views."

"Let's walk the mountains for a while before we visit factories." This was a feint to see if she would be comfortable on a mountain trail alone with someone who had disrobed her the last time they met.

I parked at a stream coming from as far above as we could see. She had tennis shoes. We made good time with no particular place to go. We came to a granite outcrop with magnificent views both up and down the mountain. Pine trees to infinity! The landscape evolved from rugged brown where we were to dark green in the distance. Glacier boulders peppered the landscape. We sat. I had a bottle of water. I took a drink, hesitated and offered it to her. Another information-rich hint of how things are going. She took a healthy drink without hesitation, without wiping the top. She handed it back and I asked the first question. We compared the differences of numbers of names for Spanish women.

The subjects, the quick sharing, the strength to present an attitude, all endearing and resort friendly.

People came to Chinchon to set the sun and imbibe heady anise. Each Anise factory offered samples to help you choose your favorite.

We visited three. I was the driver and experienced with alcohol. She had two for each one I had. My second was watering the hedge. As we headed to the third factory, we held more than hands. The smile was flashing radiance. I could see why men hungered to have the vibrancy she could fire. Nonchalantly she'd step close to my side firmly brushing my biceps with the breast I had so gingerly saved from scarring.

At her apartment, the "buzz" was in my favor. She didn't have to close her sweater. I could sit as close to her as the pliability of our skin could manage. Kisses warmed. Arms hugging. Nibbles all over non-combustible properties.

My right hand caressed our breast in common. She reached over and held me tighter to the pink. I pray it is not only liquor responding. She kissed my fingers, didn't budge when I took her thrust for a little circle. She pushed it at me for more. In a flash it was back in the bra. That was ok, I mean not really ok with me, right to go with what I hoped for next Wednesday or Sunday.

"Denya, I should look at the healing where the strap dug in. I promise no "hanky, panky". Would you like me to check?"

"Of course, that's very caring of you. You don't have to prove your celibacy every step of the way. "Hanky panky" is an interesting idiom. Could you demonstrate?"

"I will do a 'movie trailer' of that in a minute. That's a short advertisement before a movie. Could you get some antibiotic crème and a big Band-Aid?"

Re-arranged my attacker while she was gone. When she got back, I concentrated on crème depth and band aid angle. Bringing my hands both from behind her, I joined them at midriff and gave a good bounce to the breasts.

"That would be one variance of 'hanky panky'.

"I'm not drunk as you might think. And Lance, you are not the first man of my life. I see what you are trying to do to hide yourself. I know you are restraining yourself. That's the right thing for this early relationship. I'm not ignorant of the urges. If we continue, I promise I won't be shy asking to share your masculinity."

CHAPTER FIVE

Costa Brava

No relief and additional tension came from watching her perform. Relief approached with summer vacation. In Spain most businesses close in August. Denya does no lessons nor acts. I promise I will have her, resort or not. I was a water guy and she would be a water girl. I gave her a red Scuba II training book to concentrate on. I e-mailed the resort letting them know I would be delayed on the candidate in Madrid.

We arrived at the sea hotel I had booked and still hadn't been "skin diving". We had a king bed and we slept together. In that potentially auspicious setting with suggestive ceiling décor, I only got as far as lightly caressing her precipice. After dating so long, second base was not appropriate. No "diving?" I was beginning to worry that in spite of the "I love you", she may love girls, not boys.

She was able to scuba in limited areas. Second day in a wetsuit we were scuba buddies. We dove in water up to 30 feet. Reef life was rich. Forty yards off shore, under the water, was a huge wall. It dropped down to 60 feet. The wall had some lobsters and even a Moray Eel. How she handled this could be a game-changer. Solid curricula from the resort point of view.

She looked down. I was out in the deep near the surface. Her forward momentum and light current carried her away from the wall. I saw flailing of arms. She had a B.C. set carefully by me. The current had spooked her.

She was in no danger. She had doubts. Finns pounding, I arrived to take her arm in less than fifteen seconds. She made a try to climb on me to get to the surface. I had seen those eyes before. Using my lifesaving cross-chest carry I turned her away from me. Though she may try to flail, she couldn't get me. I chanced turning her back to me to see her eyes. I was much heavier and even adrenalin would not put me in danger. She came around and saw me and I could see some spark. Panic gone she got it and there was an explosion of air as she laughed into her regulator. She was relaxed again.

We kept our hands together and created a four-pointed star. Rolling out, I came up behind her and pulled her wetsuit covered booty firmly into my middle. I reached up and squeezed before my balance caused me to fall away. I took my regulator out, put my mask in a locatable place on my tank, reversed position under her gap, and unsnapped her tab. I flipped her tab up out of the way. Warm tongue, no obstruction, quick preview, no rejection. A shiver.

CHAPTER SIX

Home Plate

I had run out of patience for my masculinity. Running out of breath, I put her together again. Regulator in, mask on, there was heavy air use in both tanks. There was no way she could do this for me. Holding her breath wouldn't last the tease. What I could see in her mask approached a smile.

Showering together, both nude, was a non-starter. Celibate, except for second base, for over two months now, made me randy as a two-pecker Billy-goat. There is no way I wouldn't bend her over and take her hanging onto the shower control.

As far as I was emotionally concerned, tonight was now or never for a job offer as well as my heart. I had come to the door of her apartment in Madrid three times with intentions of breaking if off. Each time she opened the door, she was so gorgeous, I swallowed it and with a voluptuous kiss, settled for second base. This complicated my hormonal system incurably.

She showered, me in a room where I couldn't see her. I heard the shower stop and went in. I showered, even dried my hair. With a towel I walked into the bedroom.

She was under a sheet on the bed. Her breasts were breathing, breaking the surface. On her side, the swell of hips begging for a baby. She rolled to her back, hair still damp, pushed the sheet off, and waited a beat while I viewed. She reached both arms up beckoning me, throwing the towel. I went over and held myself over her. She reached over, lined me up, and pulled me down. I collapsed; wand buried.

"Lance, darling. I was so wrong. Please take me, immediately. Let it be part of my apology. Quickly, don't endure. Don't resist. Keep Yes!" She moaned a happy recipient of my warmth. She rolled to her side, breasts brushing my chest.

"Lance there is more. I told my mother about our closeness, and she cried, "No, no don't lose your heart to a foreigner. He will use you and go back to his country and forget you. It has happened thousands of times, millions of times. Don't make such a mistake!"

"My body had been telling me for a month that I should succumb. When I thought of you, heard your name, or your voice, I was damp. When you playfully, led us through underwater romance, it was clear.

When you sought out my heat under water and teased it, it was an electric torch. I surrendered. I would risk my happiness on you in spite of my mother."

CHAPTER SEVEN

No Easy Letdown

Hesitatingly I responded, "I know the time will soon come when I must return to my scuba dream. I will go. I was here so long because I accidently fell in love. I realize I can't uproot you from your blazing career. I would never. Could never. You know you can't give up such a stunning life to be a scuba diver in a jungle. I was foolish to even dream such an impossible thing. No more now. Let's love again, it's your turn."

We loved fully over and over in a hotel down in Barcelona. Flamenco: love: monuments: love: Day cruise in Mediterranean cabin: love. It's a big city, love, enough for a lifetime. I had to leave a dear one for a career one.

We returned. Tomorrow would be our last day in the Costa Brava. Prepared, it was still heart-wrenching. I was so sorry I had made her mother right. I would never label this loss of an ideal scuba partner a waste of recruiting time. I would live the rest of my life with her memory every night. One slower sweet loving tonight. All night.

CHAPTER EIGHT

Candidate Two: Madeline, Elementry Teacher, Germany

Greg had Cheryl; in Germany I was pretty much alone. My German was only for dinner and finding a museum. If she doesn't speak English, I am a boring date. There were other emergency options. Although they were dazzling and well endowed, I didn't like the idea of paying. I had been successful in university without. Patiently, but determinedly, I was searching. The Expat bar where we got Cheryl the job was basically all English, perhaps a few bilinguals.

I continued searching for a European for the resort, possibly an American woman with some foreign language plus European ties.

As flashing eyes can do, I was struck and didn't mention the resort until our second 'after-love' bubble. It was a party dress, like a teacher half-heartedly dressing for a party. It was a third-grade teacher at the base American School. Once you raised your focus, you forget any kind of dress. The eyes direct you, influence you. I could imagine how happy third grade boys and girls would be seeing those at 8 a.m. each morning. They would do anything for her. I WOULD do anything for her. I would do some serious 'any-things' for her. I had to find a conservative line that would appeal to a conservative teacher.

A casual bar-meeting, and someone I didn't know introduced her to me. No hit-line required. Maddy and

Lance. We shared who and from where. No dreaming about where we might go. Early, we established our single status.

In the depth of German winter in February, the holiday of Fasching created a cultural rebellion. People dressed as in an American Halloween. Kids were allowed early evenings. Later evenings it was trick or drink for the adults. Winters are only a mild cold as compared to a mid-west February. Many women had mini-costumes of most transparent allure. They diminished enticingly when the activities moved indoors. This is a buxom crowd. The new beige, was pink.

I invited Maddy, wearing something under a warm cape and me professional as a pirate. I soon learned "Maddy" would be inappropriate for this woman. We started down to the party center, Sachsenhausen, in Frankfurt. It was mobbed, colors like fireworks at night. Sachsenhausen in a hollow in a wind break. The beer had been flowing, pink cheeks on all sides. Many of those pink cheeks were on women, often other pinkies. There is no conservative reveler on Fasching in Germany, even a teacher. Topless was all around outside, more intense inside bars where accoutrements didn't quickly freeze.

My gaze was traveling joyously from beauty to beauty. Maddy had experienced Fasching. She got caught up in being part of another culture, especially in a raucous celebration. Her eyes tried to command mine. I was hardly noticing her. With a high growl and a flurry, she threw off the cape. She will not be upstaged in the eyes of her date, ever, or never again! What was left was the lead female singer in Cabaret, black net garters, only make-up anywhere else, Maddy no more. A voluptuous 'Madeline', worth every syllable of her name. My eyes were hers to command.

Whatever conservatism haunted me dissipated. We

whirled and kissed in all corners of the bar. The passion burst and my knees were weak. The "crush" leaped. Her eyes were glazed. As much mauling as one could do appropriately was our mission. Nothing maintained her breasts. My gaze had new focus. I had to rearrange appendages. She saw and half-heartedly tried to help. Brazen! With a constant supply of beer, we sang the traditional folklore songs with hearty loud ein svei gesufa.

The party went late and Madeline showed her true colors matching me with every dance and drink. As the crowds thinned, we caught a tram. More raucous partying. We agreed that going to my house at that hour, with bleary-eyed German driving going on, would be much safer than her place on the base. Both our eyes showed that the driving or distance was hardly the point. Cape on, we got off at the nearest stop. We hurried through the cold, damp and up to the first floor of my apartment.

We walked through the door. Turning back, the cape was waved to meld us together and the kiss passion-laced crushed us close.

I removed the cape and most of my pirate-ship. We shared the disrobing and she was again up against the door booties in my hands. The kiss crashed and control was hers. She slid right down.

We had both been alone a long time. We were crushed, teased, and implanted over and over until sunrise. The curtains were closed and we slept the sleep of the loved. This pirate had had his timbers shivered.

Sunday beckoned and I learned her intense creativity. Way above third grade! We brought our "wild" out of boundaries beyond fire. Warm holding; lovingly caressing bookended our starts. I made sure she had as many "turns" as I. Without exception.

I spent the next month walking on air, running to the base to bring her back to my place. Schedules permitted trysts on Wednesday evenings and weekends, all weekend. The melted comfort of post-firing pillow talk took us far into dreaming. I explained about my passion for the scuba operation.

Having been in Germany years more than I, she took me to the castles on the Rhine and the Hofbrau House in Munich. We frequently went to small Dorfs within a day's drive for a new beer and new beds. A few sofas.

My next trip to Central America was scheduled after her school finished for the summer. My lights blinked on and I realized I was learning to know the perfect partner for the scuba resort. She didn't scuba. As instructor I could quickly train her. A teacher would already be caring for divers, a bonus for me, beautiful.

A full summer of scuba clubs; I invited and she agreed. School person she was, she checked the Kama Sutra from the library for the summer. Some raised eyebrows, but they had been at Fasching. Her family would come to Frankfurt for a week in May; going on to other European adventures. We went south-west. Greg and I had been doing extremely well with salaries and royalties; Cheryl couldn't keep up with demand. I could easily provide the ticket. She hadn't even been as far south as Florida.

I sensed some discomfort in Madeline after she saw me dealing with most airline communication in Spanish in Miami. Spanish was mine, only German was hers.

In seven hours of jet lag, we learned our layover in Miami, scheduled to be two hours, due to someone's screw-up would be four hours. Embarrassed, since I had hoped to show her the good-times she had shown me in Germany, I headed for the bar. I had rerouted the luggage to LANSA air from TACA. She relaxed somewhat after a tall one, and I told her the joke about the airline names on these southern routes. Lansa, Lineas Aereas Nationales South America was translated to "Lost and Never Seen Again." The bigger one going into Cosa Rica was TACA, "Take a Coffin long." I need to keep my loving skills shipshape; my joke telling is poor.

We were well-oiled but irritable at the short separation between rows of seats and three on each side. It was only two hours to San Pedro Sula. We steeled ourselves to tough it out. The atmosphere was not warm. I felt uncomfortable thinking about what she was feeling. No food beyond peanuts and pay for all drinks including water didn't help matters. We still had two additional flights to get to the island.

In SPS, we had another one-hour delay. The plane to Cuenca on the North Coast was a DC-5, a plane first built for WWII. Not beautiful, it was one of the most durable and secure planes ever built. We're now nine hours into jet lag and she is not impressed. Reluctantly she journeyed on.

In small Cuenca, we exited our plane and walked over to the final. It was a four-passenger including the pilot. I could sense a "fight or flight' emotion but she delicately climbed up into the back seat with our suit cases. Her face was stone, no emotion, like she had no hope of survival.

When the plane began to touch down on the gravel landing strip for Guanaja, she leaped and buried herself in my arms, shuddering, until it stopped. She flew out, a flash, kissing the ground. Classical, of course, but I was hoping she would be working at my resort.

I got the luggage and held her for a long time. Nothing said. Eventually, Trey in one of the support boats arrived to take us to the resort. She was not fearful of boats but wasn't smiling.

Walking up to my air-conditioned cabana, she got two mosquito bites. I hurried her into the cabana and applied repellant. Seeing the shower, she was out of her clothes and into my dream. She was humming a quiet intense tone of stress even after being there twenty minutes. I was waiting to hold her. She went directly to the bed, covered herself, put some repellent on her face, arms and neck and fell asleep.

She slept all the way through until the next morning at 10:00 a.m. I had a light dinner and a heavy rum drink and crawled in and slept next to her. She started twice in the night, disoriented; lost. I was right there and rocked her back asleep.

I was right there in the morning, too. Having forgotten where she was and what she had gone through, and that I was right tight there, I got a smile and a crusher kiss. Unfortunately, things went only slightly uphill from there and shockingly downhill thereafter.

I slipped out of my cabana and returned with some coffee for her, an island fruit and a home-made roll. She was still lying down but raised up and took the food with another smile. I talked a little and she vaguely listened. She agreed to learn to snorkel and see some underwater wild life and fauna. She got up, full frontal and took another shower. When she came back, I was waiting with the repellant to cover her. Finished, I had repellant all over me.

In happier pre-flight times, she had packed some very short shorts and a T-shirt which I am sure she brought for me. No bra. Torture, only temporary, I hoped.

We walked down to the dock where both dive boats were gone to reefs north-east of the Island. I got her snorkel, mask and fins and we headed east through soft white sand. The pier was long and wide, painted white in a "T" shape, a place for both ramp-tail boats and the security to conveniently dock. There was another retired airport boat with its nose attached to an old gnarly coconut tree.

By the time we got the 60 meters to the snorkel reef, we were both soaked and she had won the wet blouse contest. We arrived at a portion of reef which had been formed long ago. A coral head had been broken off a wall by a monster storm. The wave action had been immense that rather than the length of broken reef falling to the bottom, it had been carried within forty meters of the shore. The rock was now thirty meters long by three meters wide in four meters of water. Much of the original coral remained with significant amounts of new coral and plant life. The wall was still there, 150 meters out. A perfect spot for a new snorkel experience. My eyes, of course were not as much on the coral as on the wet t-shirt snorkeler. Diving buddies must stay near each other. We fondled around a half hour surfacing for air and some maritime information from me.

Following, I came around behind her as she reached into a hole in the wall. I lunged, but too late. A wild stirring in the water with sand filling the water around me, an eel burst out of the hole, mouth open! Given any escape route, eels don't mess with creatures 20 times as big as them. Frightened and disoriented, it coursed around, grazed her calf, slimy rough skin, and shot off into the distance. She shot up out of the water screaming. I was right there, used my life saver approaches and got her into shallow water. The fright on her face was palpable. I held her and tried to talk her down.

She said, "Lance, I've got to go back. Out of the water now". She didn't use the snorkel again. She was frightened and I was heart-broken. One of my greatest joys in life and at the moment she hated it.

The warm sand by the pier was creature-free if you didn't look too deep. Nothing to snorkel for. The water was still fresh. In later summer, it was too warm and you couldn't wait to get to the thermal clime. Especially if you were in a wet suit. We jumped in and out and her face became friendly. Cautiously friendly. Then sunburned. I ran to the kitchen and got the sun cream SPF 50 to save her that pain. I should have put it on with the mosquito repellant but I was 100% distracted. Her face was a bit red, her back and legs golden tan. Delicious. We rolled around, additional supplicating caresses of cream from me, and eventually the dive boats came back. Thirty on each boat. She watched as I went and helped my captains disrobe the divers of tanks, B.C.s, fins and weight belts.

Within thirty minutes of the boat's arrival, happy hour started in the bar and restaurant. I got her there early to try to wash away her difficult day. She had a few, didn't open up to any of the divers to chat. We had dinner and went down to the dock to watch the moon and stars. Another quiet time. It was stunningly romantic and we kissed a few times. She was again in a tight t-shirt with no bra. I guess she didn't bring any.

With the sun gone and the tiki torches showing the way to the cabanas, she said, "I'm sweating. Your cabana has an air conditioner, right? This humidity is killing me."

We walked up with sweat running down her back and front. She was huffing when we arrived. She stripped and headed straight for a cool shower. As she was finishing, I went in to rinse the salt off. We passed, both naked, didn't grope. We dried and she went to the bed first. When I came, she was welcoming, but mild. We hugged a while as I was debating which whirlwind position, I could use to charm her tonight. She turned to me leading with the buxom girl's firm on my chest. With eyes and no words, she made it clear she needed me emotionally and forcefully physically, but not fast. Slow and sinuous.

Slowly, I could take her for a long ride. I did and burst. She cooed, "Your warmth!" I smoothly slid down where I could return the favor. The demand for seeding after near death may be true.

"Lance, oh god, I needed that to be sure I am alive."

We laid once again on our backs in those open vulnerable moments. I had nothing to say, but felt a hurt in the touches. She finally took a deep breath and said, "Lance, I've got to go. Not tonight of course, but get me the small torture plane as early as possible in the morning before the wind comes up. I know you love this life and Germany is just a stop on your way. I respect your skills and ability to help these people have wonderful experiences. The heat, the humidity, mosquitos, sand fleas, sunburn, fear of what I don't know, I can't force myself to tolerate even in exchange for the deep love you offer. Hold me tonight, please come with me to San Pedro Sula, then let me go. Perhaps we can communicate by skype or when you get back to Germany."

I agreed to her wishes; didn't sleep a wink. I knew I would never be able to anticipate every anomaly of an ever-changing reef. She didn't have any nightmares that I noticed. I gently moved her off to San Pedro. I couldn't force her to stay for more fear. Seeing her, I would be destroyed, too. Another potential quality partner lost.

We skyped a couple of times. I returned to Germany in October. For a while I hung out with Greg and his wife. I stayed away from the base near Frankfurt. I did one platonic call to confirm I was back in Germany. My insides still hurt from the loss. I knew who I was and what I dreamed. I hoped there would be another out there who would enjoy joining me in the same dream.

CHAPTER NINE

Futures

In the fawning pride of Greg, I was introduced to the new Mercedes executives on rotation. We had continually been forwarding ideas with my designs. Nothing was mentioned about my office on Guanaja.

We were all studying some form of business or engineering, some land based, me marine based, and Roberto Sea Agriculture. We drank beer, played hoops and dreamed together. Roberto would vacate his suite occasionally when Greg or I were "entertaining." Roberto and I had pretty solid plans. With Greg's didactic mind, he could find work anywhere. I dreamed of owning a scuba-based resort in the Caribbean and with the share of the patent could do it without parental support. With Roberto's contacts, I was soon building the cabanas, buying a second ramp boat, looking into marketing not only in the U.S. but in Europe. I went to Spain a month after Roberto. We never met again until some years later back in Guanaja.

Roberto, with good support from his family had his eye on a shrimp farm. Luckily the U.S. Senator from the south on the Cartels "Lempira payroll" wasn't aware of another bribe opportunity. The farm was adjacent to the big island pertaining to Honduras. His father struggling to operate in an ethical manner in a government inundated with drug cartel money, had been there long enough to survive. He and Roberto were both studying the options.

His Dad agreed to a year's trip through Europe before developing the farm.

Roberto was studying off and on, Castilian, at the Official School of Language in north Madrid. He spoke Spanish and English growing up. He only needed to tone his listening skills and pronounce the "theta" style use of the for z. We spoke often about the development of the resort where he had actively participated. He knew of the expansion requiring an additional woman partner and European marketing. He would, of course, support the search, but at the moment, had no idea I was attending Zarzuelas in Madrid, a few kilometers away.

It would be a year and a half later before he would recount this experience and that of a woman potential candidate he had met in Callao. It was a saga in itself.

CHAPTER TEN

Melissa: Marketing Model
Recruiting German Marketing Contract

There were several local men available to captain the ramp boats and cook and tend bar. Some dive clubs included women members and we didn't have one. I had tried and lost several in Spain due to the place they were in their careers, or their fear of underwater creatures. I think some may have been frivolous with the applications. The position would be a full partnership but hadn't drawn a mature candidate. I was still trying but now needed to concentrate on increased marketing. We also needed to extend our marketing specifically to Europe from where we had had three walk-in clubs. Our website and brochures were attracting U.S. divers, but Western Europe needed development.

In Spain, I had some joyous extended recruiting meetings for the partnership, but no serious nor appropriate candidate. I booked a flight from Barajas up to Munich. Greg and Cheryl were on vacation. I advertised both jobs, but got no sensible candidate for the partnership. The modeling contract was a whole different experience, successful this time.

There were some modeling agencies, bilingual groups on the Marienstrasse near the famous Lowenbrau Brewery. Booked in at the Lands Berger Hotel the night before, I walked over to the Marienstrasse for breakfast among many, many Germans and tourists. Parked on the sides of the Marienstrasse were scores of cars to be sold second-hand. Set back from this street were several huge buildings holding scores of offices and hundreds of apartments. The bottom two or three floors held major department stores. Kaufhof, C&A, Bauhaus to name three. Between those buildings and the cars were open air restaurants. If it were not raining, chairs were full. It was cold but sunny.

In front of the C&A store were several theater Kleig instruments. Off. I ordered a hot chocolate, large, and sat toward the back of the café near the cars. Everybody is looking around at everybody continuing chatting or starting new chats. The German, too difficult for me.

The Kleigs came on bathing the door and the front of the store in soft light. A photographer and assistants scurried out. Tripods set up and video placed. Some gay looking guys came out holding some fluffy material. Wrapped in that material was a female form. It was a little far from me to see. The boys unwrapped the female who had her hair up in some sophisticated style. No-one would see the face if that stayed where it was. Dammed if I didn't know her. No one would be looking at the face because the girl was nude except for her stilettos. She struck various poses; the photo assistant guided her and turned her according to what the photographer shouted. I thought I must have lost my lucidity.

She swayed over to the Platinum red Mercedes. She caressed it lovingly. It was shocking. She mounted the hood holding the Mercedes symbol between her knees. The movement of mounting exposed her thighs to the depths. A few men were shifting in their seats. She used her thighs to stroke other parts of the hood. The dismount was calculated to take the swell behind the male zippers to maximum. She lounged her way to the left car-side door, opened it, and bent forward inside to adjust something.

Pre-meditated booty view! Striking. Three couples went hurriedly into the building. 'Thrust' would be the word. They were the foreign tourists. Most of the German men and women alike never looked up except to smirk at the tourists in their dishabille.

She adjusted for maximum time of male survival. She got in, having a little trouble with her stilettos, which caused her legs to go completely open. She smiled and closed them slowly. Obviously programmed. Closed the door. Photographer came and took a photo down into the car from above the door. Titties turning the wheel. She opened the door, put her legs out first. Fields of thighs. Any tourist with a camera was in action. The photographer growled about copyright and put an end to that. She strode again to the fender of the car and bent over to give a hug. Leaving the booty shaking, she gave a final twerk of disrespect and headed again to the hood of the car. She laid across the front hood, looked up and met my eyes. Frozen smile. Moved on.

She got off now looking disgusted, threw a rude twerk, and headed for the muscled gay guys with her wrap.

I sat there breathless. I wanted to do something. I sat there frozen. I decided to wait and see what might happen if she emerged from that C&A door. I knew she was a model, perfect for a white sand beach scuba resort.

It wasn't long, and Melissa, now I remembered, came out of the door with a warm-up suit. Without a hesitation she headed toward my row, my seat. She took me by the hand, not much more passionate than a greeting at a funeral. "I knew from your brochure picture you were here. I saw you stand up when I came out. Walk with me. Please don't touch me now. I'll explain later. We need to leave this place now; it has to do with my advertising contract. Don't hold my hand. Try to let on this is a business meeting. Please be patient and all will be well."

I shut up. We sat at a table, she on the other side. I stumbled on what to say in a business meeting. She saw my discomfort and gave me leading subjects and lines I could use to generate a fake play of discussion. She said, "Ok that's enough."

"Now, Lance, walk with me very demurely, not too close, no touching, like I was your sister. Here's our situation. If I were free, I would have your hands and fingers caressing me all over. You were magic in Spain, now, please don't react. You will have a mountain of chances later. Listen! The bottom line of my contract here is to sell Mercedes automobiles. I am a central part of this advertising campaign. I know shit about any automobile, what I am actually selling is myself. It's more complicated than that.

If you ever had a psychology class in your college preparation, you may be able to follow this. In the last 20 minutes, I have "fucked" the Mercedes for all the heterosexual men in this audience. In their mind, and for some hours later, they will unconsciously feel that I will be part of the purchase price. The longer that lasts, or re-occurs, the higher the number of sales.

In the meantime, they saw me nude, but also recognized me when I left the building. They will all be asking themselves how they can get into my pants. I have created a bubble of existence for them. If the bubble stays in existence, chance of sales going up is high. If I did well enough, and I did, that attitude will remain in their sub-conscious and they will have an affinity to that shape of car. If they see me in any level of passionate relationship with you, the bubble will burst and sales may be affected.

Now, this is not a forever binding document. I have done my job. Their lust has been enhanced. Many are still under the trance that I will be in the car. Mercedes paid half of my fee in advance. I will go and collect the remainder tomorrow.

"Lance, what hotel are you in?"

"I'm in the Munich Lands Berger hotel, three blocks from here, up that way."

"Lance, go to your registration desk, get your key and inform them your wife will be coming soon and please give her a second key. I will be Mrs. Starr, for a while. Or, we'll see."

A quiet knock at the door, and all the tall parts of her were intensely up against me. "Lance, please settle me first. Later, it's your turn."

Cheryl had introduced me to Melissa in one of her match-maker phases when I came alone to Germany from Guanaja. While we did date for a while, I did know she was a model, but not this much of a model. I wasn't looking for a woman partner for the resort at that time. I knew she was very connected in Europe and Los Angeles. Although my resort was doing well, even a partnership would not be in her league. She left for some shoot, up in Sweden and I hadn't even communicated with her again.

A surprised but stunningly all-passion kiss; both to our knees.

"Lance, please let me stop. I have been dreaming of feeling exactly this expansion for five months. I held little hope of seeing you again unless I decided to try scuba. Relax, let me glow in your desire."

I was on fire. This was the finest woman a man could imagine, much less capture. After five months, I now realized I had been the last guy.

"Lance, I'm starting. Move the hoody away, up above."

" Before words, I responded.

"Oh, heaven. Without asking, you remember. I'm in love with every part of you. I must explode! Get out of the way at your peril."

There was no hesitation here. We had in a very few words re-kindled a now continuing relationship. She had left her rational world behind for the enthralling rush of the great release. Some women call it the "little death". They are disillusioned. It is the celebration of human heaven on earth.

She has said and now proven again her vulnerability to me. It is such an honor and privilege. Both know there is little possibility of survival across two continents with meetings only time and again.

We grasp and take what we can. This is the woman I desire to share in magnificent movement. It is the sound of the mature woman who paints my hearing. She starts with the murmur of breathlessness, breaks into intense moans, and collapses.

I celebrate, moving her into our post-loving bubble.

"Melissa, maybe we should take a nap or settle in for the night. You must be tired pretending all that trick stuff for Mercedes."

"Lance, you can be shallow. You took me to energy depletion forty times the energy used as the silly Mercedes model.

I did my best to kiss her passion, love her neck, and caress her breasts. "Lance, enough. I am not begging for foreplay after five months."

Tomorrow became the afternoon and I had to explore if we could contract her for the Starr Scuba Resort. I expected to receive no special discounts, her standard and travel pay scale. We had little time for champagne but made a date in Guanaja for two weeks later on a Sunday. I gave her the shooting schedule pending acceptable weather. She marked it up with several extended periods of re-charge time. I smiled. She was used to charging in 220volts. Grab what you can, prepare to weather a broken heart.

CHAPTER ELEVEN

CANDIDATE 4: MS Phillips

She was in 8th grade, a beauty with a rack. I didn't know what a rack was because I was only in 5th grade. I had seen a few naked classmates but they didn't have racks. I did know what a beauty was. She lived on the other side of the lake, like a distance that could never be navigated. I saw her only in our little K-8 elementary school.

If you are in 5th grade and the girl is in 8th, she won't even acknowledge your existence. You are a lower creature. She would be embarrassed among her friends if she even talked to you. I, in turn, in my emotional force field, was sick for her.

One valentine's day, I purchased a big red heart of chocolates. I went to give it to her at recess. She pushed them back at me in a nasty way and said she didn't want them. I was crushed; distraught.

My first really hurtful heart break. Her family moved away at the end of that year. I never saw her in high school. I never thought I would see her again. I never forgot her.

A few decades later, owner of a Scuba resort in the Bay Islands, I spent some of the winter in the Midwest, nostalgic. This time the trip was tax deductible, as a critical position was open at the resort. I spent most of the time east near the large metropolitan city of Milwaukee with many performance venues.

This weekend, aficionado of live theater, I drove four hours west. I was in Dubuque on the Mississippi attending a presentation of "Pump Boys and Dinettes". A moderately funny show not riveting. I wasn't constantly focused on the stage. My eyes wandered around the audience. Not thinking of her recently, I saw a woman, older of course, with a familiar profile. Her profile had been stunning as I remembered. I didn't take this seriously. I did think of her. It had been many years. I wasn't sure I would even recognize her. I didn't live in Dubuque; in fact, I lived 4 hours away near my home town where I had loved her from afar and lost her.

When she had moved away from grade school, I didn't know where she had gone. I refocused on the show and forgot about the errant thoughts.

I hadn't seen this show and loved musicals. I had driven over, rented a hotel for the night and went.

Long with two intermissions. I patronized the "in-theater" concessions when their profits go the civic theater.

I turned away from the bar, which forced my view towards the lady's room. Always embarrassed by this, I moved to turn away quickly. In the spin, my eyes were arrested. Coming out of the room was, or was it, my Ms. Phillips. Her name was Patty I remembered. I wasn't confident enough to move to her. I couldn't keep my eyes away. I'm a big guy and don't think she missed me. She didn't speak. I completed my spin and she went in to the theater. I went back to my seat for the next act. I didn't concentrate much on the play. I frequently glanced her way to try to be sure I was right. I think she caught some of the glances. I wasn't sure.

The second act ended. Another intermission. I am now certain it was her. I had had some experiences along the way and developed my self-confidence. I had missed

39

some opportunities by being shy. I was not going to miss another by being afraid to approach her. "Excuse me. My name is Lance Starr. I apologize if I am making a mistake here, my memory tells me you are Patty Phillips. We were in elementary school together."

"Yes, Lance, I thought it was you. You haven't changed much in lots of years. Your face has stayed rugged and thin. I'm actually Patty Burns now. My husband passed away five years ago and I haven't seen a need to change it."

She was about 5" 10' with long brown hair. I could tell it was lightly colored. The "rack" was still uplifting. The lines in her face expressed a long-time life of caring. Sometimes sadness. Her face had high, flat planes with a nose of character. Strong chin led to a model's long, supple neck. Her lips could express any emotion; her eyes, flashing, said much more.

"Patty, the show is going to begin soon. We need to go back. I have some feelings I would regret if I didn't share with you. Could we get together tonight or tomorrow and catch up?"

"I'm free. We could also sit together for the third act. There is a seat open next to me."

"Great, we can make other plans."

After the show, late, we made a date for the next day. There was a replica of a 1950's diner a stone's throw from the theater. She lived in Dubuque, it was walking from her house. We met for an early dinner at 5 p.m.

"Patty, when you knew me, probably not well, in fifth grade, I was awkward in my speech. Star struck! From my side, I was fiercely into you, too shy to say. I'm better now. I'll start before I lose my nerve. We have years to catch up on".

I went on about my single life traveling and living in nine different countries. Her non-verbal reactions were what I could hope they would be.

"Lance, after we moved, I ended up in Lancaster High School. After living in the Milwaukee area, this was pure farm society. There was little to do and the boys knew they were going back to the farm. They had little motivation to do school work. I knew I could never settle for the life they would give.

I did well, however, in high school and won a half scholarship at Northwestern. Although Mom tried to keep me nearby, I bolted to NU and knew soon I would be happy. I would be a sorority girl. This opened up a sumptuous social life and I would never go home again except to visit. A girl with some taste of life, I left the U alone to take a job as an accountant here in Dubuque. The company 3M had a branch here and I was there at the right time and right place. Still not a Milwaukee, Dubuque had a night life and many cultural offerings.

I soon learned that a bachelor's degree from university didn't prepare one well enough for accounting in the real world. The recruiter had seen this before, He set me up with an older more experienced auditor. In short, this Glen guided me through the bumps and grinds of accountancy in that setting. He marched me directly up the aisle to the preacher and we were married. It was maybe not that direct. We did practice some of the lighter side of marriage before we tied the knot. Not for long though. We knew what we wanted and had recognized it quickly.

She went on to note she had gotten her masters and there was a married daughter living with her son-in-law in Holland. Sometimes they scheduled visits with holidays.

Our third time together, things got more intimate.

We had started dinner later. We left soon. The moon was out. At the doorstep, I moved in for the hoped kiss. It was there. It was not one of those air kisses you see in Europe and places further east. I had finally kissed my 5th grade flame. Like a teenager, I skipped to the hotel.

I had to be out of town the next day and she had an audit she could schedule. We didn't see each other that night. The following day we headed for the diner again and talked personally. We were venturing out to what we might agree on in the world; on what we might not agree. This was an awakening of what we shared in common. The exception, of course, was watching the Green Bay Packers football.

Her late husband, Glen, although originally from Illinois was a Packer fan and clearly had little respect for the Chicago Bears. That's how his name came in to our discussion. She also commented our sleeping alone the previous night without seeing each other had been notably "lonely".

She offered this comment of feeling about the loneliness. I have always had to be the one to risk sharing such feelings. It made me nervous every time. What joy and difference to have it come from her first. Here I got a hug in, even in the diner.

It sparked my hunger. My goal changed to a man and still beautiful woman. Our male animal nature and ego cause us theoretically to want to have a child with this beauty. Together, we see how beautiful and smart would be the offspring. My theory anyway. In reality, another child at this time in our lives would not be comfortable. My mind was wandering.

For her, the hug had very intense meaning. I could sense it physically. Then it really came out. Emotionally. We had not said much about previous relationships. Her late husband, although important, hadn't come up. Until now! Thanks to the Packers.

"Lance, we have quickly re-connected. I need to share this. It is important I do this. For me, I absolutely have to let it out."

"Patty, whatever you want, I am interested in all your thoughts."

She went on to recount that (married) part of her life. They had been together many years. She talked about their meeting in 3M and how the relationship had developed. Glen knew a beauty when he saw one and set his hat with no other acceptable option. He pursued her until she caught him. He found her every joy and involved himself in sharing. He didn't particularly love opera, she did and he quickly had season tickets to the one over in Milwaukee. It took him less than a year to capture her heart and give her an engagement ring. The rest of their time together with the exception of the daughter's adolescence growing pains was all positive.

There had been some symptoms of illness a few months before he died. What happened was not a complete surprise out of the dark. The death of one she had loved so dearly was an emotional shock and grievous heartbreak.

"Lance, we woke up one morning. We shared a couple night-tasting kisses and he quickly stood up. He had no sooner got to his feet than he collapsed. I was still sitting up on the bed and thought he may have been playing some joke. He didn't move. I called 911 and tried to do some CPR. There was some little response so I kept going until the rescue squad came. For me the response had stopped. I left him to open the door for the EMT's. They took over and transported him to the hospital. They had the siren wailing and were traveling fast. I was hopeful there was still some chance.

At the hospital he was rushed to the emergency room. Shortly later, they took him to surgery. Nobody could tell me anything one way or the other. I would rather die than have to live through such an experience again.

After the surgery, the doctor came to see me. He said it had been a massive stroke. They had cleaned the area affected. Chances were small. They moved him to intensive care where I remained immovable.

Two days later in the night, I was holding his hand and felt a small movement. I went to look in his eyes and they were active, clear. Pain strained his face.

He said, "Honey, it's so hard. Would it be alright with you if I go over"? My breath caught as I realized what he was asking. Would I give him permission? I knew what had to be done. I told him I loved him forever, kissed him softly and said, "Go, darling, go to where you don't hurt." The lights in his eyes faded.

We were the last ones in the diner and all staff eyes were full. I waited while she regathered her strength. I ordered us a coffee with a shot. I walked her home arms entwined and stopped for a thoughtful kiss at the door. Bodies were seeking each other with not an inch of distance. It was not the right night to seal a relationship after hearing the tearful end of another.

Lance, she said, "I feel better and probably shouldn't have waited. While a catharsis, it leaves me bushed. I need more spirit to share other things with you. I am not blind to where you, we, are heading with this relationship. I need one day to put things in perspective, the vulnerability I would be trusting to you. An unexpected fresh new start.

Huge gear change, a miracle, Lance. Please come over tomorrow night.

I went home, got online and bought the remainder of the opera tickets for the present season.

I arrived at her house at 4 in the afternoon with my suitcase packed. She met me at the door with a glow. She had had her catharsis. There was no doubt. She pulled me in the door, nudged me against the back of it, thrust her body with every curve sensing me. She tipped her head back to see my eyes, paused a beat, and took me into a kiss vibrating my shoestrings.

We had a quick dinner. She hadn't been loved for a long time and was absorbing every nuance. Desert would be on the bed. All you need to know about a lover was intensified in her eyes and her touch.

"Lance, lover, let's not bide any more. Come gentle, slow and quiet. It's been so long. She opened and reached her arms up for me. Filmy legs around me. "I want you to be on top. Don't worry, I'm a big girl. You won't hurt me."

"Doze with me if you wish, she said, "you're not leaving this house or bed in the foreseeable future. Warmed up, so gentle, so quiet. I'm healing ".

"The visiting doctor is not done!" Entranced, I began. What a long wait for a 5th grader's dream!

I tend to be gentle especially with a woman not well known to me. Long awaited, she was wildly aroused. I will not be party to any modicum of pain in the sex act. Foreplay, do whatever you want. I began it her way. I heard her say: fast; moved my lips to the exterior ellipse of her flame and began the wave. She squeaked. I increased my velocity around the swelling center. Speed like the chariots in Rome. It was a teasing sensation and I knew she hungered for more. She shrieked and throwing her midriff in the air, shuddered, panting, swearing love words. She raised her midriff, held for three beats, exploded an exhalation; wild bursts into her relief. The look in her eyes I would cherish for a lifetime.

I moved next to her on the bed. She pushed every part of her body into my body somewhere, wrapped her arms around me, melted, and said, "Your turn. I was far beyond control, and with a new, long desired woman, managed only a few seconds. She started, throaty satisfaction, "stay in me. I forgot the stunning, full feeling."

We made the opera. It was not difficult to entice her back to Milwaukee. A full circle in a lifetime.

CHAPTER TWELVE

Perfect fit, but life grows limits

I was on a mission with this special gift surprise. I told her about the resort and the job. Accounting and book-keeping, her years of experience perfect. She leaned back in the couch on my arm. She thought forever. "

"Lance, I am torn apart. I know what I must do, for you and for me. You have re-opened a world I thought I would never see. I doubt any other man could do the caring things you did. If I were to accept, we would have to be married to go to Central America. As sweet as your love, I couldn't do it. I was horribly comatose when Glen died. I lost all desire and yearned to go with him. I absolutely could not face that again and live on.

If things in life changed, and we could be together, I would still have to schedule times alone, nights without you, keeping myself prepared. That is a selfish requirement and I would not expect you nor anyone to live that way. To ease this heartbreak that we are both facing, let me tell you that you are welcome here for a visit anytime, continuing everything we have shared together as though we had not been apart. I will not be married and you would be free to choose what we might share together. It need not be good bye. Au revoir. A bottle of champagne required upon return.

CHAPTER THIRTEEN

CAROLINE: ON SITE, Unexpected Benefits Package

It's always at least spring in the Bay Islands. It was a warm, humid return to Guanaja. Nothing was new of which I was unaware. Either a captain or Roberto was on Skype weekly.

The groups were getting larger for the spring and I jumped back into being boat Captain to distract myself from thinking about Cassandra's legs around my waist.

Two of our diving staff had decided to pursue their non-water careers on the mainland U.S. I immediately posted the positions on-line and, in the Miami Herald, and a smaller paper in Gulfport. I also posted it on the bar on the island.

CHAPTER FOURTEEN

THE ARRIVAL OF VANNA, Candidate 7.
(Walk-in)

Divers buy a package for this resort. For a set price, the flight and transfer of them, their equipment and pretty much everything to the dock is included. I had two large compressors with air included. Odds and ends of other equipment could be had if it happened to be available. (Watches, depth gauges, etc.) Three meals per day and one drink each happy hour plus cabana rounded out the package. A firm warning was given that they take only pictures and leave only bubbles. I had a picture of a guy kicked out early having tried to unearth a sea fan. A novice would not know that when you take one of them out of the water, it smells terrible. The only other difference was prices for people wishing to extend their stay when their package ends. They could stay for a week at 10% discount, but may have to move into a cabana not reserved by a coming group. Those were a little further away from the central toilets and didn't have a private shower. The meals and drinks continue as before. I had tried a 20% discount but it hadn't increased interest that much. The probability of a person or two extending increased, if at all, with a group of twenty-five or more. That's the only lasting morsel of information I gleaned from university "Probability". Got a "C".

There was one other resort on this island on the north side. "Nude.com". I was friendly with the owner and went over occasionally to share gripes and a rum and coke. There was not a lot of cross visiting because the jungle path was painful and the other resort was "no clothing permitted". The owner was a woman, Zulinda, with rotating guys as her main squeezes. I didn't visit a lot because she was such a momentous beauty (not a stitch), I would get out of hand quickly. I stayed a few moments to share selected things about my time in Germany. Good relations were important for both of us as we used the same supplier for many of our meal preparations. Legs crossed fifteen minutes, just mine, kept things friendly.

Moving into summer, a group of thirty reserved everything we had. Both ramped dive boats were full and the security boat took two guys who had dive instructor licenses. Two of my captains also had the licenses, as did I. With the captains, I helped get everyone into tanks and B.C., s.

There were two women in the group. Both were lovely and with good muscle tone, undoubtedly from a lot of diving. One was on each boat. The difference was only the choice of swim suit. On my boat, Vanna didn't have a thong; it wasn't much more. The girl on the other boat, Donna, had a more conservative two-piece suit. The interactions between men and women didn't include anything flirty. The women were "one of the guys" and any thoughts that I might be having, weren't echoed by the men. Maybe they were sisters or had been with the guys long, now being ignored. The other difference which was notable, at least on such a demanding dive, was Vanna's handling of the equipment. Diving is an equipment intensive sport. She donned the heavy gear asking me for a boost getting the tank in place. Strengths didn't appear until the middle of the dive and thereafter.

Sensible divers never dive alone. She had a partner. They had partnered before. I was diving above and behind the group, veritable mother hen protecting my large investment. Several times she saw him slide into rocks where the air valve of the tank would drift up and trap him. The diver's response is to bang his dive knife against the tank to signal request for help. He never got his knife into striking position before she was a foot away from him easing him down and out. They didn't need any mothering. I noted it and moved ahead.

Everybody is salty and tired from the equipment effort along with losing body heat to the water. They float up on the recovery ramp and friends or the staff help them shed their equipment starting with the weight belt. Vanna came to the ramp, thrust her body forward, rose to her feet unassisted and moved into the tank storage area. Like a flash she was out of her weight belt and tank and other gear heading back to help friends on the ramp. I could do that, a glance at my shoulders would make it obvious why. She wasn't rippling muscles. Only two deep breaths told of any effort. If you weren't watching this, you would miss it. I noted it and walked on. She looked up at me and we shared a glance a couple of beats longer than typical.

The next two days I went in the small boat with the licensed guys. I didn't dive; maintained the location of the boat in the current. Frankly, it is painful getting over the side of this boat to get back in. I prefer the ramp boat.

Happy hour, first drink free, happens as soon as people shower the salt off and dry up. Several mixed drinks or beers is not recommended. Alcohol and diving can be dangerous. The mildest repercussion is too many beers. You drink it at one atmosphere. Tomorrow, it will be in your digestive track at two or three atmospheres. Not fun.

We met each other's glance a few times over drinks. When we moved to the buffet, she was sitting at my left. We did shallow talk and she asked about any irregularities of the reef. I knew them very well. The fact that she knew enough to ask the question was added to my notes. Tempted, I didn't walk her back to her bungalow.

The week went on. She dived morning and afternoon. She did the Wednesday night dive, as well. She was clearly strong in condition as well as strength. On one occasion I was her buddy. We didn't always focus on the reef; occasional minor invasions of the other's space were mildly suggestive, but platonic.

On Friday, the day before they would leave, she came and asked about the conditions of extending her stay. The conversation was particularly warm. After drinks and dinner, I went up on the balcony above the bar to finish my drink and catch a few stars. No moon tonight. She shadowed a little later and sat next to me nursing her Southern Comfort Old Fashioned. We discussed some other diving she had seen and some, in the Caribbean, that she hadn't. We finished the conversation, sharing similar vibes. She leaned over and said she definitely wanted to extend her stay, gave me a peck on the cheek and headed off to the cabana.

CHAPTER FIFTEEN

Vanna Becomes Viable

I registered her stay the next morning and sent her out with a Captain in the small boat. She had taken a double tank and would spend some time at deeper levels. The captain would be in the water not going that deep. She would have to decompress at 10-15 feet and he would exert absolute control over that.

The dive went without incident and she was hungry for lunch. Only the staff would be there until the next weekend Food was aplenty. I ate lightly; sipped on a rum and coke. It was early afternoon and I would be in no trouble if I dove the next day. I didn't plan to. She floated away into the trees and I guessed she was feeling the time at 100 feet, and would take a nap. I moved back to my A/C., read my kindle and dozed. I got up before four o'clock to be sure I would be able to sleep that night. A day without the exercise of a dive, I decided to walk the beach.

She wasn't as tired as I guessed. She was toning the tan and making a momentous sand castle. I went over and sat in the sand. I added a wall to the castle gleaning a smile. I asked about the deep foray and said there was not much down that deep. She agreed and said she did see a huge grouper in a cave. The second it sensed me, it flashed and was nowhere to be seen.

I went over to wipe clean the tanks and B.C.s. As I rose, she did too and stepped toward me, asking if I would dive with her tomorrow. Well, she was paying the full price, she should get whomever she wanted as a dive buddy. There was a little more in the request about having me rather than another Captain. I agreed, glad I hadn't drunk a beer.

I walked over to the ramp boat and stepped aboard to clean the tanks. The boat swayed surprising me as she stepped nimbly aboard. Nothing was said but she watched what I was doing and mirrored it. It was my least favorite task and I had to do two boats, 32 tanks, weight belts, B. C's regulators, knives, and spray half as many wetsuits. I appreciated the help. As noted earlier, she needed no help in man-handling any of the heavy equipment, including her double tanks.

After moving to the second boat, conversation continued. We talked about her experience and I learned what I had here. She was a female version of me as per experience. Large group experience was my advantage to the moment. I mentioned my other job in Germany. She asked when I usually went there. Conversation waned and we sat glad the initial opening hurdle was behind.

Among the staff, and even with groups on site, we chose one night per tour to "dress for dinner". That had been mentioned in the brochure. Groups packed appropriately. I reminded her it would be tonight. Since she was the only guest, we wouldn't insist.

"Lance, I would like to. Give me a chance to present myself as more than a ragged beach comber. Delay dinner a half hour for me to assemble my armor."

"That's fine, I doubt there will be much jousting tonight."

Two hours later I was nursing a lemon soda and looking for the moon from a bar seat. A rustle of the hedge presented a vision with a very sexy smile. She had every reason. Low cut, open shoulders and short-skirt would get no sand in it. I compared it in my mind to her first-used thong. A mistake, I had to revise my location on the stool. My immediate thought was how 'no-bra' improved a swim suit. She had worked wonders on her hair considering the humidity. I hurried over to her with the mosquito repellant. I wanted nothing to interfere with her joy in being dressed that way.

We sat at a table and the staff sat wherever they wanted. Several sat themselves with her in the corner of their eyes. This dive-limiting drinking could be a drag. She was an enigma, much to be unearthed.

We took our soft drink up to the balcony and the staff disappeared to their cabanas. She sat close to me and we searched the skies for a while. She gently took my hand.

"Lance, will you still be able to dive with me tomorrow?"

"Of course! I've been behaving my drinking all day to be prepared. Do you have some area you would like to explore"?

Her smile suddenly reset to devilish as she replied. "Lance that could be a loaded question. I'll let you off the hook only this time. Explore the East reef!

A pause! I did not need any pause.

She quickly followed up, too late, the flirt was set. She would like to go to the East of the island where the licensed divers went the other day. And Lance, if it's necessary, here is my dive instructor's license.

After all I had seen her do, I had not noted that. I should have guessed she was beyond a novice diver. She had saved her partner innumerable times, right in front of my eyes. Then, the foray to 100 feet. Actually, that was probably more of a disqualification. All her help with resetting equipment on the boats would pay her penance. At long last after searching in Spain, Germany and the Mid-West, I had found my partner. Ironically, after all the effort, she just appeared. If she was interested?

The next evening, I put my arm around her. There was no stopping a kiss. She moved in closely molding her mostly naked body to me. We were not exploring now. There was no holding back. The kiss continued with whispers and finally the French. We went from a brush to a passion to an attack. Down at the bar Alexa played the "Unchained Melody". There is an emotional body-clock that chimes when you know you must stop. At least the first night. Our clocks were close to exact. I moved my lips reluctantly away. She put a big wet one on me and feathered over my cheeks and face.

"Lance, don't wear your wet-suit tomorrow. We won't be playing below the thermal clime. Speedos should be enough. I'll want to see your license. She quickly rose disappearing into the dark.

I sat for a while, wondering if this had really happened or if it had been a dream. My German Cassandra crossed my mind. I knew there was nothing better nor poorer. It was style. I could never force an end to Denya's family and career. The third-grade teacher would collapse. Melissa was living another financial world.

Guanaja Defense

CHAPTER SIXTEEN

Vanna and Lance Submurged Intent

> There are many ways besides a signature to signify continuing intent<.

We didn't hurry to get started. We needed no boat or staff help. We had a tank caddy and put our equipment on it making it easier to jockey it to the point we would gear up and submerge. I was wearing my speedos as commanded. I also wore a t-shirt to reduce the pressure of the tank against my back. She had the t-shirt as well; the thong was the one described on her first boat dive. For a while I avoided thinking about that. I mean I had high hopes, but for a while her licensed Captainship was calling the shots. I had my license laminated in plastic. Whatever might happen, I was heartened by the fact that she was a "kick-ass" professional diver. The job was advertised on the back of the bar.

She floated over to me, regulator suspended; snorkel affixed. She took my hand, pulled me off my feet and hand-in-hand we sculled out to the deeper part of the reef. We arrived at the hill of reef that boded the coming of the valley on the other side. I watched her skill in maneuvering in the small current that washed us. Her judgement was flawless and I am a professional judge of that. Her license was not a photo-copy of some nefarious dangerous diver. I had seen those, too. Sent home on the next plane.

57

As further proof, she basked in the sand waved up as a ray made its escape, inspired, no fear. She avoided putting her hand in any cave that could have an eel that wouldn't enjoy being wakened. There was a depth of experience here. A half hour on the tank of this and we floated to the third valley. We dropped to 20 feet of the 30 there and she stopped our progress. She floated up until we were mask to mask. She made the contact and we pantomimed a wet kiss. She turned me upside down so I could pantomime fun for her sliding the thong away. While I was so involved, the speedo fled. I could hold my breath for a long time. It turned out she could, too. Yup, licensed. She was no longer exploring when she turned us around, still limber and she slipped herself onto the unavoidable projectile. I knew the time-limit of this for a woman, in short order, much of my tank was empty. That is, both my tanks. I guided her to the surface where I promised I would return the favor.

"We'll see if you are as good as your word."

I took her hand, this time, firmly, and we skittered on the quick side up to my cabana with A/C. Seldom did you have a day with her that you didn't need it. Out of the water, anyway.

"I promised you something in the water after you drove me to salty ecstasy. Equality is the driver, it's your turn first"

She responded, "lover, you have a license for this?"

I ignored her and turned her upside down. More comfortable and sensitive out of the water. We spun through wind-mill turns before we fell into the post loving moments of vulnerability. A/C helped but no need to dress. Women may get tired of men adoring so earnestly. But, I'm sorry. No, I am not sorry.

Resting my gaze on Vanna, my mind was running

pictures of different futures before my eyes. As most women could, she knew there was something behind that gaze. Eventually, she knew she could and would find out the source.

CHAPTER SEVENTEEN

Contract For Vanna

"Vanna, the desire you are unearthing at the moment is challenging my concentration. I could lay it out and disastrously offend you. There is no doubt about how we feel about each other?"

"Lance, Mr. Dork, have you not witnessed my response to you. I knew how I felt about you since the first day you helped me adjust my tank. I am much attuned to the value of a touch. I am not an unexperienced 18-year-old girl with stars in my eyes and no maturity in my soul. I can see your arousal endlessly. I am never impatient at the time you spend watching me. Nor will I ever if it comes to that. I have no doubt. I knew what I desired when I decided to extend my stay. You're such a gentleman, you probably didn't catch on until I pecked you on the cheek and asked you to dive with me. The nature of the dive was in my mind before I slipped my thong on that morning. Get the long-belabored point?"

"Vanna, I will surge ahead trusting in your response. I will go to the bottom line of what I desire. When I get there, please give me a chance to re-phrase anything that offends. I will try to be clear."

"Vanna, I would like you to stay here indefinitely as my partner and my lover. We would live in the little air-conditioned bungalow when we are here. Together. Any package deals or resort policies that affect you are burned. Any household things you want to bring down, I will negotiate shipping on a banana boat. What may be the most difficult is to decide how we will get a salary. There is no question in my mind that your skills are well above those of the present water staff. I would be surprised if there weren't many other experiences you have to bring to bear on our operations. I would need to get your thoughts before we, you and I, get something fair."

"I mentioned my job in Germany. I limit my time there as much as possible. It often goes two to three months. I cannot imagine being there without you that amount of time. I have an apartment there where we would live most of the time. Any other living would be in a hotel or perhaps a night or two with my dear friends, Greg and Cheryl, in Munich. Can we live with these parameters keeping our options open about marriage?"

"Lance, you must have been staying up late at night thinking about all this. My response is "yes". My passport is good for four more years. Since I am not a citizen here, I should not be on the payroll. We can explore options. The previous time I had in Germany was in closed, restricted places. To see more of it would be wonderful. I also can read your mind about what you worry might offend me. We know each other and neither will be trafficking the other."

Vanna continues, "I feel silly in even mentioning that. In fact, I'm looking forward to honing some of my skills in that area. Oh, we can make that one of my contractual demands if you feel you have too many of your own. Are we done yet with the contract? We are long beyond the end of our post-love non-lucid bubble time. Let's make a new one."

CHAPTER EIGHTEEN

Supply Trip and Rueger

We made supply runs to the mainland every two weeks. It was a two-hour ride if waves permitted and wind was not against us. Vanna went with me this time and weather was perfect. The bottom of the boat was not comfortable enough for loving. She dressed the island-girl outfit with short skirt, white lace along the bottom seam, white socks and tennis shoes. It had to be an industrial strength bra and the pinks appeared no matter what the blouse or top.

Vanna was an immediate favorite of everyone we saw. The owner of the supply store provided a money exchange service which gave a generous exchange rate and you could cash personal checks. I am a major customer and with Vanna on my arm, we had many invitations to tea or beer, sometimes Southern Comfort.

Life in the country had taken on a somber atmosphere due to the drug traffic and the deaths directly involved. It was on the mainland, but had migrated to the main island. My island was an hour and a half by boat on a good day from that island. Tourism there had taken a hit. I had never before considered safety other than air embolisms or nitrogen narcosis as issues in the diving world. News and friend's anecdotes made me reconsider. I went to a mainland sports store and found I could buy a pistol if I had the cash. I had one and when Vanna became dear to me, I got one for her. While the supply people were loading the boat, I showed Vanna what I had purchased. I asked if she had experience. She, too quickly in my mind, said yes! I was doubtful but knew there was a gun club a few hundred yards into the mountains. We could walk and did.

The target area had a sandstone cliff that would absorb any stray bullets. We were alone. I could comfortably; not hurriedly, set her up with the luger. I took a few shots with my Colt as she watched. I asked if she would like to try and she agreed. The targets were bulls-eyes thirty yards away. I had hit the target at some place each time. Vanna set her stance, raised both arms and fired. The bullet hit the outer rim on the right side of the target.

"Lance", she said, "I think this one is pulling to the right. Let me adjust the site. Her next shot went into the left outer circle. She said, "Ok, I've got the angle for this gun at this distance." She fired five more rapidly and hit the center every time.

I made a mental note: This woman manhandles heavy tanks and diving equipment, dives as an instructor, captains a huge dive boat, dives each time, and is the unseen 'diving buddy' for groups of six or more. She is a strong swimmer with live saving training. I had witnessed that as a twelve-year old boy panicked when his old model B.C. disconnected in open water. Now, to my mental checklist I had to add "crack shot".

The day had started sunny and our ride over was relatively quick. Walking back from the quarry, we were drenched in a summer squall. The wind came up. I had been here before. I hurried over to the supplier who was already unloading the boat. I quickly borrowed his pick-up and drove to the edge of town to reserve a room in the only decent hotel in the area. After a drenching, Vanna, in her sailor girl outfit, looked a succulent course. She was waiting in the lobby-bar of the hotel on the square which would not be one I would book. A few men were sitting around, playing cards and back-gammon. They weren't watching their cards much at all. I paid and immediately hurried her out. A quiet sigh of disappointment.

The boat would be secured to the dock. There would be no hard bottom to interfere with passion tonight. I had often recommended the hotel to divers missing the morning plane due to wind or storm. A bottle of imported champagne arrived as our night-cap.

CHAPTER NINETEEN

Shrimp Defense

We were going to leave for Germany in two more days. We invited Roberto for dinner. He was a trusted friend with power of attorney if needed while we were gone. Over the years he had been much more than that.

He was looking downtrodden when he arrived. We noticed immediately and pursued whatever problem before serving. I quickly offered a glass of his favorite scotch. "What is it, my friend?"

"You know, Lance, that I have a shrimp farm and a dolphin riding business.

"Been there."

You know my island base is infested with drug dealers, big money narcotics peddlers. Not peddlers, major shippers. Recently there has been a larger than normal influx of shady businessmen and their radicalized thugs. Since they bribe all the police and government employees, there is no law nor enforcement. They have three power boats. Big motors. Two go out and rip the shrimp out of the beds. This happens at least once per week. They load it into an even bigger motor yacht and take it to the mainland and sell it to the people who have been my customers for years.

I ask why they have changed suppliers. Some don't

even speak. Finally, a long-time friend explained that they have families. If they don't buy from Don J. Mondo Do, they may' lose track of their children'. There is no police nor DEA nor government protection. They are forced to buy or something terrible may happen to their family.

I have gone and talked to the police chief who 'guffawed' me out of his office with arrogance and smirks. "We'll look into it" is the answer. Absolutely nothing happens. I have gone to mainland authorities for the same smirk. And the same nothing happens. I keep going higher and they are all in Don J. Mondo's pocket. I don't have proof, but I am certain even the president is corrupt.

I have no other place to go. I am going to lose my shrimp business. The dolphins don't make enough to pay the bills. The utilities bills to me have been tripled. Do you have any ideas? I'm dying!"

"Roberto, I do have a couple of ideas. I'm leaving to Germany in two days, but can do some research before I go. Any action I can take will have to wait until I return. I will try to limit the time in Germany as best I can.

Lance: "We can't solve it tonight. Meet Vanna and let's eat and maybe drink more than usual. I'm not diving tomorrow, tank anyway."

"Roberto, because I am gone to Germany, doesn't mean nothing is happening. From here on in, don't ask me what I am doing or not doing. Its better you don't know. Trust in our friendship and that I care and to my limit of power, I will help. Now via con Dios."

CHAPTER TWENTY

Vengeance by Night/Shrimp Fields

Later that night I spoke to Vanna. "Sweetheart, if I am going to help Roberto, I could use your help. There is some danger involved. I will try to limit it, but I will love you the same either way, whatever you decide. I wasn't aware of the seriousness of this when I made your contract. I had only heard a couple snippets from Zulinda, who evidently was underplaying it."

"Lance, tell me the plan?"

"I don't have it completely figured out, but I don't think we can take Don J. Mondo Do openly. Whatever we do, we must avoid it being traced back to us. It could lead to losing my resort to fire or whatever he might plot."

"I think the weakness in Do's operation, or his crony's, is with the smaller boats doing the night raids. The larger boat that extorts the restaurants may also be a doable target."

"There are two things we could do to start to sting him tomorrow night. We will need the cordless re-breather systems and the two small one-person under water diver transports. I have the transporters docked under water on the west side of the island near the gravel airport. No one should know I have one nor were. The re-breathers are on the top shelf in the tank room. Have you used these?"

"I have used the re-breathers extensively. I have played around with the transport but not seriously."

"Every-day I'm finding out more of what you can do. We need to have a big talk one of these days…. maybe in Germany."

"Tomorrow night, after dark, we attach the diver transports to the smaller rescue boat. We attach the small, quite electric outboard to the transom. Full black dive suit, two underwater lights and two variable crescent wrenches. Two pairs of pliers; a dive knife. Black plastic camouflage to cover the safety boat. Only for major emergency, put your Luger, loaded, in a plastic sack."

"Here is what we do. The boats have 100 horse motors. They will be outboards. Two, one for you and one for me. We must do this as quickly as possible."

"I'm going to guess you know what a pliers, a crescent wrench, a drive shaft, a cotter key, and a shear pin are?"

"You're right. I have no experience, however, of firing a pistol from underwater to a land-based target. I could throw a knife."

Muted shock in my eyes, I responded, "If we should have to fire a pistol, we will be out of the water and probably diving behind trees to save our skin."

"Let's go inside with the A/C, less apt to be heard. One other thing we will need is a small part of a centimeter measure. Are you still sure you want to risk this?"

"I am not prone to changing my mind after I commit, but continue with the plan."

"We drag the transports behind the security boat, boat covered in black, we in black full wet suit and black charred cork on our faces. Using the electric motor, we go to about one-quarter mile from the bay where the boats are moored. There we moor dropping anchor.

There is one support you are unaware of. A mutual friend of Roberto and I is an adjunct officer with the U.S. military stationed near the extra-long Cuenca airport. His field is drone management. We had a dinner with him and he showed us some things he probably shouldn't have. At the time I never dreamed that I would need him for protection. I called him after Roberto explained his worries. He will be a major protection for us. Except for a serious life and death situation, he will only provide intel. Roberto is ready to trust him with his life. In an emergency he might help. His call sign on this military radio here is "Songbird". Ours is "Birdcage." I'll alert him at the half-mile point."

"At the quarter mile point, we anchor the boat, discharge the transports, and ride in underwater. It should take ten minutes one way. We'll have another ten minutes to remove the shear pins and measure them, down to the smallest millimeter length you can read. Measure especially length and diameter. Make note of any anomalies. I'll measure and wrap the ropes mooring the boat around the propellers, just on my boat. I'll come back in my transporter to get you and we'll leave as we came. That is the basic plan. I'll check with Songbird at noted points to see if there's any reason to abort."

"If you need any directions on how to remove and replace the shear pin ask me now."

"I'm fine on the shear pin. I'll keep my hair under the suit hoody."

"I think that's all for tonight. If you are still ok on this, let's go to sleep. We'll have a 24-hour day tomorrow. Or, if you are feeling some stress, I could do something for you to get you to sleep easier."

She answered after dropping her hand, "I think I am ok, but you surely aren't. "

"I'm always like that with you around."

"I deeply appreciate that. Come here now. An easy one, don't try to do a fifteen-minute marathon."

I stretched muscles and rose. Stretching Yoga has applications other than street fighting rapists. She pulled me down, midriff up, captured, and took me home, her eyes flashing. I ignored duration and flew free. It surely wasn't five minutes; no marathon. I caught my breath and laid down beside her.

"Lance, I changed my mind, short but complete."

I went quickly to her lips, bursting passion, dropped to her breasts. Lips on one and warm palm on the other, she held her breath. I skipped the midriff but thighs landing on swelling fire. Ragged breath, the A/C was on and she bested it with sweet vibrato middle C. A sweet success-announcing sound.

Lance breathes, "We'll be getting back to this tomorrow night."

"Lance, there will be a changing of mind. About the marathon, that is. Please be careful. We could be easily caught under surprise wilting fire tonight."

The wind had increased into the one-digits We arrived at the anchor spot in an hour. We had left at 1 a.m.

"Songbird, this is Bird-cage. Do you read?"

"Five by five, captain." He knew me well, but anonymity was the word of the night.

"Do you have infra-red up? Any warm spots? Over."

"Negative, I 've been monitoring the spot for two

hours. I think they ran a robbing raid before midnight and are home drunk. I'm watching for thugs, though. Check back 10 minutes into the mission."

"Roger, over and out for about 15 minutes."

Vanna had her hair hidden and we made short work of disconnecting the transport. We had our tools and gun over our shoulders as the electric motor kicked in. Removal with measuring took five minutes, too long. Total thirty minutes. Our B.C.'s was empty, we made no waves. No warning from Songbird. A bit of luck. Vanna's eyes were tense, business, combat wary in every direction. She well realized the delay and was prepared for a violent response. Dumb luck which couldn't happen again. We would be back here.

CHAPTER TWENTY-ONE

Mondo Threat, Demise

In the middle of the second week after the swipe at Don J. Mondo's poaching boats, Songbird called. "We have three intruders approaching your pier arriving in probably fifteen minutes. Three aluminum boats. Over."

"Roger that, we have two of them on surf reader."

Vanna went down the hill to my right, Weatherby hidden. I was at the bar with a pistol on a shelf, shotgun concealed under the fruit.

Don J. Mondo Do was maintaining a place between the intruders. Cowards foment insurrection, don't ever lead it. Here's a guy who knows he owns the police, gendarmes, lawyers, judges, the Senate, and other officials above and below. He can do and kill whoever he wants in Times Square and drink to it with champagne.

"Songbird, Mondo is coming toward me among the others. He has a shotgun. One henchman is in a clearing below where Vanna is standing. The other is 20 meters to the right of the first also in a clearing. They both have American assault rifles."

"Roberto, get over behind and below Vanna. Unless she misses, don't give away your position. If I get into trouble at the bar, you have to save me. Put a wall of lead in front of the bar. I'll be cowering low behind it, in the fruit cellar. There's a guy with an assault rifle up from you behind Vanna. She knows it."

"Vanna, Mondo's got a shotgun. If that comes up, it's my problem. You shoot the guy up the hill, duck and take the guy in front of Roberto. Roberto will cover if you have trouble, but I'd like to depend on your speed in the first volley.

"Birdcage, we have them on screen, guns also. If the least happens, they will go to jail for illegal weapons. But there is no sheriff nor judge. Protect yourselves. We have the green lens operating, say burst if you feel you are about to get shot."

'Songbird, if a shot is fired, Vanna will take the one out downhill from her. You MUST take the one nearer me in the clearing. If I say burst, it will be because Don J. Mondo has leveled an obvious threat at me, my business or my workers and families. I will surely say "burst" and dive below the bar. Be right on top with finger on your trigger. A second late and I'm dead. You can't mistake or think about the fading democracy. His shotgun will injure or kill me even behind this one plywood thickness of the bar. Please don't hesitate! Over"

"Roger, we know our business! Over"

The green lens was the killer option. Nobody but Vanna and I had any possibility of seeing it.

"So, Mr. Starr, maybe it's the former Dr. Starr! We meet at last.

I said nothing, meeting his glare.

"I've had a few accidents with my shrimping boats recently. You wouldn't know anything about that, would you?"

Why would I know anything about that? As far as I know, you have no shrimp farms.

Ah, Mr. Starr. That is where you are wrong. On my island, if I want a shrimp farm, I take a shrimp farm. The easy or the hard way. I will take the dolphin business if I want it, too.

Again, I said nothing hoping Songbird was recording.

"You don't leave clear tracks, but I know you are causing these delays. Late delivery of shrimp can cause spoilage. I don't tolerate losses."

"There are courts who indicate ownership in a civil matter. Take it to them."

"No, Mr. Starr, on this island I am the authority. The police and courts are manned by people who agree with my claim. I am also the judge and jury on what is now your late island, here. You are guilty of damaging my shrimp farm equipment and will not have a chance to do it again."

The shotgun came up, I yelled "Burst' and dived behind the bar, head into the fruit cellar. The BOOM, and I grabbed my shotgun and rose to whatever might be developing. The remains of the top left of the bar were tatters. The only shots I heard were from Vanna's Rifle.

Songbird beat Roberto to the draw. No, it was Vanna. Songbird's burn had come in seconds too late. I was alive because of Vanna. She had taken three out in a matter of three seconds at 180 degrees apart.

Peeking over the bar, I saw Mondo on the ground, a small plume of smoke under his chin. One rifle, one drone. There was no trace of blood. His gun had flown over his head. His face was set in surprised rictus.

I hurried to hug Vanna and thank her for saving my life. Her shots had been perfect. I also checked to secure the passing of the victim of the green flash.

"Roberto, I need you over here ASAP, for sure now. I need help."

"Lance, I'm back in the channel, didn't even get a shot off. Will be there in ten."

Roberto was in shock seeing Mondo deceased.

"Roberto, he and his henchmen tried to kill us. Between us, we managed to survive. The fact that you didn't get a shot off doesn't mean you weren't a critical life saver, particularly for me. I need your help to dump their three aluminum boats, and their bodies."

"I need you to devise something that will sink those bodies and keep them down for several years. We'll see if Songbird can help with the boats."

Roberto responds, "We'll attach the U.S. armaments, guns and ammo to Mondo, et al. The water out north east of the island is over 400 feet deep."

"Songbird, this is Birdcage, over. We have three aluminum boats to move north-east out of sight and circulation. They are empty of any cargo. If we pull them over to the east of the island, can you drill some holes and light the gas tanks?" Over!

"Birdcage, there are no bodies in them?"

"Songbird. I am unaware of any bodies. For sure not in them."

"Ah, very interesting, your short memory. Maybe it's shock. We'll deep six the boats. Bring them right now. I don't want to face being late for dinner. Out!"

"Vanna: "Can you go over to those ruined engines right away? Take any Styrofoam out so they sink fast, and stay sunk. I want what scum remains on the mainland or Roaban to know any threats or actions they make to hurt will be met by huge repercussions. I want to do it immediately on the day they sent their "Mondo". I want him to disappear on the same day that their damaged engines disappear. I don't want them to use them again to destroy us. Tow them over outside the north wall beyond what the tourists can see or hear and Songbird will make them vanish."

"If any of you folks think I'm a little unhinged here, remember I came within 3 seconds of being killed 20 minutes ago."

"It continues to be urgent that we leave no evidence, and move fast. Vanna, maybe it would be better if I come and we do it together, or if you are concerned, I can do it alone. I will check with Songbird, but don't expect much extra security from them."

"Lance, what part of 'I'm not going anywhere without you and you ain't going anywhere without me.' do you not understand? Given a half hour, I can destroy those bodies and boats beyond any recognition."

"Thank you. My lifesaver of tonight. We need to complete this because tomorrow we need to meet with Zulinda from the other resort. I think we'll need her help because that larger boat continues to poach shrimp two or three days a week."

After dispatching Don J. Mondo and his cruel crew, Vanna and I briefed Roberto and Songbird about our now delayed, but pending return to Frankfurt. With the need now for a new Don J., we should be able to do what we needed to and get back before they were re-organized.

CHAPTER TWENTY-TWO

Enter Rayban Hernandez

Rayban Hernandez was by far the richest young man in Sambo Creek on the Northwest coast of Central America. It was a bitter-sweet reality. His dad, Octavio was an icon to him as he was growing. He was the man who taught Rayban to fish. He taught many other things that had to be shared to feed the family. Rayban had a younger brother, Octavio Jr. and his mother worked as housekeeper and cook for one of the banana management families. Rayban was too young to realize the survival struggle of the family, a time when Dad had to catch fish every day to put food on the table. When Ray reached age 13, mom got the housekeeping job and together they bought a moderate fishing boat. No longer forced to fish with plastic-line from shore, there was time to offer guided tours to men who came from the U.S. with big money. Dad knew the waters of the Caribbean after forty years. Boat tours were offered as well. There was no option; Rayban had to work on the boat. And that's where he got his name. His name was really Francisco. Initially people called him Paco. One of the tourists forgot his sun glasses on the boat. They were wrap-around and Paco never went out without them. The RayBan sun glasses became his name, Rayban.

Occasionally, Rayban's father had to travel to the capital to fight the drug lords of the Bay Islands and northern coast. This fight wasn't yet of the bloody type, but the lords through bribed lawyers and judges persisted in raising taxes and increasing commercial fishing license costs on all but the drug lord's lackeys. Not paying a bribe to the lords, small businesses fought a losing battle at least in the short run. Octavio hated the trip for this but it was the only thing to keep his family functioning. He also distrusted flights being flown into the country's Capital. The runway was perfectly acceptable for a DC-7. To accommodate the larger 727's and 737's, a runway bridge had to be built over an existing highway. Years of graft had siphoned huge sums out of the government by the drug cartels. Needed renovation lagged and many other places were becoming dangerous, as well. Even with that, pilots had to approach at minimum speed and flare out to get down in available time. Fog often exacerbated the difficulty. The dependable DC-3's and 5's only flew the north coast routes. Buses were often more dangerous. They were seriously overcrowded, sometimes fell off narrow mountain roads, and frequently were forced to stop by lord thugs and the people robbed of all possessions.

This day Octavio flew. He always bought flight insurance. If the worst happened, at least his family would be taken care of. The combination of worst-case conditions, high level wind, ground fog and wet runways developed causing the worst catastrophe. Getting low enough lost the minimum seconds needed to get to flare. Octavio's plane crashed onto the road bridge below and he was in front of the wing. Below the front of the wing, there were no survivors; neither the pilots.

Rayban returned at sundown with a full locker of fish and two well-heeled sport fishermen. Unusual, there were scores of people on the city dock. Rayban jumped to the pier, secured the boat and turned into his mother's sobbing arms. His brother was standing there in shock, tears streaming.

"What?"

"Francisco, your father was on a 727 airplane that crashed at the capitol airport at noon today. There were some survivors at the back of the plane, but Dad was in the front. Rescue workers found some of his belongings, but he had passed." Rayban gathered his remaining family in his arms and his mind relived Dad helping him learn to ride a bike, play a large fish, prepare fish, handle a boat and on and on, a lifetime.

Survival left little time for grieving. Legally, there was only twenty-four hours to perform the funeral ceremony. Rayban went fishing or touring only half days for a week. He stood near his mother as friends came from all over to "give you my sincere condolences". He was sick of hearing that over and over. The numbers waned and his mother could suffer her grief alone and with the two boys. Sores would begin to heal as much as they could and there would be some other old woman or man appear with "condolences", reopening the wound in my mother's soul. He could see the shivers moving through her face and the drooping of her shoulders. When you learn of a death, if you can't avoid going to it, get it over with, and discard those meaningless words. Use other words. Ask about the future, plans, changes, things that should now be considered. Help with the future is the only you can give.

Two weeks after the death, a cartel crafted silk suit appeared at Rayban's door, pure imbecilic lieutenant. From torture to bittersweet moments, he informed us of the one-million-dollar flight insurance my dad had purchased. "Sign this form and we will calculate the expenses and taxes and deposit the remaining proceeds in your bank account." He might as well have said, "Bribes" as expenses.

I had observed my dad fighting these crooks. For years. The lords, early in their coup of the government had re-instated death tax. Of a million dollars, they would change the law again against my father's will.

"We will sign nothing today. Give me your card and I'll call for an appointment."

Friends and clients had often urged me to get a lawyer if anything of any value to the druggies should develop in my life. I knew my father's lawyer and family. They lived in the suburb of Pedro Sula. I called and heard a cry of grief. A more measured voice took the phone. It was Felipe, my dad's old friend's son. I told him who I was; he knew immediately. We had been classmates in high school. He also had read about the life insurance. He knew I had a large inheritance coming. I told him that I had called to retain his father's help with the will and particularly how to protect the large sum. I learned of the cry of grief. Felipe's father had been on the same plane. Our old friend and lawyer, gone.

"Rayban, you still have a lawyer if you would trust me. I graduated from LSU law school and passed the bar exam for the U.S. and here. After passing the bar, I worked in a law office in Atlanta, 'Jones, Crawford and Race' as an intern. Being black is still a problem there, as you have probably experienced here. I guess a conquistador got in the mix with some green-eyed beauty of a great-great grandmother. My DNA black is dark brown. As sick as that is, the green eyes and the good wardrobe my dad could supply disguised my Afro-American roots. I eventually worked my way up to a trusted level in the firm.

I was aghast at the corruption and dodges of law they practiced. Bribery was the name of the game. Corruption is rife in the U.S. system if you get into bigger money. They call it Lobbying. It is more expensive than it is here even with the drug lords attacking us.

A corrupt president pardoning his white-collar lackeys up north. We never learn the prices and favors that pass in the smoked filled back rooms. I came under scrutiny from my own firm because I avoided this. Using the excuse of my father's death, I am now back here. I am still on what's considered "good terms" with them, but I can't imagine what favor I would ever ask of such racist, evil people."

"Well, Rayban, a disturbing story for someone offering to be your lawyer, but that brings us up to date."

"Felipe, could you estimate the costs I would need to provide for you to do several things. One, to avoid as much as possible damage the cartel could try to level at me, secondly, avoid any frivolous costs they could use against my business. Finally, get my million-dollar inheritance out of this country so no other taxes can be manufactured against me. What would you need? A fair price. I don't want to take undue advantage of our friendship."

"Rayban that's a tall order. I can't give a definite cost until I study some options, many actually. Unfortunately, that includes the U.S. while this president is permitted by the Republican Senate to abuse the laws of the constitution and even decency. I'm not sure I could solve this before he gets voted out. My guesstimate would be a retainer of $10,000 plus in the range of an additional $50,000. I would include the retainer in the $50,000, but dealing with a million dollars could take it above that. I will provide an item by item description and if there are options, would not carry them out without your pre-approval.

"Felipe, I am a fisherman with no university degree, but much expertise in the Caribbean. Enough to provide for my mother and brother well; for a family of my own as soon as finances, and the right girl comes along. You were an excellent student for the years we were together. I trust in the fairness that lives in our ethics between families.

I think, in the interest of avoiding taxes by showing investment and costs, I should find a much higher quality fishing and tour boat. Potential tax expense deductions. The boat my father fought and saved for a lifetime, was surely a big step forward for our family. I'm young enough to see the surging technologies and am capable of handling an excellent boat into that 21st Century world. If I should be cheated out of my money by U.S. bribery or local drug lord licenses, I would at least have that and the fine living it could provide."

"Felipe, I would like to move on that as soon as possible. Before any corrupt cartel or corrupt government can block me. However, I would like any financial guidance you might have considering all the other technicalities before I make the purchase."

Without putting any local collateral in jeopardy, Rayban visited north coast marinas and some on the Pan Handle of Florida seeking the right price but also the most advanced technology. On the internet, he found one in the Cayman Islands. Felipe knew the abnormal private account activities of this island. His Atlanta law firm had been frequent clients. He drew up detailed contracts and bill of lading to secure the purchase.

CHAPTER TWENTY-THREE

Starr Resort Communications Center Attack on Rayban, East of Guanaja

With monthly visits to Zulinda, our exotic resort neighbor, we operated business as usual. Three months went by with no harassment nor anything else.

We settled into an evening of "no-dive" planned for tomorrow. A couple extra drinks on the veranda. We were beginning to move off to our lover's bedrooms when the emergency radio channel blared. There was a cruiser to the east of Guanaja out of control.

We ran down to the bar to communicate by emergency radio. We called with no response. I went to the dive boat to use radar technology to locate the call. We continued calling and after 10 long minutes, we got a response. It was Rayban from Sambo Creek, who all but Vanna knew because of his beautiful new boat. He wasn't lucid. He garbled, "Thief, attack," stopped. His voice, "Concussion. I'm lost." Other wounded sounds with pain.

Vanna called, "Lance, you have him on radar? Is that the guy from Sambo Creek?"

"Yes, his name is Rayban and his cruiser is the "Octavio.""

"The radar is on the dive boat. Let me get the radar up on the rescue boat. Get three more people down here, and Vanna, get the pistols and ammunition."

We loaded up with emergency items. Vanna drove the boat and I followed the radar. A boat captain repeated calls time after time. Garbled messages flew through. He tried to give us his location. I said, "I know exactly where he is." I handed the luger to Vanna and pushed the Colt into my waistline.

"Rayban, are you alone?

"Alone, please help, I'm dizzy!"

"Rayban, are your lights on?"

"Red top, red pot, red...."

"Say again Rayban?"

"Vanna: Call Songbird and see what they have."

Lost in the ether, "Starr, I think I see you on my radar."

"Songbird, this is Birdcage. Call sign "Birdcage please. We have an emergency call from a boat registered to a Rayban. It's the Octavio. Can you locate?"

"Birdcage, this is Songbird. We have the Octavio. We have you, also. Unable to see what emergency is from here. You are less than 30 minutes out. Over."

I grab the rail for balance. Lance throttles down and I drop buoys and secure the two boats together. I start on board the boat and Lance warns me to let him go first. That's a non-starter and I leap aboard with my hand on my Luger. The only thing I see is Rayban, on his knees, head between them. Lance joins me with a concerned chauvinistic smirk, but quickly scans the rest of the boat. I focus on Rayban.

"Songbird, this is Birdcage. We are aboard Rayban's boat. It's very new. Ray has a concussion, but there is no sign of loss of blood. Unless he has something internally.

He's dizzied, but improving.

"Vanna, I shudder to ask, but did you also have nursing along the way?"

"I worked as nurse on a battleship for six months."

"Now don't tell me you are a doctor, too?"

"I took a lot of anatomy in undergrad, but didn't go to medical school. Parents couldn't afford it and I couldn't stand five more years in school."

"Can you see if Rayban has a concussion, or something else?"

"I know that. Sailors get them frequently on low gangway ships."

She raises his body to see into his eyes, which are closed. She takes my light and opens one eye, shines light, watches, and opens the other similarly. She runs her hand over his arms and legs and feels on the stomach. She double checks the neck and upper leg.

"His eyes are dilated, but mildly responsive. He has a brutal concussion, but he is fighting back. There is no noticeable internal bleeding. We can move him onto his back, but no more movement. He needs quiet rest, so don't try to ask him a lot until I see more activity. It will take at least a half hour, but we should have one of the captains keep a constant watch.

We wait. I go through the boat from engines to stern seeing only some scratching from force on the fish off-loader. No, it is forced and is still open.

"Songbird, this is Birdcage, over."

"Standing by, Birdcage?"

"Songbird, the captain is here and presently alive. Vanna notes a brutal concussion but some mobility returning.

His eyes are closed and show dilation anomalies. He tried to speak on-route but it was garbled. No bleeding other than a scratch on his head where somebody hit him with something. Vanna and I agree he needs to be treated by a doctor. The closest available is the company one in Cuenca. Vanna can take our security boat and I think I can manage his. It's new it may take itself. There is some damage indicating theft in the fish unloader, but that won't impede movement. I will run this full out if it doesn't irritate his body. You could try to get a doctor to meet us, but the only ones I know are in the drug lords stable and I doubt they will bother because Rayban is a capable competitor. Call the hospital directly to prepare them to meet us."

"Roger, Birdcage, out!"

"Vanna, let's get him on a cushion with his feet up. I want to run as fast as possible and there is a chop. We need the cushion to absorb the vibration. "

"Roger, that. Do you want me in the other boat? The captain can continue to observe here."

We ran at 23 knots for forty minutes before he stirred. We were another hour out. The security boat was having trouble but followed our running lights. I slowed and got Vanna back on the cruiser with Ray. The captain ran the security craft.

Occasionally he tried to talk but lost his breath. "We got, "attacked, dark, stole fish," and he faltered. Vanna caressed his forehead with cool water, but he was gone for another half hour.

"Songbird, this is Birdcage, over."

"Birdcage, we have both your boats on radar. You are one half hour out. Roberto is ashore and will meet you at the banana boat dock. It is empty. You see a large liner off the dock? We have talked to the captain and he can't land for six hours; reducing port fees."

"Thanks, out"

Ten minutes later Vanna said, "His eyes are flickering, having trouble maintaining focus. Rayban, can you hear me? Lance, you should come here. He doesn't know me. I can handle the boat."

"Rayban buddy, can you hear me? It's Lance from Guanaja. He turned his head toward me and squinted finally getting focus. Rayban, this is Lance, can you hear me?"

"Yah, better than I can see ya.

"That's ok. You have a concussion. Vanna, my partner is a nurse. You'll be ok, but we are taking you to a doctor to double check. Rest now."

Rayban, anger, adrenaline driving him, "Lance, I can't rest. My boat was bordered by those drug thugs. They dumped my flounder into a net next to their boat. Somebody hammered my head and I went out. Their boat had no name as I could see. I tried to call Songbird, but collapsed. As I went out, the only thing I saw was a red can or coffee pot hanging on the diesel exhaust."

He didn't talk again as Roberto loaded him into his jeep. Vanna moored the boats away from where the banana boat would dock and I got a taxi to Sambo Creek to advise his family. They came right back with me. I dropped them off at the hospital and headed back to join Vanna. The younger brother, now a teenager went to the mooring with me and took the Octavio back to the pier in Sambo Creek.

Roberto called and said he would stay with Rayban until the next day, or whatever was needed.

"Songbird, this is Birdcage. The Octavio was boarded by drug thugs. The hold was off-loaded; stolen. He had flounder so I guess they took the catch up to Gulfport to sell at the wholesale market. They shouldn't have arrived there yet. Can you see them to confirm that? The only description we have is a red can or teapot hanging on the exhaust. Can you get in close enough to identify something like that?"

"Stand bye, Birdcage. We can identify the make and color of your girl's shoes. That's classified. No trouble with a teapot."

I was red-faced looking back at Vanna. "They'll pay with bruises at our next dinner."

"Birdcage, this is Songbird. You were correct on the heading of the pirates. We got the teapot and they are heading back to their liar on the big island. We have several identification marks on the boat. We may have to discuss any response. Things had been going well for quite a while. Maybe they got a new Don J. Do. Do you have any word on Octavio? Over."

Vanna answered, with anger in her voice, "Songbird, they hit Octavio very hard with an oar or something. His concussion is not minor. If he had fallen overboard, they would have smiled and let him drown. Did you tape your contact with the crook's boat? Oh, and keep your invasive little camera above my neck. Over"

CHAPTER TWENTY-FOUR

Repeat of Loyalty

The sun was up by the time we returned to the resort. The boat captain went to his bungalow. Vanna and I had a 'Bailey's and wrapped each other up, until 3:30 p.m. the next afternoon. Then we were quiet, wrapped and re-wrapped in several layers. She not so quiet.

A stunning wake-up call but even after, I could sense anger in Vanna. I rolled next to her in our usual emotional bubble.

"Vanna, tell me what is stressing you?"

She grits her teeth as she said, "Those bastards would have left him to drown. They left his engines engaged. Evidently this new design slips the boat into a circular trajectory when there is no sense of push or pull in some pre-programmed circuit. Barring that, it could have crashed on a reef or rocky shore and exploded and burned."

"Lance, I was internally hesitant when we first fought back at the druggers, sinking their boats and killing them. I participated but felt some guilt. I had left jobs of similar violence, perhaps because I hadn't been personally convinced of the worth."

"The personal value became abundantly clear as Don J. went after you with his shotgun. I was watching; everything changed. At that second, I had no doubts.

My response was drilled in, habit, not thought. After his atrocity to Rayban, I held him in my arms, my personal arms. He was in serious shape. I didn't indicate any of the things I was doing to treat him. We could have lost him. It was touch and go all the way to shore. Lance, if you have any doubts, I personally will lead a revenge strike. I now understand how vulnerable we could be if the lords get definite information about us. We have no choice but to leave no survivors nor evidence."

"Vanna, you saved my life tonight, come into my arms. There never was nor ever will be a doubt about you."

"I have been scheming and planning all night about what we can do. Let's wait until Songbird can send us the video. I think I have a plan we can mount the next time Ray takes a load of flounder north."

CHAPTER TWENTY-FIVE

Dinner in Sambo Creek,
Vanna Meets Rayban, Lucid

Two weeks after the rescue, Rayban had gotten through his dizziness and invited all of us including Songbird to a Sunday Dinner. Vanna and I came together leaving the two boat captains to cater to the 20 divers there for the week. Rayban's mother was busily scurrying around making hors d'oeuvres as starters while Rayban grilled large fish, some Sea Bass and some Sea Bream. He offered a fish-shish, which was a filet flounder deboned and twisted onto a skewer like a shish-kabab, onions and tomatoes impaled, as well. Fish-Kabob!

Roberto was there. I was reluctant to involve him in this revenge response, but with at least three bully pirates who would likely try a heist again, I needed the manpower. Vanna met Rayban for the first time out of concussion. We had an enjoyable dinner with Songbird being gentlemen and super accommodating with Vanna. Lots of fun, but she consistently dresses giving no escape for a male eye. Not Zulinda, but not an iota less dangerous. I could remember when I first met her trying to keep my eyes up. Songbird was struggling while I no longer had to get permission to ogle. She gave it back looking down, not up, at me.

After digestives, I politely wished Songbird good night and said we had some other things to discuss that perhaps they would be better not to hear. Kisses on both cheeks all around and Vanna, Rayban, Roberto, and I huddled away from mother and little brother.

I reviewed the information Rayban had remembered and that Songbird sent in the video. There was no doubt we would recognize this motley crew if we saw them, even in fog again. I laid out the plan for the next night that Rayban would be heading north. We couldn't necessarily wait for fog because these guys were on an evil run and flounder was big money. Rayban would advise us the day he would leave.

CHAPTER TWENTY-SIX

Vanna and Zulinda Tangle, Zulinda Wins Verbal, Vanna Wins Form

Rayban had three sport fishermen to guide, big money, low overhead. It was a week later he contacted me. He said he had a full catch, but had to take it north at night or the hot Caribbean sun would spoil it. The wholesalers bought mostly in the mornings, anyway. Advantageous for the pirates, but we would be prepared this time.

I asked Roberto to come over on the afternoon of our response. I asked him to bring a gun if he had one. He had several. I advised Songbird of our night journey. We napped in the afternoon. Octavio informed us of his departure from Sambo. Our resort was two hours into his journey. We began to radar monitor passing ship traffic.

CHAPTER TWENTY-SEVEN

Face-off: Zulinda and Vanna

Aware from the resort radio of the coming action, Zulinda appeared at the top of the path from her resort. They both knew her very well, in a sense loved her very well. Roberto was still there with Rayban returning to what he expected would be additional planning with Zulinda. Vanna faced me across the table, eyes burning. She immediately left. Zulinda was, as always, naked. She insisted that her clients mirror that, or leave. She modeled her signature behavior.

There was a pregnant pause after which I reviewed what we were planning. Zulinda had been here three years before I even started constructing Starr Resort. I had known her most of the last two years. Striking she is, I couldn't keep my eyes down every minute. It never went beyond that. As distracting as it was, she could have information useful to what we were doing. After a few minutes into my review, Rayban surely needed to prepare his boat. Likewise, Roberto suddenly needed to load his armaments. They had both been close with Zulinda, but were not immune to her presence.

In a personable way, eyes up, I introduced Vanna to Zulinda. Vanna had short shorts and bra under her top. The air crackled between them. I jumped to clarify more. Vanna is my love, camp leader, and my dear partner. She has saved my life and soul several times. Vanna, Zulinda is owner and operator of the Nude.com resort down through the jungle. She had been running her camp for several years before I cleared the hill for ours.

Zulinda commented, "three years."

"We have used the joint Cuenca supplier to improve efficiency which has improved our profits, but largely our security. With Zulinda's cooperation, we were able to clandestinely install the trip wires for what has become a much-needed security device."

The atmosphere cleared a bit when I introduced Vanna as my love. Anytime I said anything complementary about Zulinda, tension increased.

Zulinda followed, "By the way, I had Sandy return the unneeded wire and here's the refund."

"Thinking, now they're warmly chatting about a guy I know nothing about," Vanna quickly rose and went to the back of the cabin.

Before I could begin to discuss the cooperation, I needed with taking out the remaining trawler, Vanna returned. Nude, not even shoes. If I should try to describe the look in her eyes, I would be in trouble forever.

My speech halted, Zulinda stood and said, "Vanna, you are gorgeous. I could never have held a candle to you."

My heart in my mouth, Vanna took a breath and quietly responded, "Thank you". Zulinda answered, "Vanna, I feel some tension between us. In my lifestyle that has happened before. It is obviously because I prefer not to dress. But let me say this again, "You are beautiful hot, molten heat. Since you now will be with Lance, I would like to be friends with you, too."

Vanna, "I appreciate that, and I know you knew

each other long before I arrived. You, too are lovely. It's impossible that some relationship didn't blossom with you two during that time. Are you about done?"

This was a blatant attempt to mark her territory.

Zulinda is no dummy. She stood and said "Yes". She started down her path, thought, returned and sat.

I had nothing to say about this. I was worried. "Vanna was deadly."

Zulinda said," Lance, we need to clear the air here, and it would be best if I do it, or at least start it."

She turned to Vanna and took in the blazing anger.

"Vanna, for many dangerous reasons here, we need to be friends. I want to open that door. I am not competition nor is your resort competition to mine. It's obvious you have either imagined some erroneous ideas, or feel endangered. You need to know some facts."

Vanna snapped back, "You mean about the three years you were here while Lance was building the resort or other times after that. I don't have to imagine. If that's what you want to say, forget it!"

"Vanna, your reaction is understandable. This time, it is mistaken. I heard Lance tell me you are his love. I have never heard those words about any other girl from him. That is evidence enough to put these worries to rest. We have never had a relationship develop that would include that. Over the years I have had two strong ones with men that enjoy my life style. I trust I will be testing that again, soon, not with anyone you know."

This wasn't only about a verbal clash for Vanna, she had disrobed to 'out-sex' Zulinda. Obviously, I picked up on that, and obviously I kept my mouth shut.

Zulinda struck back again harder than I had ever seen her. "You need to settle down and listen to me. I'm not going to leave here until this is fully communicated and you can do what you want with it, or him."

Zulinda continued, "My resort was growing and busy. I wasn't worried about our resorts being in competition. The whole auras are different. For two years, he never even visited my resort, never came over the hill. During his third year, the Cartel waited in hiding and over two months stole all his incoming supplies and mine. At that point, he came to suggest some ideas. This was the first time I even met him. I don't take strangers to bed."

"We agreed to share boat captains to jointly make and defend, if necessary, the incoming supplies from Cuenca. It was working; neither of us had to be directly involved. I didn't see him for another year. Later, a short time before you came, he stopped to coordinate other shipping business. He told me about his trips to Germany. I enjoyed that because my grandparents still live there."

"We agreed to formalize that and he now comes once per month to share any info regarding what we're facing here. For your edification, in every inter-camp meeting, he has been fully dressed and I have been fully nude. Our friendship is platonic and what we know of each other is only what I see when he is wearing the thick corduroy to protect himself from the barbed hill. I have come over three or four times outside of the formal meetings. We don't even share a drink. I come because he is reluctant to come to the nudist operation.

If you hadn't in anger, repressed your feminine wiles, you would've intuited I came tonight because I am concerned that Rayban is involved in a dangerous operation. Rayban is a man I am learning much about, both with and without clothes.

I am not interested in an apology. I can understand the conclusions you could draw. As I said in the beginning, I am interested in your friendship. If you want to say something more, let's do it, otherwise, act supportive in our challenges."

Zulinda waited for a beat, and turned down her trail.

CHAPTER TWENTY-EIGHT

LANCE SOOTHS

The eyes were not great but I took Vanna by the hand into the bungalow.

"Lance, why didn't you tell me about this?"

"It never crossed my mind. There is nothing notable to tell."

"Lance, you are interested in sex, feeling what you do with me, I assume you would at least have a casual tryst with such a tall beauty."

"Vanna, you have heard her Force's holy truth. If I know the real you, you'll at least, over a day or two, accept it and we'll forget what wasn't even there to remember."

"I don't usually comment on this, but I did have lovers for various amounts of time while I knew Zulinda. Before you. I wasn't crazy horny. All ancient memories. You also might note that to avoid any wallops from you, I am sending you to do any and all inter-camp processes with Zulinda."

"Finally, and before we rest and go to dinner, for me there was, between the barbs, some pleasant truths. I doubt under the circumstances you considered these on a resigned, rational level. Through the steam on the sidelines, I could see viscerally the fierce love thoughts you have for me and I for you. We have talked about this and are grounded in our love. Selfishly, it is a security that is good for me to see occasionally. Now, let's wrap up for a while, quietly, because we have a risky mission in the offing."

I said no more, she relaxed and also said no more. Caressing her along her midriff, brushing her breasts, I woke, stilled and laid in question beside her.

"It's time to go if you still feel like it."

She turned and with every unclothed inch took me into a kiss on the pillow that could have seriously delayed the mission.

CHAPTER-TWENTY NINE

Project Flounder: Avenge Attack on Rayban and Flounder Theft

"Songbird, this is Birdcage in the resort. Project "Flounder" is underway. Expect Octavio in our waters in two hours. Could you inform us if anything is launching toward us from the Drug Island to our West? Over?"

"Roger that, but their boat may not be as fast as Octavio; may match your security boats speed. We may have to inform Rayban to coordinate his speed accordingly. Birdcage, stay off your radio, we will contact the Octavio. Maintain radio silence. This is shaping up to be a night of patchy fog. Evidently the thugs have a mole in the Sambo creek area tipping them off. Too much chatter may tip them off, over"

"Song bird, appreciate advice, but my security boat is a ringer. I brought it on a Banana Boat. It has a Chevrolet engine capable of up to 22 knots. Pirates are at around seven. "

"Birdcage, careful, their boat was running 18 knots when it was empty on its way home last time. Out."

"Roger, tell Rayban all this, out"

Vanna, Roberto, and I were pondering using the ramp boat for more inertia, but it's not that fast. We'll have to use the security boat. Vanna, please get the pistols and shotgun.

Sometimes before these dangerous activities, Vanna and I get heightened emotionally and meet in heat wondering if it could be our last time. In the end, the physical and emotional stresses were greater after the event than before. It was more stress-relieving to celebrate it then. Roberto was there anyway. I didn't want to influence him to take a run down to see Zulinda at Nude.com. I needed him and his cruiser.

Octavio was about 30 minutes east of us and heading north when Songbird alerted us of a pirate launch. "That boat has three thugs; our facial-recognition confirms the same crew. But, Lance, they are heading at 18 knots and will meet Ray more north than west of you. You need to leave now. I'm informing Octavio. Maintain radio silence. He knows you're coming. Be aware, we predict a fog bank stretching from one mile south of the contact point to a half mile north. We are providing friendly situational information and know nothing of what you may or may not be doing. Songbird, out."

"Pedal to the metal, Vanna." Eight cylinders took us to flank speed in 15 seconds. The boat was one of the long thin canoe style crafts that frequented the Bay Islands, usually fishing or hauling freight. A similar delivered my supplies. It could not plane off, but the power increased the speed to 23 knots depending on wind and wave action. The wind was against us, but mild.

"Vanna, the fish conveying machinery is on the starboard side. We need to go to the port."

Songbird, "Birdcage, we estimate crooks will arrive 1 to 2 minutes before you. Give it all the propulsion you can. Crooks are sporting pistols and battering rams; one American assault rifle. Songbird, out"

Rayban had the same information and was trying to stay ahead, yet let us catch up from the southwest.

The thugs were on a north/north east trajectory. Ray may have to carry the initial blows, but he would not be caught unaware and would fight to the death to project his Octavio. He had a knife but no gun.

"Vanna, I see the pirate boat. It has only second's lead. Roberto, boat hook in right hand, pistol in left. Don't forget your tiller."

"Vanna, hang on to the tiller, but access the shotgun. Yeah, keep your pistol in your belt."

"Vanna, bring the boat right in on Rayban's wake. Pirates have moved to three feet. One jumped off on the bow. One on the transom, one still maneuvering their boat. The one on the bow is moving toward Rayban, probably the one who cold-cocked him the last time. Rayban is aware, but with the height advantage, the bald guy may get the club down too soon. Vanna thumbed off a double tap. He staggered and Rayban drove the knife into his throat. Pushed off the starboard machinery side of the boat, he was fish food in the propeller of the conveyor.

Vanna was exchanging fire with the bald-winged guy hiding behind the transom. Roberto swung our parasail seat over to hit the buoy Ray had dropped to between the boats. I jumped aboard and baldy was in a crossfire, body parts soaring in several directions.

I popped up to check Vanna. The marauders boat was 30 meters port and 20 meters aft of her driving our security boat. Roberto had fallen back 40 meters with his 100 MERC whining to catch up. The thug was trying to control his steering but firing off pistol shots at Vanna and me, some going right between us. I could hear the whiz. Rayban was cursing, "Not my boat!" He began swerving it to avoid rifle fire. My balance swerved the opposite way.

"Vanna, you have the angle, I don't."

I could see the venom in her eyes as she raised the shotgun. I gave her half-hearted cover fire. She put the first slug right into the tubing forcing water vapor into the engine and diesel fumes out, flames licking. She immediately realized the danger.

Vanna, "Lance, Rayban, get out of here, full speed north. NOW!

Roberto head EAST, pronto. Hurry."

The bald, blond guy was ducking from my cover fire. Vanna, rose up again and put the remaining slug into the base of the boiler. A fire licked at the blond. It bloomed.

In the Octavio, I screamed, "Vanna, get down and go flank out of there. Get away, go west, upwind! All it's got, 23 knots."

As she turned and pulled quickly away, I fired another double tap into the alien boat but saw only the holes and damage I had done with my pistol. One of Vanna's slugs had pierced the boiler which erupted with a whom. No other movement. Engine pieces peppered her waters.

"Songbird reacted, "Oil and gas on the water. Withdraw if you are anywhere nearby. Out!"

"Camp radio now".

I had heard all I cared to from Songbird. Better for the Republican lackey of Don J. Mondo not to hear.

Vanna erupted, "Every-one, the boiler is sinking. Set your autopilot and get down."

Ten seconds after her last word, a red, rushing circumference of water and fire breached the surface.

"Sitrep, everybody, Rayban and I are fine."

"Roberto here, I'm clear."

Vanna: "Had to dodge part of the flying transom, but it missed."

From "Songbird, FYI: the crooks ran their engine too far, too fast and the boiler let go. Will check for survivors."

Lance, "Songbird, we would surely confirm your sighting

and conclusions."

"Interesting, Birdcage, one of the crooks blew up onto the bow of the Octavio."

Lance, "Songbird, missed that. Maybe he was knocked out and fell off. We'll see if he drowned. If he was wearing an American Assault Rifle, it would have taken him right down. This is deep water. Out!"

We knew he was already being digested.

Smelling more diesel and some gas, I washed Rayban's sodium-light over the wake. It was blue, white and sometimes pink. Some of the petroleum had surfaced after the explosion.

"Octavio, do you have any emergency flares?"

"Of course,".

"Get up to flank speed before you throw one back. "

"This is Lance, on camp radio. Check the surface of the water near you. If you see bluish tinges, drive directly into the fog bank to the north. Go immediately, schnell!"

"Vanna, how far away are you from me?"

"I haven't been able to see you in the fog for over five minutes."

"Ok, change your heading to north-east".

"Roberto?"

"I saw your running lights about three minutes ago, lost them. Am proceeding North, I see the end of the fog bank, over."

"Rayban, quickly take us north until we get out of the blue surface diesel fuel."

"Vanna, veer north, top speed. Everybody, if you are not five hundred meters into the fog, inform immediately. Otherwise, there will be a fire bloom around you in two minutes."

Vanna," In position",

Roberto, "Out of danger."

"Rayban, fire that parallel to the surface over the stern toward the south."

Crackling, cooking, burning, no such explosion as before. It continued hot for five minutes then broke up into small area fires. Detached blond hair floated below the surface.

Lance on Camp Radio, "All craft, carefully return to initial point of enemy contact? Take your torches and search the area for any bodies or any evidence that could be a problem for us. If you find something, come and get me from the Octavio."

After ten minutes the area was scoured; Vanna approached.

Lance next to him at the wheel, "Rayban, I don't think we need you anymore. If we think it necessary, we'll debrief when you return. Be clear about what happened here: Three men with pistols and an American assault rifle waving, pushed their diesel engines too hot for too long. Their boiler exploded leaving no survivors. Song Bird will confirm that. But Rayban, we have a serious loose end here. Do not try to take another load north until we talk."

"Roger," a hug, and I jumped into our boat, Vanna driving. Roberto followed, calling, "Lance, over where the boiler exploded, burned blond hair. Other body parts remaining."

"Roberto, take some wire and wall blocks. Check for any guns or knives. The hair sank, I'll weight the other pieces."

Roberto, "Area is clear, with one exception. The red teapot."

"Thank our lucky stars you noticed that. Songbird saw it. We know we got the right assassins. It's going to be connected to the brick and follow the crook to Davy Jones Locker."

We arrived at dawn. With more light we scoured the boat and found some minor pieces that may or may not have been of any evidentiary value. Knowing Roberto had been feeling guilty about the fight at the bar, Lance called him over and expressed his appreciation for backing Vanna, saving her at one point and with a hug showed how much his protection of Vanna meant to him. He also whispered thanks for catching the red water pot, saying "you may have saved our booty on that one." He re-filled the tanks, Roberto peeling off to nap with Zulinda.

Vanna and I hurried up to the cabin and once inside wrapped our arms, drew deep breaths and still dressed, went to our knees and fell to the bed. Asleep in minutes. Shower would wait till morning till we had more energy.

CHAPTER THIRTY

Vengeance for Roberto's Shrimp Theft Loss

We had taken a small chip out of Don J. Mondo's shrimp theft and extortion gang, but more had to be done, and sooner, not later. That was why I shortened our time in Germany, and why I hurried to see Cheryl. I explained keeping the details vague should any trails lead Don J. Mondo to Europe. I did show her the measurements of the shear pins and contents of their composition. She knew immediately the hardest metal that would do significant damage to the whole drive shaft and gearing of a 100 horse outboard Motor. Titanium. She offered to make the pins of that. I had the tools in Frankfurt to do this as well. After discussion, we decided to have her cut them and mail them to me in standard German mail. Building in a cut-out for her if Donny J. came sniffing my way. Machines even from the same manufacturer leave different scratches not unlike fingerprints. I didn't want to make it easy for a Mondo technician to unearth a comparison. Cheryl made them and instead of mailing them, dragged Greg out of his trance to come up to Frankfurt for delivery and dinner.

He managed to last one night. They hurried him back to his big 'thinking' chair. Vanna and I stayed a few days more for German folk dancing, and Sauer Braten. I showed up in the Mercedes office in person for a couple days and Vanna topped up her wardrobe with garments that would only make it through one night or less with me.

Roberto had for many years been integral in covering for me, finding equipment for me, and even in a military fashion, defending the resort with me. I didn't want to make him wait three months for relief. I packed the small cylindrical destroyers in a hidden check-in bag. Vanna and I spent the 12-hour trip looking at options to insert the destruction pins, and also break the back of the trawler that had extorted shrimp sales on the coast. She said she'd deal with it. These asides of hers reminded me we hadn't had the big chat in Germany

On the flight from Munich to Miami, I contacted Roberto, gave our itinerary, but asked him not to see us nor call us after we arrived. No direct contact, nothing on sea coast radio. I didn't specify. He knew.

After a two-day jet lag decompression, we set the plan.

"Vanna, whatever we do, we need to do it all on one specific night. We'll never get their proverbial 'pants down' twice in a reasonable time frame."

"Unless they are drinking which they usually are."

"No, too chancy, and it's critical we remain incognito."

"The shear pin tactic will work on the 100 horse motors, but not on the trawler. Do you have something for that? Or would you prefer if I took the trawler myself?"

"Lance, how many times have I saved your life in the last three months? Do you know how to mount an underwater limpet mine, for remote control? Sometime when I am deep in my cups and of high spirit with Greg and Cheryl, I will convince you why you should have no stress for me. Now, I will have to make two trips, one alone to the trawler and one with you to the 100 horses."

"Ok, ok, we go on the first moonless night. We need to reconnoiter a few nights to locate a pattern."

"Lance, I will need the underwater transport. You wait for me with the electric. When I get back, we will go directly to cripple 100 horse bays. Things will remain quiet from our point, until my gifts on the trawler or the 100's pull out to rip and ruin."

"Take whatever we have that you need. I will bring the shear pins with an extra, if necessary. Be sure to pack a flashlight."

The moon was waning. We left at 1:00 a.m. three nights later. We could never be faulted for being too close, but we slept seriously tight those three nights. We also monitored the usual movements of the three craft.

We started from the dock in the rescue boat in normal gear. We had not informed Songbird, nor would we ever consider the straps the corrupted Congress had tied behind their backs. The new interrogator was still there.

We throttled down to and affixed the electric motor for the trip to four hundred yards off the trawler. As usual, it was moored on the seaward side of the huge cement block that once-upon-a-time had provided glee for the non-cartel kids. Nobody noticed aboard but Vanna waved my concern off and slipped into the salty water. She had a single lead weight that kept her mask above the waves when she wanted.

The heart-throbbing waiting time settled in for me. I put out two spear guns and sound-suppressed pistols in plastic zip-lock bags. In stress, I swayed forward and backward in the boat. Fantasizing what we had and what we might lose. I realized my short wave-length sways might carry to the shore. I froze and put on the remainder of my wet suit.

Without even a heavy breath, Vanna wiggled over the transom. I sighed in relief. We held a quick hand and she pushed me to the throttle. Her expression was combat mode. It was a "see, I've been here before look." Quiet as the night our electric carried us to the head of the bay.

"Lance, I heard some noise on the shore but nothing on the trawler. It could have come from the block where the 100's are docked. I'm not sure, but be super careful. Give me my titanium pin."

We cut the electric motor and anchored five hundred yards from our targets. We would need the submerged transporters until and unless we sensed a security presence. We disconnected and launched them quietly over the transom.

We slipped in pulled by the transporters. No extra lead weights necessary. No moon hovered over our mission.

We stopped at the prow of our respective target boats with the transporters silenced. We signaled that we had the tools and the pins. We slipped to the sterns of the boats where the motors were affixed, I to the starboard craft and she to the port.

As I lowered my face a second time toward the prop, my hood pushed a slight ripple to shore. All hell broke loose. I had the old shear pin removed, centering the "ringer". A shot rang out and I heard the splash inches from my head. I couldn't see Vanna, but she was surely head down. Another seriously ugly ragged bearded head came thundering out of the trees. He spotted Vanna and lined up to fire. Ducking a pending bullet, and firing, my spear went through his stomach, with not even a grunt. I fought to get my pistol out and the guy that shot at me was going to win the race. I ducked under wondering if I would be dying when I came up. The shot was again set off course by the water. I popped up to face the muzzle of his pistol. Right at me. A pfft sounded and he was in the water next to me, bleeding the red sea. I looked for Vanna. She raised herself above the side of the boat, small relieved smile, and finished the shear pin insertion.

We quickly met at the prow, affixed lines to a leg of each cartel radical and towed them out to the electric boat. We got in the boat and took a deep cleansing breath. Too soon!

The motors of three boats growled into operation. We had the moon on our side, but they had search lights. The trawler was cruising along trying to locate our camouflage. The 100's were darting about in every direction, outside the shrimp reef, disgusting oaths spewing. Over their roaring motors, our electric was invisible. We also couldn't hear each other. Twenty-five per cent of the shrimp bed was nestled between islands which faced the concrete pier where we had changed the shear pins.

Vanna urgently pointed, I understood, and headed feinting into the shrubs lining the island. Both 100's saw us. They ramped up to full throttle, engines whining, ragged beards brandishing smuggled American-made assault rifles. Heading directly into the shrimp reefs.

Side by side, within a second of each other, the propellers with the titanium pins ripped off bending one of the other two props. A second later, a flash, a screech, a ripping of metal and an explosion which hurt our ears. We ducked low. They hit shallow reef, the pins held, another propeller gave out bending a third. The drive shafts seized, flaming into pistons and cylinders. Housing spewed out of the back of the motors taking partial transoms with them. With the centrifugal force still pushing, two guys alive but bloody tried to glide their remainders out into the sea lane where the trawler patrolled to get picked up on their way to threaten shop keepers. The mangled parts of the 100's reached the lane, but the trawler ignored the drowning rag-heads. Such loyalty among cut-throats.

The 100's were down. The trawlers were leaving. Vanna, with iron determination pushed her first button. The prow submarined and they needed bailing. A limpet under the gas tank erupted starting an intense fire. Two singed black faces ran to douse the fire. The limpet under the pilot house decimated the center of the boat still above water. Three bodies of carnage. The pilot fell forward to the fore-deck free into the water, flailing, dragged under by his assault weapon and ammunition. The fourth limpet exploded. No chance, no remains to dispose of.

"Vanna, do you have anything else" The wreck is still floating. With a dark look, remembering what these people had done to Rayban and many families, she lifted her black box and triggered. The last limpet had been targeted for the front of the trawler.

We had made a lot of noise and now had to move quickly. Three stops. Vanna drove and I jumped in where I was sure there was no armed opposition, which was nowhere. I pulled the Styrofoam float bars out of each of the boats that would normally keep them afloat. Not wanting to leave any evidence, I threw them to Vanna. We were at the 50-foot mark now, with the bonefish clouding the water rushing over the channel in the reef. The only evidence left was three bodies and blue-green gasoline on the surface. We attached them to the two others and headed to the four-hundred-foot depth two miles north. Vanna tossed a flare across the surface and the blue-green was yellow-gold and then none. We headed out with our muted engine.

We slept around the clock the next day not mentioning our mission to anyone. Our love and passion and stress and fear exploded. She made me feel much better. Her sounds said the same. Decent, selfless human life, survived from evil.

CHAPTER THIRTY ONE

Subsurface Demolitions

Reclining in the Captain's chair one night, Rayban thought he heard an explosion well off shore in the direction of the Bay Islands. He relaxed again thinking that if there was a serious problem, he would pick up notice on the sea-band radio network. It was ten minutes later with no notice on the radio, two more explosions sounded. Nothing followed on radio, Octavio felt obligated as a concerned sea community member, to investigate and offer safety to any people in danger.

Nothing was shown by this point on radar, Octavio headed in the direction he estimated from his knowledge of the area. His crew assistant was home in bed. He fired the huge cruising engines not being able to add sail to speed. If asked, he would guess that the sound came from west of the Bay Islands. He headed between them. It was not a short journey but he could make it at 25 knots in less than two hours. The fog was like a scrim before the stage lights come up.

His radar was top of the line, but there was nothing pinging in any direction. On this night in this fog, there was no available technology that could help him. His gut instinct was that he was in the general area. He knew the bottom of most of the Southern Caribbean with a blindfold. He knew he was west of Guanaja and east of Roaban, the drug island. There was a huge undersea wall that dropped off to 150 feet and went straight down for an unknown distance. He was a scuba diver and had dived this wall to 130 feet which is sport diver limit. He had given himself another 15 feet below, but there was nothing.

Using all of the technology available, he dropped the "magnetic" fish finder. He knew it was accurate only to 90 feet, but what's to be lost. The boat on remote moved north to south above the steep drop-off. The wall moved mostly north and south, but as nature seldom agrees, there was occasionally a jog to the east or west. Actual depths were running at 150 feet. His finder indicated that. He had little hope. It had been a long day at sea and he was beginning to zone out, but suddenly saw what he thought might be the outline of a completely desiccated hull teetering at the edge of the wall. It was out of focus, with no bodies nor recognizable artifacts visible. It was not from Pirates of the Caribbean but he lost view of it as his boat moved under remote control. Maybe he was so tired he was imagining things.

He had heard no radio traffic. He put the boat on radar-driven cruise with no sail. There was no major reef nor obstacle between here and Sambo creek.

He reclined again in the Captain's chair with hope of a doze. According to his instruments, he had traveled a mile and a half when another explosion erupted.

By now, he had on record the latitude and longitude of the phantom boat. He programmed the target point and set the engines at full. He arrived in forty minutes, activated the fish finder, and cruised the wall from south to north. There were a couple of familiar looking rocks, but no sign of any boat. No sign of anything although it was at the edge of the wall and anything could have washed over that. Or maybe he had been hallucinating. He thought he saw a flash of red running lights to the north, but they disappeared quickly; he ignored them. As he pre-set the returning parameters, he thought he heard a small engine leaving the area to the north. He saw no running lights so decided to get home and get a good night's sleep.

CHAPTER THIRTY-TWO

Aboard Starr Resort Rescue Boat

"Vanna, I can see it on my underwater radar. There is another modern-rigged cruiser in the area. I have it on satellite radar. I have an idea who it is. He noticed the sunken trawler we put down but weather conditions forced him for home. I think it will fall off the cliff in a matter of a day or two. The shrimp piracy mustn't pay well with such a rusted trawler. Let's get behind the airport island, no lights and idle for a few minutes. Be careful of the weather. A northerner can bear down in twenty minutes. You may not even see it at night.

Resort crew, turn south-east and we'll meet at the dock. Go ahead and light your running lights. The new cruiser is pulling into Sambo Creek. My radar indicates there is no-one to see us.

We had a full group of divers and all Captains available. On the surface, all was smooth, but those who had been involved in security backup activities were waiting and wondering. I thanked and dismissed them and radioed to Roberto. He came for breakfast with wonder in his eyes. Off in the trees, Roberto said to Lance, "I have technology, too, and I know what you did for me. The bombs on the cruiser were obvious if you were listening for them. The 100's are also a danger and I didn't hear anything from there. I know I can't ask any more."

Lance quickly replied, "They're gone, but let's not discuss this any more for a long time."

It was like the Revolutionary war. We were using the tactics of the revolutionary fighters against a huge enemy. We hit and retreated to hide. We couldn't ever win against the drug lords and the country army in a direct fight. As inconspicuously as possible we had put the shrimp thieves out of business saving Roberto's future. The bombs weren't inconspicuous, but we had no craft to take that trawler out quietly. Clean-up left no evidence or clues. Any court case in an uncorrupt U.S. court would throw the charges out. We operated business as usual.

CHAPTER THIRTY-THREE

Back in the Nest, Lances Resort

As we relaxed from our first relief of the day, we settled into our emotional bubble. Vanna, "Lance, this doesn't leave me with a great sense of joy. It does leave me with a much greater sense of security."

"Perhaps not joy, (you are where I find my joy), but I do agree with at least short-term security. I don't see any liability for Rayban. I am also proud of how brave our group faces these horrid, dangerous thugs. As fiercely as our spirits have fought, we have to keep focused on how they may be coming. We have the trip-wire fence and the surf alarm. I think we need to consider other options."

"I ordered the CCTV cameras and we can set them up after a day of rest and/or relaxation. They would be more dependable if a policeman or judge would even enter them as proof of anything against the Don J. Do Mondo. As much as it may represent the middle of the previous century, I think a dog, a big dog, could be a huge protection. Finally, for now, I think we need to keep a pistol or shotgun in our bungalow. Keep carrying the electric tazer in your purse, with pepper spray. I will continue to keep open channels with Songbird. I think I have protected them from any culpability with our responses. I should probably call them. Come over here, maybe a little bit later."

After we spelled "relief" again, we dozed and a strange bird call erupted outside our cabin.

"Don't come out. I don't need you to see my eyes."

Roberto off to catch a load of shrimp. Bye! The way he loped off down the hill, I think he had a real good time with Zulinda. I remembered hopping and skipping like that. Different girls. If ever, now was not the time to mention it to Vanna.

CHAPTER THIRTY-FOUR

Sambo Creek

A week and a half after the boiler explosion (limpet) event, we met again at Rayban's home. He had been doing some tours and four sports fisherman guides. The fish guiding was reaping thousands of dollars in an average month. The all-inclusive package was $500 per half day, $950 per full day. Ray knew intimately the fishing fields. Some his father had used. The fishermen always went home with satisfying catches.

Rayban said, "I have to thank you for dodging me and my cruiser in the (limpet) boiler explosion event. When I heard several explosions, I was tempted to go back in case you were in trouble. There could be other ears around so we referred to it as the 'boiler event'.

"No trouble, Octavio, we had you on radar while you were out. I didn't want you to be seen with us near the resort. We turned off our running lights. The weather helped and you didn't see us. We left well enough alone"

"Rayban, could we speak very privately for a minute?" He took us into the parlor he had renovated with some of the earnings. Don Felipe had been watching all improvements and maintenance carefully for maximum bribery or tax savings. He hadn't cleared the majority of the life insurance yet.

"Rayban, after the first boiler went down and your attacks continued, I realized that someone had to be informing the drug thugs of your shipments. The distances are too great with too much fog for them to guess and catch you out there. There is someone in Sambo Creek getting bribes for hurting you.

If a white-face like me is seen nosing around, the mole may be spooked. You're going to have to get support from close, definite friends. I suggest you use Zulinda's resort and breakwater as feints a few times until you can get scent of who is directly talking with the thugs. It's going to be a white-face drug connection because Don J. would never have any Afro-Latins working for him, other than golf caddies at illegal immigrants' slavery pay. Have your friends get it around town you are planning a long haul. I will get Zulinda's permission. I'm sure she will cooperate because we have lost some supplies by robbery at gun point. In fact, we are running some supply trips jointly with her boat captains. With arms. Rayban, you are going to decide what can be done with whoever you catch. There is no lawyer, nor judge that will punish or stop this. If you need support at that point, call me.

CHAPTER THIRTY-FIVE

Manatee Conservation Issues

All our night-time security activities went unknown to the client divers. Business was above average. And then came Bucky. He was a deep brown Chesapeake Bay retriever. He immediately warmed up to the resort guests. That was a problem. He was critical security and had to sound an alarm when a thug with a fire arm appeared. Roberto had sneaked him over to the resort. He had to come to take him back for more complicated training. Bucky needed some appropriately timed "mean".

CHAPTER THIRTY-SIX

Warning Attack on the Manatee Defense

Rayban served me a double Captain-coke. The conversation bothered him. Between the points of the small peninsula sheltering Sambo Creek outside of the breakwater and the first docks, lived a pod of Manatees. They don't move much, got very fat and were fun to watch. They eat sea grass and algae, are not carnivores. The non-cartel teen-agers sometimes play with them. Try to ride them. They roll over and dump them off. Tourists request them by name on the Bay tours.

Rayban Hernandez saw them every time he returned to his home inside the breakwater. Recently, he saw a dead one. They have no natural predators at these depths nor are they of any food or other value. Not a normal occurrence, he began to monitor the area.

Within a week, a canoe type-diesel-centered boat drifted to shore. Three older pirate stock teen-agers jumped out with tridents and set to jabbing them and worrying them, hurting them. Laughing and evil, interns for the next Mondo mafia Don J.

From his boat Octavio called them to stop. They ignored him. He set his throttles half forward, maximum wake and filled their boat with water. Cursing, they left only to return two days later. They saw Octavio coming and pulled their boat way up on shore. His waves had no effect. Octavio turned around and came out to our resort here to see if we had any suggestions.

We concocted a plan. Fewer would have to die this

time, hopefully! The next time Octavio saw the young evil-doers, Vanna, Roberto and I took our supply boat to an outcropping three hundred yards west of the manatee's nest. Bucky, our Chesapeake Bay retriever, stayed to guard the camp. Octavio went near their boat and warned them again to stop. With even more filthy language, they blew him off. He had his radio on so we could hear the invective. Octavio headed back toward Guanaja, the island of our resort. They had had their warning.

I put on the rest of my wet suit. At sundown, I would be invisible until I got very close. Staying under water, I moved to 15 yards away and shot the taller guy, who was gleefully stabbing, with my spear gun in his thigh above his knee. Warning, comeuppances! Unless I hit the artery, he would not be in mortal danger. They had cell phones so they got transport to the town hospital. An hour later, I checked with my hospital contact and the young punk had been treated and put on crutches.

Daddy pirate went screaming from bar to bar, helpless again because we had left no trail. Rayban had retraced his path coasting outside the breakwater headland. We waited another half hour, putted along to his boat, secured ourselves in the fish machinery, and headed in tandem at 28 knots back to the island. Only one discernable object. Only his running lights. Songbird's drone could have tracked us but they knew nothing of the conservation efforts that had gone down.

Our helpful contact with Songbird had been transferred to Costa Rica. His replacement was wedded to the rule book. He had been the one we had called when pirates were massing to invade the island and he said his ROE didn't permit him to intervene until they were actually on the island on private property. He was also the one who refused to interdict the Don J. Mondo because a later invasion fight was over and Songbird could not pick up a now non-combatant. Songbird was the one to call us a week after the conservation strike and ask us to come to his office. We chatted before we slept that night. Ray had not been called so we wouldn't mention him at all. A fishing expedition and we knew it. He knew it.

"I called. The meeting was at the military office. I wasn't treating anybody for lunch in this deal. Roberto, Vanna and I went. The atmosphere was ice in a climate of 95 degrees. I wasn't starting any conversation. The ball was in his court.

"I assume you know what we have to discuss here?"

I responded, "I do not."

"There was an assault on a young man out near the manatee nesting grounds late last week, Lance"

We looked at each other with steely feigned ignorance.

"What, they were assaulting the Manatees? A fisherman reported seeing a dead one floating there a couple of weeks ago."

Brainerd, you may refer to me as Mr. Starr and "I know nothing of that. We have been out on the island for two weeks now and today we are doing the usual supply run. We came over here first so we haven't heard any gossip. At this point since you ordered us here, I assume you plan to charge us with whatever it was."

"No, don't get ahead of yourself. I'm doing an investigation."

"Why out of the clear blue sky are we 'people of interest'? Somebody, maybe a drug thug, has something against us." I continued, "Wouldn't be the first time and based on no shred of reliable evidence."

"You have some evidence, some gut feeling we are secretly behind whatever happened? What did happen, inform us!

"Somebody shot a fishing spear through the leg of a young man."

"And why would someone do that?"

"We don't know why?"

"Were there any markings on any Manatee indicating human brutality?"

"We don't know. The local police were involved and didn't indicate anything."

"How many young men were involved?"

"Three."

"Any of their parents on the police force?"

"We don't think so."

"Do any of their parents have cartel businesses the police need to work with or purchase from?"

"Not that we know of."

"Then what in the name of incompetence leads you to suspect us. Ranger Brainerd, I am done doing your work for you. You are putting credibility on a club of cops who have their lips so glued to the drug cartel bosses that only major surgery could remove them. If you don't know that, the lawlessness rampant here on the north coast and islands is understandable. I have been here over six years. I have communications with a few people who speak to others and thus to everyone on the coast or islands. I know you haven't gone once into the American bar/restaurant. Nor to the best quality restaurant, nor to any dance festival, or concert.

"If you did that and had any awareness, you would know what this culture is, and is not. In that process you would learn that I and my associates involve ourselves only in self-defense from these thugs you are incompetently blind to. Hopelessly, we report any other theft or damage to our environment. Their bribe-driven police arrogantly ignore us. And now you question us?"

"You can be sure that every family in Sambo Creek knows we're here. Probably half of Cuenca. Some of them even know what happened. Those Manatees are part of their financial future. These young aspiring pirates will end up with much more hurt than a wounded leg if they continue. That's not a threat from me. You have a wider community to deal with, and at this time, good luck! You have no credibility!"

"Vanna and I are not married. There is no law involved forbidding testifying against husband or wife. Take her in the other room, ask what you need, and be done with it."

He came back flustered. Behind his back she had a devil smile.

I said, "Ok, this sham is over. I encourage you to choose your patsies more carefully next time. Very carefully or you will be unable to purchase any goods and services, other than from the cartel, from any store closer than San Pedro.

'Sorry, flight to SPS fully booked. Sorry, the bus is filled. Oh, we're out of fresh eggs. No sausages made today.'

"You need to act to protect the community's financial future, not harass decent people trying to make a life in this drug-driven failed government. The only jurisdiction you have here is the good-will of the people. You need to recognize your enemies. In this region, you have many. Good afternoon."

Only that round of the desecration of the Manatees was over. It didn't end there.

These cartels are so inherently evil, they want to destroy even if it pays them little or nothing. Their poor little crooked teen-ager had an injury. The saga of the ghostly bone spur fisherman was entertaining the bar rooms of the entire north coast. A few knew. A few guessed in their beer. Every cop had a big enough bribe from Don J. to sweep the spur under the sand.

The ignorant and obsessed criminals considered it a point of honor. Their creativity beyond an attack of force was empty. The bars were full of the boasting and threatening. Juan and our Railroad Street communicators had us completely up to date.

Rayban pulled up to our pier on his way to Gulfport with flounders. We scanned his route with the resort drone and no criminal activity appeared. We checked the sea radar. Clear.

CHAPTER THIRTY-SEVEN

Continued Desecration of the Overweight Manatee: Impending Saga of the Errant Bone Spur

"Lance, Vanna, thank you for the notice of clear passage, but I am concerned again about the Manatee situation. These brainless vandals have gotten it into their head that the Manatees are the ones who have caused the problem. The vandalism of the young punks has been lauded by these fools. Juan Railroad says they have set a date to go out in force, a dozen or so fanatics, and destroy every Manatee and the nesting grounds. The department of natural resources is populated by the drug fool's friends, they know, and will plan to be on the other end of the country in the Mayan ruins during that week."

"Rayban, via my Railroad Street raga-muffins I've had that information since last Friday. We've been discussing what we might do to protect and create a legend that will continue to maintain that protection. We have a plan, but you will be integral to carrying it out. You have time to finish this delivery, but stop here on your way back and we'll finalize."

"To create the legend we want, this plan will need to include several synchronized parts. Unfortunately, to embolden its credibility, with this criminal population, there need be some fatalities. There will be no children included by these guys. Their manhood has already been called into question by the injury of their demon offspring. The skill level of the operations people and the bravery and survival attitudes of Sambo Creek will be strong enough to launch it."

"Rayban, in a status of reverse racism, you need to choose the darkest black volunteers from Sambo Creek. Darken their teeth. You need to meet those privately two or three times to coordinate the actions. Rayban, to give this some imagination and thus lasting relevance in the community bars for years, I will need to use a plane. We already know the department of natural resources is in collusion with this cartel desecration. From the Railroad Street kids, we know they will be in Copan at this time. I will be sending Roberto over there with Pedro Gonzalez and his two-seater Cessna. I will advance the costs of gas and pilot, but Rayban, I need you to speak with your association of tour groups to reimburse some when they can. Finally, Rayban, we need to run Sambo and Copan Ruins in tandem. For reasons you will learn later other things are in the mix. They need to be obvious that they are related. We will need you to evac. us to Guanaja from the area immediate after the action. Prepare to attach our boats as we did before.

Three days later, Vanna, two boat captains and I gathered five spear guns, one as a spare, and stationed two pistols in the gunwale of the security boat. Roberto went to Guanaja airport to fly to Copan. Rayban delayed, then launched from Sambo Creek break-water to amplify communication if necessary, and be ready to pick us up.

Actions by the thugs were reported to Bird-cage camp radio by Railroad Juan on a 15-minute basis. Rayban, in communication with the leader of the Sambo Creek group, his younger brother, got them immediately from me.

The beginning of the approach came as our Chevy engine settled from full throated glide toward a landing point 100 yards closer to the nests than the last time. I informed Rayban. His volunteers were on their own, except for emergency communication. They had heavy black tarp sacks to blind crooks and to avoid any recognition. The black forest attack group were cautioned not to speak or make any sound.

The boat captains, Vanna, and I in black face and black wetsuits swam below the surface toward the nest. A Manatee unhappy with our proximity rolled over away from us and under the bank. I raised my head to listen and could hear a few explosive cries and strikes in the dark forest.

I hurried us along. We needed to be at the main nest to stop any injury and combat the first marauders that might get through. We aligned ourselves, below the surface, parallel to each other facing the shore. Vanna and I had pistols in plastic bags at our waists should worst come to worst. This was not intended to be part of the plan but if things went south, the resulting plan could be the worst.

All hell broke loose as the first thug in the forest cried out and was muffled. He had seen nothing. Other cries and ensuing muffles continued. There were a dozen and a few got closer to the shore, but were still in the grasp of black phantoms stalking them.

We maintained our positions now with our masks breaking the surface. The plan was to wait and take out the first four that came to the nest. In the forest, back cloth bags were shoved over the heads of the white-faces already captured. Their rifles, pistols and ammunition were thrown into heavier gunny sacks. The darkest of the dark, so we couldn't make a site error, collect the sacks and dragged them over next to the boat.

The ruckus in the forest had quieted but we could

hear tripping thumps of boots coming toward the shore. Four of them came bursting out of the brush with automatics at full bore. We were literally inches above the surface and suffered no casualties. There was no debate about defense versus offense. Without rising to a dangerous knee, we each put a spear in each midsection. They were immediately face down with their automatic's yards ahead of them in the sand.

I pulled my pistol, removing the plastic, and moved to stand up. I raised to fire when out of the brush came a phantom so dark, I could hardly see him in the shadows.

"Lance, stop, it's me, Ray's brother. Don't shoot. "

"Ok, ok, relax, Octavio. Come and help the drivers' put hoods on these thugs and drag them to the boat."

Octavio Jr. raised up to come help and a crash came out of the forest on the west side of the nest. One step into the clearing, he was white. Then he was down, face buried in the sand, automatic two yards from my feet. He blindly reached for the American assault weapon. I was out of balance trying to bring my pistol to bore. I would never have time. Vanna did. One double tap. Love those damned Seals!

"Octavio, bag this guy and take him over to the boat. Reggie will be there with three more."

Vanna stepped over to me with a look of relief and love in her eyes. Our eyes met for three beats, then we jumped to get back to the boat and out of site.

The Drug-lord's bounty: the ones who would never be found. Rayban eased up next to us and our four extra-body-boat plus guns and ammo. We secured the two boats firmly and without any running lights, headed at 30 knots toward Guanaja. We headed a few hundred meters west of the island, then north for four miles and

200-foot depth. With hate, American guns and ammo, the thugs went to visit Davy Jones.

CHAPTER THIRTY-EIGHT

TV, Radio, and Social Media

Once more on Guanaja with the captains shooting strong relaxing liquids, I called Octavio Jr. for a field rep. Rayban, sitting next to me, was relieved to hear his brother's voice.

Octavio Jr, with relief in his voice said, "Those drug guys are down where your boat had been. The bags are still over their heads. They didn't see anything after we took them down in the jungle. We didn't have to kill any. We didn't speak so there is no voice to recognize. You have their guns and ammo. The fish are eating their clothes as they sit naked in the water at high tide on the beach. I think we should bind their wrists and ankles so we have plenty of time to disappear home. They'll get free in a few hours. Wonder what story they will be slurring in the bars tonight."

"Good idea, good leadership!" If anybody asks any of you anything, you know nothing of what happened tonight. Your families will confirm you were home in bed. To make a long-term aura of safety for the Manatees, there are other related operations in play now. When you hear them included in the legend someday, you can have fun embellishing and exaggerating the story. You will indirectly continue the safety for the Manatees. But you weren't there!

After checking with Octavio Jr, I contacted Roberto

in Copan. The three jeep vehicles the department of resources drove out there had been pushed into the river overnight and their drive shafts and pistons were rusting. "There will be some surprised corrupt officials in the morning". In plastic in each vehicle was a message. "Saga of the Phantom Bone Spur, Confederate Version: 'The Manatees are a natural resource to the financial health of the North Coast. Your blatant attempt to collude with criminal elements and white supremacists to destroy them is known in every home. You may be liable to reaction from residents of the community. Your drug-controlled police will never be able to protect your disgusting actions from the thousands here who have a financial and emotional advantage from their presence. You are the brainless lackeys of the Don J.'s lords in this allegory. "

Finally, I called Juan of the Railroad Street regulars. "Do you have the sticky messages to put on the department of Natural Resources mail boxes and front doors?"

"Yes, half done, will be up by midnight."

"Can you get the other simpler forms in and around the bars?"

"They are already up. Generic pages on the bars, also."

CHAPTER THIRTY-NINE

Manatee Legend goes Viral

"Juan, can I talk to your sister about the Facebook and Zoom pages?"

"Yes, unknown person, she is right here."

"Yes, I'm here, Mr. Unknown person. But we hackers always find our person. We collect kisses in exchange. Facebook and Zoom are up. I also uploaded the form to Twitter, the code name there is #Lanna. Lance and Vanna, get it?"

Lance smiles, "Got it. Now, our major purpose here is to make this evening's actions into a saga, a legend of the invincibility of the Manatee. We want it talked about over beer on the north coast and islands. Even some publicity on the Panhandle might help. If there's an elementary teacher willing to include it in his/her fantasy curriculum, it would be great. Knowing a friend of a friend would work here. So, use your imagination. Every Manatee will have a kiss for your forehead."

Later the next day, Roberto returned to his island and Juan of the Railroad Irregulars reported the shock in the hung-over crooks. Many who had not participated in the raid were recounting the myth with the greatest of embellishment. The Manatee saga had succeeded getting long lasting results.

CHAPTER FORTY

Second Run for Octavio

Octavio had announced a fish delivery trip and I was standing by at Zulinda's. This was a fake delivery trip that would go only as far as Zulinda's on the south of our island. Octavio's friends would be watching and Songbird and I would be monitoring by radar. Zulinda had quarters for Rayban for the night.

Vanna marched me right back to our cabin proving that the joy there, was more relief than any stirrings I might have popped from seeing Zulinda, Au natural.

CHAPTER FORTY-ONE

Just an Accidental Slip on the Trigger

Two weeks later a gas-powered boat came around the east end of airport island. Two men in Hawaiian shirts. We already had them on drone camera. Song-bird had checked in as well. They could have come from the Floating Suburb or the Drug Island. No black drone I could see. Bucky and Vanna with a Rueger ran down to what could be the landing point. Vanna held in the brush, but Bucky took down the first one that hit the beach. Vanna and I had seen no guns, so she told the one still standing to lay down right now. She got Bucky off the other; put him haunches down immediately. They were squealing. "We're from the Artificial Island, why are you attacking us? We can get a lawyer for assault."

"Yeah, you get a lawyer. You can get one from the mainland who will sell you right down the river to the drug cartel. Now let me see some identity. If you have any weapon, put it on the sand or your hand will be bleeding into the surf. The identity confirmed them as from the Island. I called Captain Brearly to confirm. Up on your knees. What are you doing over here at sundown?"

"We got bored and decided to have an adventure. "

"You have adventured onto a deadly no trespassing zone. You were one second from getting shot. There are two resorts on this island and if you want to set foot on either, get on the internet and buy a package tour. There is another island, Utila, west of here. It is mainly disgusting but you can visit. Now get your boat and get away. Where is that boat from?"

"We borrowed it from the animation office on the Neighborhood Island."

"I'll check that out. The last boat of this size came to attack and burn this resort. They were dispatched.

Looking up, shuddering, the 'adventurers' saw rifles with scopes focused on them from the nearest ramp boat, three on the path in the briars, one on the upper deck of the bar, a tripod on the tower.

"We are extremely sensitive. You are lucky!"

CHAPTER FORTY-TWO

The Sambo Traitor

In our emotional interlude we smiled certain how warm a welcome Rayban had received. Roberto was gone on the mainland getting Bucky advanced lessons. I rolled over face-to-face. Devine every time!

We had to do four more fake trips before Rayban's team located the traitor. Zulinda smilingly provided lodgings and breakfasts. Vanna kept me well entertained, under her finger (s), occasionally letting me go as far as the drone on our tower.

Rayban's culture was different from the others on the mainland. They had techniques that I was unaware of. However, the end result: the traitor was not seen again. We did another fake trip and there was no launch. Communication would be down for a while. Rayban said that remorse was an important element of their cultural response. The boy showed none. His family had no financial need.

A month of three trips north had no attacks. Octavio told me that another neighbor boy was seen on the sly with a thug. When the thug left, one of the mothers who had witnessed the event, took the boy and thrashed him severely and having his attention, explained the whole illegal situation. Octavio was an icon hero to the boy and realizing he could be putting him in danger, he broke down crying. None of this happened behind doors;

this kind of information quietly, but quickly, spread throughout the community.

I was trying to decide a safe time to re-set my contracts in Germany, specifically in Frankfurt. With the setbacks we had dealt to the drug lords, I was anticipating another attack of some kind at any time. I stayed. I also pursued additional security. I had to pursue back-channels via Roberto. While Songbird had been supportive beyond their mandate, it couldn't continue to be expanded. I knew of trouble from a Senator from the south confidently pocketing "campaign donations" in Lempiras, currency of the 'Lords". His whole party would have to be voted out of office before I could be safe. I needed that technology of back-up and now, I needed it from Germany.

It was dangerous to pursue this in the corrupt business 'failed gun control' and government atmosphere in the U.S. This train wreck president was surrounded by ass lickers that could directly hurt my career, future, and life.

I contacted Greg in Munich on encrypted technology media. No hackers had developed ways of beating that yet. Within 24 hours, Greg had located the drone system I would need along with the apps that evolved it from defensive to pro-active. It would come via Roberto temporarily in San Pedro Sula. He could access it from cargo since veterinarian Alicia wasn't closely monitored by the cartel. Bucky was completing his training. He would transport it hidden in the shrimp boat which would be bringing Bucky back. With help from Carl from banana research I should have it up by the weekend.

Up on our island tower with alarmingly powered green lasers, we tried another 'feint' fish run to Gulfport. Rayban stopped and hid with Zulinda. Once again, I was removed by Vanna from Uncladbeach.com and thrashed into rapture in our little cabin.

As I was caressing her, I reflected that a little jealousy was providing some hot results. She was now leaning down very close, firm pinky to chest and using me to send her off to shriek-land. This position giving her control of my chest, and, well, my triumph, was taking us together into ecstasy.

Two hours before sunrise, I checked radar for any launch from Drug Island. Rayban had used another source to plant a fake trip. As he calculated, the false information got to Don J. Mondo. I launched my drone and targeted its infrared. We located the wake. I called Songbird.

"Songbird, this is aerial Birdcage. We have a wake leaving Drug Island in the direction Rayban usually takes. They will find nothing tonight as Ray is being hosted by Zulinda. I don't want to interrupt any of his activities, so could you confirm the Drug Island launch, over? I will power down and switch to land based radar. I'll maintain ground radar monitor until two hours before sunrise. Perhaps we could meet for dinner again and delineate ways to keep us from interrupting each other or running into each other. Over."

"Laudable, you're keeping Rayban's engines from cooling. I suspect Zulinda makes you redundant. Congress is cuckolding so many sycophants, our activities should be lost in the corrupt ether."

" Birdcage, we'll be glad to have lunch. Don't worry about any in-sky collision. Military grade drones fly up to 10,000 feet, way beyond what your bird could access. We could review "defensive maneuvers" which we have unofficially monitored before. Frankly, after the destruction wracked by the 'Unknown Islands Revenge' person or group, we anticipate terror at any time. If you feel you are a target, harden your defenses soon. Out."

"We've got tripwire, surface alarm, CCTV, Drone defense and offense, and Bucky. We are low on assault weapons which we know they use. We need two more noise-suppressed rifles, 300 Weatherby. We may store but avoid using RPG and hand-grenades. We should at least mention the situation to Zulinda. Out."

" Starr group, go to camp radio."

"Vanna, could you dress, or undress as needed and go over this with Zulinda?" I don't want to come back hog-tied by you tonight. I have to set the drone for monitoring radar if our ground unit powers down."

"Roberto, could you get the rifles and ammunition, both regular and tracer. One set of infra-red goggles would be good, too, although we have it on two of our sniper rifles."

"Ladies and gentlemen, this assault of theirs will start either early morning, or late evening. What they are preparing bodes an attack in two or three days. They will be forced to come by boat and will want to use sunrise or sunset to camouflage their movements. Keep them off shore for as long as possible. Start with rifles with regular ammo. Second clip should be tracers. Don't doubt for a second, they are here to kill us. You cannot hesitate." If they have a new Don J. Mondo, take him out immediately. There is no iota of a chance anyone will take him to trial."

"I will go down and see what the boat captains are willing or able to do."

I had been dreaming of some draught German beer and providing some lovely carved ceilings for Vanna to ponder as I was pondering her. But I was feeling it in the breeze and in my bones. The destructive forces were forming. Railroad Juan was restive, anticipating. I had not taken any dive groups for that month.

CHAPTER FORTY-THREE

Major Attack, Vanna Hurt

Roberto, Vanna and I had agreed that if this raid took place, and if we survived, we needed to take the fighting to them. Roberto had bought the shrimp fields and in closing received maps of all the lot lines on the island including the large fort. I flew the drone over at altitude and located the room large enough to hold armaments and ammunition.

Vanna said, "We are dealing with a large group of greedy bastards, and we can't go in there and expect with our small numbers we can neutralize them. I can devise explosive charges that will equalize our chances. These should combine with what they have in there and bring that part of the castle down. The drone is powerful enough to take what we need in two trips. If the time comes and we see them moving our way to attack, we send the first drone load as they are leaving the shore. Lance, I assume you can deliver the load right on target. The second load must go immediately so you can get the drone back to support the battle.

Songbird had sensed it first. Bucky began growling patrolling the beaches. Roberto, this time, had been jogging in place, so to speak, at Zulinda's. I called him back and told her to prepare whatever she had. Rayban was heading home for the evening after collecting "$2000" for the day. He reversed at full plane. Distances involved put him in Zulinda's cove with minutes to spare. I went down and recruited the boat captains. They got suppressed-fire rifles from the boats. They had been wearing pistols on their belts for a week now.

I went through the thickets and thorns to the top of the hill between the resorts. I sent the drone to surveil. Songbird had called the beginning. They came back concerned that there were seven boats coming mostly manned by three crooks apiece. My drone called five boats headed for the dive resort and two toward Zulinda. Vanna was on the ridge of the hill to the west. Roberto was at the veranda at the top of the resort. I informed Vanna and asked her to forward the information to Zulinda.

"Songbird, they are definitely on their way. Can you begin support? Over."

"Birdcage, staffing change, we can't respond until we confirm they are actually feet down on the island. Over".

"Songbird that will be too little, too late. Turn away. Look somewhere else. Go hunt forest fires or something in the mountains. Brainerd continued to be a pw congress sucker. The guy we needed was in Costa Rica.

I focused the laser green and demolished the gas tank on the first skiff. No noted survivors.

Bucky stormed along his usual patrol path then disappeared in the quickly gathering darkness.

"Rayban, are you in position?"

"I'm anchored at Unclad, all guns on deck".

"Rayban, if you're alone, urgent you repel boarders. Hold for me! I am waiting until the second skiff is 30 meters from shore. Drone is set to green. I will focus on gas tanks. Upon the first detonation, fire at will, fire for effect."

"Zulinda, they will be visible coming around the

point in three minutes. Still two boats and six marauders. I will fire at their controls and tank. Within 45 seconds Rayban will strafe your beach. Get behind your bunker on the west end. Get the others down. If I'm late, start 300 magnum rifle fire. Rayban, immediate support!"

The first invaders were decimated by the boat captains. Roberto hit three from the veranda. Then a flash out of the dark, Bucky went for the throat of the first invader staggering from the burning boat. A scream but the crook was still alive, losing blood. He turned to bring fire on Bucky, was blown backwards by a shot from above. From 100 yards. And died. Vanna turned away.

I joined Roberto and the captains to finish off the five remaining crooks, late off their boats.

"Vanna, sitrep on Zulinda?"

"Some of the crooks have made it to her beach. Rayban has them in a brutal cross fire but there are places to hide. You may need to calm Octavio, he's panicking with every bullet sent to protect Zulinda."

Reluctantly, surprised I had to correct my Seal. "Vanna, this is not the time to calm Rayban. I'll get to him when it's not so dangerous."

Lance To Zulinda, "Zulinda, Vanna is on the briar path. How can she help?"

"Lance, I need her. My clients were warned and are dressed appropriately, two with pistols. That is far from enough"

Zulinda to Vanna, "Vanna, Lance says you are in position. My clients are not dressed. Please move quickly to the small house on the right side of the beach. Vanna, get rid of all your vestments. Fire on anybody who is dressed."

Lance, "Rayban, continue to cover Zulinda and look for marauders with any kind of clothes on. "

"Roberto, Bucky has another late-comer in his sites. Back him up, quickly. I think there are two crooks that have gotten into the trees behind you. Send Bucky out there!

"Rayban, sitrep on Zulinda?"

"All clothed people are dead or debilitated on the beach. Nude ones including Vanna and Zulinda are walking around checking for any dropped firearms. "

Lance to Songbird, "Only one repairable injury. The Don J. Do Mondo is making an escape right now across the airport channel. Now that he has attacked us, can you finally do something? Over."

"Birdcage, our ROE does not permit us to interdict fighters in flight. Sorry, over"

"Who the hell is writing your ROE, Cruze?

"Songbird, turn your congressional corruption-driven drone and your heads away from the field of battle. For the meagerness of your help, you better go again and check the mountains for fires."

"Rayban, strike your sodium gas floodlights and start a recon trip along Zulinda's beach continuing promptly around airport channel and along to our dive pier shore. We need to be sure we have no loiterers lurking with arms. Protect yourself, I think there may be two up in the forests near the path between resorts."

"Roger that."

He made the oval turn around the point and a bullet pinged off his windshield. He looked up the hill and Bucky was wrestling the neck away from the brute who had fired. Roberto in the woods fired and the crook stilled, death rattle audibles through the forest. Then from behind him, Roberto was under fire. He dived to the ground unable to see the shooter. He jumped toward UncladBeach.com and a thicker tree. A bullet missed his ear by a finger. He was wondering if this was going to be the time and the place. He heard a rustle in the thorns and tried to turn. A suppressed 'thwang' bullet went out over his head. Still alive, he looked up the hill and a crook fell sideways from behind a tree, gun-in-hand. Then he didn't. Roberto looked behind thinking he had been hit and was in heaven. Vanna, completely in naked camouflage, lowered her gun and reached to help him up. She scoured and hunted for any scratches on Bucky.

Roberto went on and Vanna went back to Zulinda's. She strode over to the little shack she had cleared earlier. She recovered a knapsack.

Vanna, on camp radio not connected to Songbird, "Lance, where is our target? We can't lose this despicable Don J.? Songbird will not help."

"Vanna, wait 60 seconds. Our ROE is "survival". She hit the button at 58.

The drone ordinance put Don J. Mondo directly under the concrete column of the armory. What was left of him looked similar to Bucky's droppings. The drone came back to me for re-armament. If any, there would be limited communication with Songbird. Somewhere I couldn't locate, there was a Senator "on the take." You could get two lempiras for a dollar, so it was worth the subterfuge.

CHAPTER FORTY-FOUR

Vanna's Wounded!

Roberto, in the blur of Vanna's beauty, had seen some blood on her shoulder and back. He followed her to Zulinda's beach and saw her set off the armory explosion. Bye, Donny J!

Roberto: "Vanna, you're injured! Lance, Vanna is bleeding in two places, not heavily but Rayban, can you bring the first aid kit. Vanna. Sit down!

In the background of Roberto's radio call I heard her chewing him out for bothering. "It's no big deal!"

I agreed with Roberto, Vanna bleeding was a big deal. I grabbed the remote drone control and flew through trees and barbs. When I got there, the screen showed Zulinda gently lowering Vanna's glorious front face down on a towel. Rayban was coasting up on the sand jumping off with the military first aid kit.

Zulinda assertively said, "I've got this Lance, float down, relax. Vanna, lay still. Rayban, give me the local anesthetic, antibiotic and the butterfly Band-Aids. Vanna, this will hurt for a few seconds until I get the local anesthetic applied. Vanna was still tense even after the cream was in place. She could see my face hovering by her side when she turned her neck to her left. I was watching my facial expression on the drone screen or she could see my worry. There was a three-inch laceration on the upper left side of her back. I could see it was not deep, but I struggled to hide my worry about the amount of blood. Perhaps the butterfly Band-Aids, several, would keep it together. Zulinda cleaned the wound; applied the antibiotic. Girls knowing girls, she told Vanna that it would heal with no scar. Vanna was still tense.

I looked and on the towel in two places there were more splotches of blood. We would have to get at the injuries but now couldn't have her lay on her back. Zulinda gently helped her to sit up on the log. On her left shoulder and for an inch under her arm, was another laceration, this one also not too deep. Three regular Band-Aids and antibiotic would serve. Hidden under the fold of her left breast was another instance of blood. Zulinda gently raised the nipple so she could see. At first glance it looked like the entrance wound of a bullet. We had to ask.

Vanna said, "I thought so, too, but I sensed and applied pressure. I felt no metal in the wound. As I was stripping and running to the beach, I tripped on a log and fell flat on my face. I think my uncovered breast hit on a piece of shale which temporarily embedded itself in the wound. When I jumped up to start running again, it dropped off."

The wound was not deep, but Zulinda cleaned it carefully and applied some antibiotic. Again, she specified, "No Scar." However, we were out of butterfly Band-Aids. A minute later, Mickey Mouse was peering out from under her breast. She couldn't see that and nobody was in the mood of laughing out-loud. We had the distasteful task of removing and hiding 13 bodies.

Bucky was sure of all the locations so we affixed them on 13 ropes to the transom rail of Ray's boat. We towed them to avoid getting any blood on his deck. Critical: leave no evidence. Went out to the 150+ foot depths, wired rifles and American pistols to their owners, and committed them to Davy Jones locker. Finally, we policed both resorts for incriminating evidence.

We sent Rayban back to his work. He now kept the rifles in his boat. I ministered faithfully to Vanna's wounds, certainly more pleasure for me than for her. Finally, she pushed me on my back, and in my view, Mickey Mouse was no longer there.

CHAPTER FORTY-FIVE

The Meshkitia, Floating Island Suburb

We took a four-day run down to Trujillo at the east end of the country and a few miles north of the Meshkitia province. The Meshkitia is essentially a swamp. Some gringos set out to fish there but were driven back by mosquitos. Some unusual primitive art comes out of there being sold in the bigger town on the north coast.

The reason to go to Trujillo is the healing of wide white sand beaches and the mild winds coming in off the Atlantic. Specifically, it is the place for a novice wind surfer to develop his or her skills. I grew too tall too late and balance has never been my strong suite, even on water skis. I had purchased a surfer which I learned the hard way was too long and heavy for me. I took it out and fought to keep my balance and let the wind carry me along. Vanna in her typical Uncladbeach.com bikini lounged on the shore chuckling. She was in an unspoken, continuous competition with Zulinda who would be around, but not often. Too much trying to get up, I concluded it was the wrong surfer for me. I took it over and put up with the constructive criticism with laughter from Vanna.

"Ok, you go and see if you can do any better." She pulled it over to the surf line, standing up already, moved it out two meters so the balance fin under the board was off the bottom, jumped up, settled the boom for her height, and went out for thirty minutes never falling. She didn't grow too fast for her balance.

"Your scuba, handle boats, blow them up, nurse, and are a crack shot. Where did you learn to wind surf?"

"Right here. I watched what you were doing and realized the changes needed, picked them up along your way. Changed them."

We went back to the lightly populated hotel and I demonstrated some of the skills I had picked up along the way. Any amount of noise was ignored by the guests and thrilled at by me.

We wandered over to the stand-alone local's restaurant "shack". It was one of those that look not too good, but the food is a knock-out. We sat outside on the beach chair and added a cold Salva Vida beer.

All day we had been concentrating on the wind, the sail, and the surf. We succeeded in repressing our cartel worries. At the restaurant our eyes wandered further around. There was a narrow channel at the end of the peninsula. Something out of alien comic book rumbled in. Off to the right of that channel was a small island or homestead. Walking around for a different perspective, we found huge metal ramps stowed above surf line. We went back to the chef of our restaurant who gave us the full explanation.

It was technically an island, but one the size of a good size suburban neighborhood. The chef said the captain of the moving behemoth had stopped in for meals a few times asking questions about where he could moor his monster and have a mooring that could support a bridge so residents could drive their cars off for day trips, shopping, or tours. The people in the Mesqitia province had voted down the idea of having it parked there. The chef knew about the Starr Dive Resort and he knew of the Bay Islands as well. He also knew well the inroads the drug cartels had built there. I asked if he had a phone number from the "island". He did.

Vanna and I went back to the beach chairs in front of our hotel. She still had that Unclad.com bikini. With the excuse of an evening wind coming in cold, I hurriedly escorted her into the room and back up against the door. She kissed me hungrily and eased herself right down. There are some very alluring activities that can be done from this position, but I carried her still joined back to the bed. She stayed on top, used me according to her desires. I was happy to be the "boy toy. Her wounds were healing nicely. I could now get myself back to lucidity and talk about what I had pondered.

We lay observing the rustic ceiling with the fan washing over us. It was that temporary time bubble when inhibitions fade and we give voice to emotions and seldom spoken dreams, sometimes a gentle kiss or two. Always the truth. We have to watch the energy buildup of these kisses or experience a double-bubble.

"Vanna, that's the first time I saw that island. I had read about it and Roberto mentioned something about it in passing. I didn't internalize anything about it until I saw it today. I got the phone number and think we should call the captain, introduce ourselves and get together and welcome them to the country.

Vanna muses, "Fine with me, but that wind surfing wore me out. Come over and wrap me up."

CHAPTER FORTY-SIX

Floating Suburbia

I got on the internet and found several such populated mobile, islands, many in Asia, at least two in the Caribbean; some being built in The Netherlands.

I called and introduced us and the resort. The captain sounded bored and was happy to invite us to lunch. We walked over the metal bridges and a sailor guided us six blocks into the neighborhood where the wheel houses, captain's dining room and his bedroom were located. He was in a beach chair in the shade of the bridge. He was, except for a pipe, the mountain of a man you would welcome to be your captain. He was a no-nonsense guy with a large round face on six feet five-inch body. Huge hands with rough, sea-claimed skin; receding hairline but always a mariner' cap. He was piloting not a ship but a neighborhood for a large corporation so his dress was crisp and proper. The eyes could give him away. The black pupils could go grey and sparkle if the situation was humorous. Solid black and glaring if things were going wrong. Vanna immediately brought the sparkle.

Although the resort was 1/30th the size of the "neighborhood", we were both captains with similar responsibilities. Lots to share. One important part of that was the drug spider legs crawling most places. The other was where the neighborhood could come to rest, for a long time. I described the possible location where a mooring could be renovated for vehicle traffic on and off. The main drug Island, Roaban had a runway long enough for big jets. People who could afford to have a home on this seaworthy land mass could easily have at least a small private jet, or a big one. The north shore was wide enough for several mooring/ bridges. There were some decent restaurants on the Drug Island, but heavily under the thumb of the drug lords. A very short plane hop or catamaran to the mainland offered other bars and eateries. The Copan ruins were a comfortable one night overnight stay away.

I met with Roberto who owned the shrimp farm and whose father had some contacts in the government and made the introductions for Captain Brearly.

There was the expected 'bar fight' from the drug cartels. The bottom line was that the "island" would have to pay inordinate taxes, clearly obvious bribes. The next to bottom line was that this world-huge corporation was of a higher stance than even a joint group of cartels could threaten. With their own renowned lawyers and aggressive security, the taxes were brought into line. Felipe, Rayban's lawyer, hidden in the background, gave valuable consultation on the state of the failing government. There was animus in the cartels.

Upon the 'Artificial Island's slow, inertia-controlled arrival at the drug island, Vanna and I invited the captain for dinner at the resort. I had spoken with him several times as the legal wrangling went on. We had met for drinks and dinner in the bigger town of Cuenca. Now he would see the resort and get an earful of the brutal attacks and blockage we and other businesses had been experiencing. From him we did not hide much, including size of decimated forces. We also highlighted the huge building/fort he would be moored nearby. It was the pimp-Lago of the high Don J. Do Mondo. Brealy listened, not showing much concern. We would soon learn why.

One pleasant side of the dinner was the surprise that

a lovely young lady, darkly tanned, from the region, hopped out of their arrival boat. It's pretty clear that many of the big boned conquistadores had inserted some of their DNA into the population. The hair had remained black, but thick and shiny. The eyes also were brown, but with golden speckles that communicated mirth. The obvious trait surviving was the presentation of the breasts. Norwegian for sure. Long legs and excellent command of English: Maria Fernando Cardenas Brearly.

Three weeks after the arrival and mooring, all the rich and famous friends and family of the island dwellers flew in and attended a monumental gala dinner and dance. Dressed to the nines, the humidity soon corrected that mistake, but there was powerful A/C in the essential places. Planes arrived Friday and Saturday freshening up/some snorkeling hosted by Vanna and I, and the ball Saturday night. People slept in on Sunday, guests leaving in the afternoon. Planes jockeying for line up on the tarmac gone by 6 p.m.

Monday morning the first bomb went off on the ramp leading to shore. The captain called me to consult. Against my better judgement, he decided to brush it off and ignore. The bomb was not professional nor very damaging, quickly repaired. The following Sunday late morning, the second bomb went off leaving a scratch on the heavy boiler plate on the front hull near the water. The captain's wife, Maria, called and urged us to avoid using our drone on Thursday night. No explanation.

CHAPTER FORTY-SEVEN

The Explanation: Black Uniformed Swat

We did use our drone to surveil Black Bird Tuesday and Wednesday. We saw his black drone above us watching, watching. We powered down when we went to bed Thursday. Bucky was on alert doing his rounds. At three in the morning, we heard the thump, thump of helicopter rotors. Vanna, always alert, waked me. We hurried up to our veranda on the top of the resort with binoculars. On the castle, East and West side, were two helicopters; guys with black clothes and helmets. They went inside the Don J's Mondo fort/brothel; we no longer could see other than a shape occasionally. We began to hear explosions which flashed out the windows. They traveled around the decks and gun shots rang out. A moment later, six of the SWAT types stepped out of a door of the east side of the fort. It was no longer time for a flash-bang. Two heavy metal grenades into the room.

Vanna narrated play by play of this causing me to wonder again about her past. No more rifle fire from there. On the distant side of the now decimated structure, two more shots were heard. Two double taps responded. Some barked orders and yelling civilian-style rang across the water. The SWAT people boarded the helicopters and left. My airport sea radio had registered no request to land nor take off. Bucky had been leaping around barking excitedly; he couldn't control himself. He couldn't tell if SWAT was friend or foe.

Speculating, we went back to bed. Actually, Vanna knew, wasn't speculating at all. Bucky had to sleep with us.

CHAPTER FORTY-EIGHT

The Clean-Up and Deadly Warning

At 6:30 a.m., Maria called again and woke us up. "We are sending a boat for you. Would you please come over now? You heard the noise last night." I looked down at our dock and Captain Brearly was on their security boat with one other armed "Island security" guy. I waved and hurried down, first asking if Vanna wanted to go. She wanted to sleep in, "been there, done that. I know what happened. Two much interruption last night."

Brearly didn't want to talk much at all in the boat. We went immediately up to the bridge. We found three security guards, and two pirates. One was the Don J. Mondo. He was obvious of mouth and dress. Huge khaki shorts on a bigger butt.

The captain addressed the lackey. "You have a chance to live tonight, maybe longer if you take me seriously. You go back to whatever Davy Jones candidate is out-ranking Don J. Mondo here, and inform him of everything that happened tonight. Tell him I can call that in at any point I feel it is necessary. If I should be hurt or killed, there are two other officers who will do the exact same thing. He may have a billion-dollar illegal drug business, but he has locked horns with a trillion-dollar real estate business. This group of nameless-faceless owners will literally crush anyone interfering with its success. If you are ever seen in this area again, we will assume you are an enemy combatant. I recommend you go to the mainland and get a legal job.

At that, Don J. Mondo blurted out, "You will not do that. If you persist in this, I will bring down such a fantastic, fantastic force of attack, if you live you will have nightmares for the rest of your life."

Brearly dangerously growled, "If you leave here, you will bring back "Hell's Attack. Is that right, real fantastic, and I quote you, fantastic destruction?"

"That is fucking right. You will not know where nor when it is coming."

"Will you be coming with it?"

"I will be fucking leading it."

"Probably a thinking man should try to mitigate effect of that attack early on. I can immediately reduce the coming leadership by one."

Brearly turned so Mondo was in front of his lackey. He brought his pistol up, black in his eyes, and shot him in the head, the blood and bones splattering the lackey.

Looking at the lackey, the captain said, "You can tell your 'sleeping Donny J., or whatever, that, too."

He nonchalantly walked back into his office. We ignored the janitors cleaning up the mess. He asked me a few details about my counter attacks, offered coffee. Maria brought the coffee and stayed. There was a lot more here than a coffee server or North Coast Bed Warmer. Later, I informed Vanna.

They both walked me back down to the security boat. Maria got on the boat next to the driver. She had a 300 Weatherby on her hip.

I waited to leave for Germany for two weeks. No peeps from anywhere. I would be relaxed in Frankfurt. There was a new sheriff in town.

CHAPTER FORTY-NINE

Germany, Another Reprise

We flew vagabond's choice, visited the airports of New York, Toronto, Ireland and Munich before landing in Frankfurt. Thank goodness for free airline drinks. Vanna wouldn't ask that again. By the time I had the pleasure of seeing her complete Venus, both the wounds under her breast and under her arm were pink traces. The deeper one on her arm was still red, but not infected red. We called Greg and alerted him we were in-country and would come to see them someday.

Vanna remembered her large shopping venues. In one month, I had four serious Mercedes concentration evenings. Any wounds were long forgotten although we didn't move from the room, mostly the bed, for four complete days in the new time zone.

CHAPTER FIFTY

Vanna's Mysterious History

After that heavy month, we ran down to Munich to catch up with Greg and Cheryl. Friday night heavy with beer and pork, we brought them up to date.

I had forgotten to have the big conversation with Vanna about the experiences or training that led her to be so multi-talented. I thought it might be nice for Greg and Cheryl to know. They were my family here and Vanna and I were seriously sweet on each other. The conversation started, as always, with limited answers to general questions.

I complained. She relented.

"After boot camp, and serving four years in the Navy, I got an undergraduate degree on the VA plan in Biology with Anatomy as the required minor. I got the license as a Nurse's Assistant. For eight months I worked in the medical ward on a large battleship. Absences and illness on the part of some doctors required me to perform duties above my normal training with grueling, sometimes panic-stricken hours of over-time.

"I registered to enter medical school, but could not face another five years of theory. From my experience aboard ship, I realized the rank and file treated doctors as their pawns. Without any choices given, they were sent around the world. Their life was arbitrarily limited by the next echelon of administration. I had intense training and experience but didn't want that external control."

"Application to the Navy Seals became available to women. I was accepted into a new more demanding form of boot camp. I faced the harsh treatment women were getting for entering a field that had been only male. I fought back and pushed over any obstacles put in my way. Of a group of 100 candidates, I was one of four selected. I joined a group of five men and specialized training ensued. I trained in scuba and extensively in both land and under-water demolitions. I labored on the pistol range. I joined in several dangerous overseas missions. Part of the training was in the new technology of drone warfare. Having played computer games incessantly, I enjoyed and surpassed minimum capabilities. Advanced knowledge of jeep and car repair is required of every Seal. I served four years, but although beholden for my training, I burned out on the death and destruction. I can't get away from it completely, but here I personally see the evil."

"I came to Central America with a Scuba Club, met Lance; here I am. Does that that answer your questions? Oh, I also trained on small and marine engines, gas and diesel."

"Wow, Vanna that is amazing. I can work more effectively and safely with you."

Vanna retorts, "As of now, Lance, you're not under-using me. I have some uncomfortable thoughts about removing those thugs, but from what I see of their savagery, there is not a correctional facility that could touch them. Even if there were an actual legal system."

"We should head home?" All computer script for Mercedes apps up to date and employees re-trained, we headed back to the warmth of Central America.

Compared to the third-grade teacher from the Frankfurt base elementary school, Vanna was frivolous in returning. Roberto had been in the usual bi-weekly skype contact and things were better than ever to see.

CHAPTER FIFTY-ONE

Caribbean Return

The captain of the "Island" became a good neighbor. His wife, Maria, didn't dress as risqué as Zulinda so Vanna was quick to warm up to her. I reflected for a moment on the strikingly beautiful women associated with Greg, Roberto, Me, and Brearly. They were breathtaking. We were definitely above middle class in finances. Are we unknowingly living the decadent lives of congress and the president's temporary trophy wives? Those interludes with Vanna debunk anything we might think of her, compared to the president's present trophy. Ours have advanced degrees in difficult fields. No, we're well above that swamp, now desecrated to a chess pool.

Brearly did take an unreported walk over to Unclad. com to meet the owner and establish amiable relations. Maria got a big surprise when he returned.

Roberto had increased dive groups, which certainly was good. There were still some snipping aggressive irritating actions from the cartel who hadn't replaced Alicia's father-I-law, deceased menace. Brearly brought me up to date. A bomb was placed in the water offshore of my beach on the airport side of the resort. No damage, it could have destroyed my future in one fell swoop. I went livid to Brearly. He said, "We're having some problems as well. We cleaned out that fort when you were here before. The problem is centered in the large apartment block south of it. Give me a night to ponder and get some home-office feedback."

I returned to the resort and surveyed all the intruder devices. I even checked Bucky's health. Having a protection device out in the water 30 meters from shore or pier was not feasible.

Vanna was bright and recovered from jet lag. I told her about the problem and that I had shared with Brearly. She wasn't letting anything dampen her returning spirits. "Fine, Lance, you've done what you can tonight. We'll get some news from the captain tomorrow. If you need to worry about it, you can start then. Let's go up to the veranda, share a champagne, and celebrate my shopping. I have some things for you that we may need to open later.

The things she got for me were really for her to wear. She'd have them on for 20 seconds.

The things for me were underwear more suited for German winter. Some pieces were designed not to block my frequent targeting exits. These would not hinder her access to whatever she wanted. A little champagne and frivolous enjoyment of anything in a bed where we sleep unclothed. I found her and she found me and I forgot all about the drug thugs.

The captain called and requested we meet in my cabana. Vanna was there and listened in. The corporation had added up cost of vandalism repair. It crossed their limits by too much and they said either he would fix it or they would. That is not really a "choice" statement so he told me to take down my drone again at midnight, Wednesday. He said he had many pieces of Intel tracing the repeated damage to that block building. The building was only thirty yards from Roberto's shrimp offices.

CHAPTER FIFTY-TWO

Black Security Returns

Vanna and I had several love meetings during the days in advance. In our relaxed emotional bubble after joy, we discussed the ramifications of the impending defense response. As much as I respected her concern for people, I had seen too much lawless damage done by these radicalized thugs, whole families' frequently. Without any uncorrupted legal system, there was no intermediate method to stymie this.

We put the drone down at bed-time and wrapped each other up to try to sleep and avoid the blasts that would surely ensue. We put Bucky directly into bed with us.

I went over the next morning to see what needed be done. Vanna didn't want to go. Somberly Brearly said, "Lance, It's a disaster. The building was full of armed resistance. Rocket propelled grenades, 55 mm machine guns, and bullet proof vests. They are gone and our SWAT cleaned up somewhat but we need your ramp dive boats to transport the remainders."

I called both boat captains and with the help of a dozen security guards, we weighted and sent the bodies out to the 200+ feet hole, this time a mile west of the previous. It was not discussed again.

CHAPTER FIFTY-THREE

R&R

The remainder of the winter season was the finest we had had in several years. The drug thugs had lost a great number of their attack boats and personnel, as well. The "Island Captain" had sent some gruesome messages about bothering his clientele. The bloodbath of the apartment block was one, and sent a shock through the community. Some cheered, but many were disappointed that their country had become so lawless that these revenges were the only push-back to crime.

We garaged the drone; the Artificial Island had their own to share if needed. I locked up the pistols and rifles leaving one rifle to each captain. Rayban had gone to Trumpland and traded a Weatherby for an assault rifle. Zulinda had some armory that I wasn't even aware of. She had been dealing with constant harassment six years before I had even started construction.

We flew the most direct flights to Frankfurt and went to ground at my apartment there. We took some side trips beer and white wine tasking. She went jovially clothes shopping and I napped. One weekend day, we drove out into the countryside and found a huge circus tent set up in a field. The parking lot was full so something interesting must be going on. We bought tickets at the tent flap and were directed to benches without backs. Our beer order was taken and then we waited. Eventually a waitress appeared with plates of steak, potatoes and the piece de resistance, asparagus. It was all you could eat, so I headed straight for the mattress when we returned. Vanna went shopping.

CHAPTER FIFTY-FOUR

Inappropriate Behavior

Two weeks later we went down on a Friday night. It was the most raucous I had ever seen Cheryl and Greg at a party. In their front room Cheryl had put out enough food for two dinners. Cases of beer cooled in the basement. Digestives lined the wall above the TV. They had other guests, one out of military and the other, Denise, salt of the earth well experienced in dealing with buzzed military fellows. Raucous in their languages, Vanna was embarrassed by the crudity when sex came up. They were ill informed. She tried to tolerate it with some Aqua Vit but we left early via Lyft to Frankfurt.

The flight to Miami was late, as typical, so we missed the connector to the island. We stayed the night in Cuenca in the better hotel on the outskirts. A delight awaited us on the island.

CHAPTER FIFTY-FIVE

Surprise Visitor

Back on the island for two days we arranged and cooperated with Roberto to get him back to farming shrimp with a vengeance. He wanted to take us over to his operation 'to see what he had' perhaps created, an unexplained twinkle.

We unbalanced my way out of the dingy and looked up near his house. A woman in a modest bikini was rocking on the porch. Roberto took Vanna's hand and walked her up the hill with me following. At first sight I thought it was Zulinda and they were going to be married. She wasn't naked. Closer, it wasn't Zulinda, 6" 5', but a match with blazing green eyes. I didn't know her at all.

"Roberto?" I was frozen expecting another jealous strapping back at the cabana if I looked astray. I think he took Vanna first so she wouldn't notice any 'discomfort' on my part. I'll admit nothing. "Roberto, who is your friend?" She moved over to him leaving no doubt as to whom she was claiming here.

Roberto started, "Lance, you know her but have never met her. Vanna, I have never talked about her during the time you have been here. I'll let her fill you in some day when you have time. Any guesses, Lance?" Hint: one only, she is Peruvian."

"Oh, you told me a saga years ago, about a pale lady from Kathmandu, but I forget the name, oh, is it Cindy?

"Yes, it is, Lance, but I am no longer the 'white lady'. Roberto's caring put that behind. On the island here, I am now the bronze lady. My English is also better due to Roberto's motivational skills. For any official purposes, I am Cynthia Maria Espinosa Martinez and now Fernandez, Cindy.

I'll quickly bring you up to date from the time Roberto and I lost and met each other. It was in Madrid after my illness from Nepal. Roberto took my care personally and nursed me back to pink/health. I was working in a software scripting company. That was my only lifeline and I had to stay when Roberto came back to his farm. Six months later he came back to see me. After one afternoon, we knew that together we must be. I resigned, took him to Peru to meet my family. We married and here we are."

"Roberto, with knowledge that you have an extra bedroom, I think we should stay tonight. I'm overwhelmed, and so proud of you Cindy, even though I've never personally met you."

Roberto had handled the introductions so deftly that Vanna had no qualms about staying. As usual, the women retired to their allotted corner of the porch. Watching their non-verbal communication did Roberto's and my hearts good.

The following day with our next joint adventure scheduled, we had a drink with Captain Brearly. He was bored again and anxious to get some U.S. mainland time with his honey. I was expecting her to be plumping up in the front anytime, but maybe they thought they were too old to deal with teenagers in 13 years. Maybe they didn't want to put her body through such difficult stresses, and the huge lumbering leading up to them.

Vanna and I were taking the dive boats out, giving the boat captains some relief. We soon worked off the good German pork. Four weeks we took ten daytime dives and a night once per week. We were exhausted from the intensity. Something could go wrong with a novice diver's B.C. trying to level off. This resort had never lost a client and that was the minimum reputation I intended to maintain. Some sleeping drug thugs did not agree. We would see some them in the distance probably causing somebody somewhere some frustration. The good captain evidently set his limits. These mini-pirates looked like products of long-time inter-marriages. Darker brown than an Afro-American with never combed scrawny braided salted hair. Sometimes an albino spot. Every chin pointed and ready to spew filthy anger.

The pressure had lessened for Roberto. Together, he and Cindy could be found out propagating shrimp. We had them for dinner or vice versa every two weeks. We learned of the famous 'Ceviche' of Peru: white-fish cooked by acidic lime juice.

Vanna gave a giggling un-stripper as she dressed. Already in competition with Cindy. I resisted and she left the cabana with Bucky to search for any items that might have come back on the bodies or firearms from the skirmish Brearly had while we were gone, items that would implicate us in any of the incidents. We had cleaned Rayban's boat the night before.

Vanna and I got into our 'night-hug" formation. We didn't wake until 10. Both dive boats were out. We went to sleep till noon. I had my own unique breakfast and we went hungrily to 'lunch'. I noticed that Bucky was not around, but figured he was on patrol after the fire fight the previous morning. Or maybe taking a well-deserved nap.

CHAPTER FIFTY-SIX

Smoke-Eaters: Fran's Boys

Fran mused, "When you are around these firemen as a group, you lump them together. You see them as one entity, not individuals. They have memorized each other's every move. A well-oiled machine! They have some things in common as most firemen must. Drenched in testosterone, if you focus on one at a time, you are struck by their abs and their rippling shoulders. That explains why they hit so many home runs on my 'Fran's Pizza Team'.

CHAPTER FIFTY-SEVEN

Fran's Phantom

I felt the soft crush on both my thighs as firm unwavering lips kissed up into a slippery of smooth damp. Then they were gone. The stalkers adoring my toned flesh softened and curled toward my thigh gap flowing on the warm film of my outer lips. The sensation of exposure did not alarm me. The sensitivity flowed further up and around my pulsing center gliding across my midriff to the base of my breasts. It coursed in circles around the buxom mounds. Roaming up the sides of each, it caused the nipples to shrink into hiding. A continued coaxing brought them back. Exploration returned its lower advance across the midriff to the pulsing heat of my sunflower. The feeling of capture by some unknown force excited me and I involuntarily began to sail to joy.

I sat up, with a start and a cry. I felt the bed. I felt no-one next to me. I was not lucid. I was in full arousal. With vibrating hand, I swiped the dampness controlling my heat, my hunger, forcing it to my right. I crashed in delight; tension dissipated. I fell back, head to pillow.

I woke up, in consternation. It was the "O". I died the glorious little death. Oh, sweet stars, but who was involved? Through my bleary eyes I looked and felt for a man in my bed. Widowed young, not a frequent but possible event. I saw a face there, but reached, finding nothing, just a memory, or a pre-cognition? There was no-one, only a face and an unusual twist of covers and pillows. I called out and got no answer. I got up to check the rooms in the apartment and found no sign of anyone nor anything. I sat again on the bed, wondering. I organized the pillows and sheets and saw some unexpected wrinkles and patterns in them. Taken close to me I decided they were the cause. Something in my mind wasn't satisfied. Another streaming flash of face. With more mundane dreams, I finished my night. The next morning, I hadn't forgotten the dream that had taken me all the way all alone. What did it portend?

I was up at 5:30 a.m. to get to my restaurant, Fran's Pizza, and deal with the inventory and tax forms. Few people were hungry for a pizza at that time of day, so I had few interruptions, except my visions flashing a dazzling phantom.

On a beer motivated unanimous decision by my men, I chartered a bus into the resorts on Key Largo and on to a Caribbean Scuba Resort. There were some inner agreements among these hotels due to the nature of tourists coming and going to the area. We occupied rooms in three different resorts. Spring break was bursting out all over and there were lots of scantily-clad co-eds cutting strays out of my pack. I couldn't help but feel jealous that my days of being the scantily clad co-ed were probably over. I was still young enough to have a baby, or two. I had some very delectable firemen and expected they would be keeping 'hands occupied', stress-free. When they were not down 30-40 feet keeping 'hands off' gorgeous coral fields flowing into the distance, that is.

I rented an 18-horse aluminum boat with two of the guys and about killed us all. I hit a reef with a propeller and broke the shear pin. We were swaying and rolling with a gentle sea, my Mexican-American fire fighter green and hanging over the railing. I saw in a first aid kit a spare shear pin. No Dramamine! I jumped into the moving currents of the reef and tried to pull the old pin out, remove the bolt to the drive shaft, bend the cotter key, inset the new pin and secure it down. I got as far as removing the bolt. Attempting to insert the new pin, a wave hit me and the new shear pin dissolved into the reef. Pins gone, no other boats in our area, out two miles into the Atlantic Ocean. No cell phones. No way would you ever find a pin like that in the reef.

Reluctantly I moved to get up into the boat, nervous about my approaching sea-sickness. Not looking anywhere in particular other than to the center folds of the craft, I gazed and there, God or Allah or somebody had dropped another shear pin into the crevice. Easing myself back down to the reef, with spider fingers I grasped that pin and in the fear of nervousness, moved it as slow as a tug into the spherical opening. In short, saved, back on Largo, we got on our knees and kissed the earth. I never got to dive in John Penne camp Underwater State Park. But Guanaja was still ahead.

Heading back to Miami airport to fly on to San Pedro Sula and Guanaja, we were thankful for our green, now brown again Mexican-American fire fighter. With his Mexican Spanish and eye-watering girls checking out his exterior environs, we moved right through. I took the opportunity to call Vanna in the camp and review Lily's special care. Vanna sounded winded and seriously tense. We would get to the island in 4-6 hours. Maybe.... after Miami and two other airports.

Having only seen a small picture of Lily, seeing the whole package, Vanna would realize chaperoning would take precedence over training. Although Lily had practiced in a shallow lake, chaperoning did in fact soon become the norm.

CHAPTER FIFTY-EIGHT

Dreaded Attack

I was dreaming of some draught German beer and providing some lovely carved ceilings for Vanna to ponder as I pondered her. I was feeling it in the breeze and in my bones. The catastrophe of having an attack at the same time as hosting a group loomed. The destructive forces were forming. Juan Railroad had checked in with eye-witness facts. Anticipating, I had taken only one dive group for that month, Mukwonago. For the first time ever, on the second night before the Mukwonago group would arrive, I got an urgent radio call from Brealey, the captain of the Artificial Island, Floating Suburbia.

CHAPTER FIFTY-NINE

Company-Sized Cartel Attack

B rearly, "Birdcage, we've got bogies coming in from the mainland and others from Drug Island. There appear to be four diesels and a half a dozen under-water transporter. ETA, one to one and half hours. Biggest attack ever. The transporters are heading toward Zulinda's beach, also two diesels. I may bring in two helicopters. Over!"

"Black Bird, contact Cuenca airport and shut down all Guanaja flights until further notice. I know your clientele moguls will have influence there.

Roberto, Vanna and I had agreed that if such a raid took place, and if we survived, we needed to take the fighting to them. Roberto had bought the shrimp fields and in closing received maps of all the lot lines on the island including the large fort. I flew the drone over the fort at altitude, and located what appeared to be the room large enough to hold armaments and ammunition.

Vanna said, "We are dealing with a large group of greedy bastards, and we can't go in there and expect with our small numbers to neutralize them all. From the pictures, I can quickly devise explosive charges that should combine with what they have in there and bring that part of the fort down. The drone is powerful enough to take what we need in two trips. If the time comes and we see them moving our way to attack, we must send the first drone load as they are leaving the shore. Lance, I assume you can deliver the load right on target. The second load must go immediately so you can get the drone back to support the battle.

The time was the worst possible. Songbird sensed it. Bucky began growling as he patrolled the beaches. Roberto was behaving at Zulinda's now he was married.

I called him back and told her to prepare whatever she had. Octavio was heading home in the early morning after collecting "$2000" for the day. He reversed at full plane. Distances involved put him in Zulinda's cove with minutes to spare. I went down and recruited the boat captains. They got suppressed-fire rifles from the boats. They had been wearing pistols on their belts for a week.

I went through the thickets and thorns to the top of the hill between the resorts. I sent the drone to surveil. Surprisingly Songbird had called the beginning. I had stopped communicating with Brainerd long ago. They came back concerned that there were seven boats coming mostly manned by three crooks apiece. My drone called five boats headed for the dive resort and two toward Zulinda. Vanna was on the ridge of the hill to the west. Roberto was at the veranda at the top of the resort. I informed Vanna and asked her to forward the information to Zulinda. I had long ago got out from between them, even in battle.

Lance feels Songbird out, "Songbird, they are definitely on their way. Can you begin support? Over."

"Birdcage, we can't respond until we confirm they are actually feet down on the island. Over."

With a building rage inside, I wanted to drench with curses the congress who controlled these drones with such worldly unawareness and stupidity. I held my tongue and didn't respond to anyone.

Vanna replied with more patience than I could muster, "This is birdcage, all the help as soon as you can would be welcome. We'll defend and clean-up. Standing bye."

"Lance, I'll call Zulinda."

Lance adds, "Octavio, are you out fishing, yet?"

Quick response. "I'm out and I also saw your Mukwonago tour group in Cuenca airport. Brearly closed it. Be there in a half hour. Automatic weapons, rifles and two small depth charges prepared."

"Roberto, bogies coming from shore and Drug Island. Approximately ten craft, maybe twelve. Bring the RPG's. Artificial Island is responding with two helicopters. Hurry over, buddy!"

Now an hour of waiting. Octavio arrived first and took station on the east end of Zulinda's beach. The beach was composed of several bamboo roofs, a toilet, and two changing rooms with no walls. If it's a nude beach, why have walls on a changing room? There was one concrete building with roof where the kitchen was located.

Vanna had reached Zulinda who was crawling out in her sans-dress, dragging the latest guy also disrobed onto the sand. The two got the other staff who herded the clients up in the trees toward Starr Resort.

I was back on the drone, honing in on the underwater transporters coming from the Drug Island. The green laser was charging directly off the big generator.

Zulinda, a true vision, body whirling down to where she had a bunker with weapons such as I have never seen off a military base. Her staff arrived and she handed out weapons and sent them to the most effective firing positions. Some went to the trees; three to sand hills in front of the kitchen.

"Vanna, sitrep?"

"Birdcage, one submersible tried to slip by. Trey hit it with an RPG, I am 'shooting gallery' the others. One other diesel has a remaining thug ducking and screaming. A suicide runs to our beach. Oops, SWAT flattened him.

"Vanna, you've got to defend the west of our beach. SWAT has to move east. Give the boat captain the other RPGs. Do you have a suppressed rifle you can give Trey? Follow in case any thug resurfaces. Put Trey back on your shooting gallery. We could really use Bucky here."

"Black Bird, do you see the suicide boat heading toward our dock? Support please."

"Black bird, now you see them, green ray, now you don't. Some clean-up will be needed before your clients hit the beach in the morning. I've decimated any floating object near Zulinda."

'Thank you, Black Bird, much obliged"

"Zulinda, Sitrep."

"Lance, all but one down. One got away into the woods, coming your way. I've sent Tim after him but it's hard to run through the barbs naked. Expect him. Big scar on his cheek, unruly blond hair. He's gonna be too close to use the drone."

"Got it! The thug also has thorn trouble. He'll never suffer from that again. Over. "

"Vanna, could you get Trey and Boat Captains to help you get the bodies into the tug boats. If you need more room, use our security boat. Tow them around the corner well north of our dock while we clean up here. We have so many, and a Mondo. We'll protect Octavio's cruiser with a canvass tarp to make the Davy Jones Trip."

"Lance, Black bird here, it's done with one injury on our staff. One boat captain has a flesh would but the bullet missed the bone. Vanna or Zulinda can handle it. We're here to clean up the beach.

Lance, "Black Bird, "Our Valhalla load is going soon. Do you have any donations? Over"

"Birdcage, one of our guys got it in the arm. He's patched up and will be fine. If it turns out I have extra refuse, my chopper will follow your boat to the deep. Get some sleep now. Out"

"Black Bird, please reopen the airport for Mukwonago Tell them not to authorize flights to Guanaja until after three p.m."

"Roger that, Birdcage. Out."

After dark with the lamps glowing distantly, Rayban and Roberto scouted the beaches and nearby wooded areas for any munitions or objects left from the fight.

Vanna and I got into our 'night-hug" formation and didn't wake until 10. Both dive boats were out. We went to sleep till noon. I had my own unique wake-up and then we went to 'lunch'. I noticed that Bucky was not around, but figured he was on patrol after the fire fight the previous night. Or maybe taking a well-deserved nap.

CHAPTER SIXTY

Delay in Cuenca

Delay in Miami, one hour. Nothing new. Fran expected an hour, maybe two. At two in the morning, without explanation, they put us on two planes and re-routed us to Cuenca. A bus there took us to a hotel on the main road into town. There they left us, so we went to bed.

Breakfast consisted of refried beans on deep-fat fried plantain and Nescafe with or without milk. The meal went slowly as did the bus on the way back to the airport. Following the palms and pineapples on each side of the road, slow as we were going, I saw very clearly, we passed the entrance to the airport. No one except me reacted. The driver said nothing, even to our Spanish Speaking fire fighter. I surged up out of my seatbelt to get to him and get some explanation. All the driver repeated was, "somebody coming". "Good time".

My group was beginning to react and I had no doubt we would soon have a burly fire truck driver doing a U-Turn back to the airport. The driver turned left quickly out onto a service road and stopped among acres of pineapples.

Bus stopped, a short but fluent, intelligent native of the north coast, hopped up and said quickly, "My name is Juan Olivera. Due to some services, I provide for your island host, Lance, sometimes associated with the railroads, he calls me Juan Railroad. Today, I have a more delightful pleasure of taking you on a short side trip before we head to the island. It is unusual and the full explanation you deserve is that a celluloid on one of the air compressors has worn out. The part is available on the mainland and will be installed in time for dinner tonight. In the meantime, we have some pineapples to taste, a romantic water falls to cool us off and wine with lunch. I know this may come as a shock, so I am giving your leader a copy of my Honduran I.D and my U.S. visa to establish your security. I assure you this will be a delightful day, so hop off the bus and let's get into some juicy pineapple tasting.'

With promised style and cooking skills, Juan provided a memorable day. The romance of the waterfall was muted by my being the only woman and a couple of the guys already married.

As the sun went down, the winds luffed and mosquitos took over the area. We hurried back to make the flight before the wind changed again.

CHAPTER SIXTY-ONE

Fran Collapse-Phantom at Starr Resort

The resort was on a different island than the runway. The boat that picked us up was shades of the ghosts of Key Largo. It was diesel and the boat captain who picked us up, familiar, probably knew every meter of reef within miles. We arrived at the three-prong dive boat pier, 'ungreened', and unloaded.

Lance and Vanna along with two dive boat captains and another handsome driver staff member welcomed us. I was balancing Lily and organizing her suitcases so didn't pay attention until Lance spoke. He had a deep voice that demanded attention.

"Welcome, Fran, we thank you for your service, firemen", Lance greeted. Juggling hers and Lily's equipment, Fran glanced up to smile at Lance, looked over his shoulder, lurched, and fell to her knees. Huge eyes. Ragged breaths! A dozen fully trained EMT's surrounded her. Lily, spread legs with swimmers' thighs, raised her back to her feet. They checked whatever could be checked with her clothes on and Roberto's Cindy stayed with her in the bungalow shared with Lily.

Vanna saw the other woman Lance hadn't had a chance to welcome and surprised at her developed feminine body said, "Welcome Lily, I'm Vanna." Smiles met smiles but Lily was dizzy in the jungle-meets-beach surroundings."

The firemen and captains carried the equipment to the ramp boats and the cabanas. Lance put everyone to a nap and promised to wake them for happy hour and dinner. There would be no tank diving today but they could snorkel out toward the east end of the island if they couldn't sleep.

Concerned, but Trey made a point of being the one to settle Fran and Lily. He brought the slough of suitcases they had up to the bungalow. Cindy was still with Fran as she focused into the muffled light. Trey smiled at Fran who jerked and tensed again, fell back, and closed her eyes.

Fran reacted to all the mauling and whispering going on around her. "Look, we don't know each other well enough for all this. I have talked twice to Vanna on the phone and only have met Cindy now. I know what I told you about your Trey, and I am not insane. I own and manage a successful restaurant with one other waitress, Lily and a cook. Lily's sister comes in to help if we expect a crowd. I am charming and endearing with the customers. I do all business operations, auditing, ordering, and inventory. I've been married but am now a widow. It was a heartbreaking loss. I date occasionally. That's enough for you to know to take me diving. Sorry, I guess the jet lag made me a little irritable.

Vanna brought Lily up to their bungalow where Fran had cleared her eyes from her second siting of Trey. Cindy stayed a few minutes to settle the two into camp life.

The next day Vanna met with Fran to learn the idiosyncrasies of Lily. Lily, who had developed into a mouthwatering beauty had, in her early teen years, some malady in brain development. During early years and for some time into the teens, there is a series of growth spurts that enhance brain function. For Lily, the spurt that normally happens at about 13 years didn't, or didn't complete itself. Her geometry teacher was first to notice it. If functioning, it would enhance Lily's ability to imagine and, in her mind, see three dimensional shapes. She could imagine those shapes opening to their component parts. Perhaps related, she had some trouble manipulating the four most basic operations on numbers: adding, subtracting, multiplying, and dividing. She had no interest in a career in mathematics so the teacher gave her "CA", credit awarded on her course list which gave her a high school diploma. With the advent of calculators, Lily, after repeated drills, could get answers needed most of the time.

Her mother passed away and she fell to the loving hands of her older sister. The sister was running Fran's Pizza restaurant so Fran could get a vacation after her painful loss of a young husband and get Lily out to see there was more than Mukwonago in the world. The sister had been with Fran since graduation, developing a plan for a pizza restaurant in teen-aged plagued downtown Mukwonago. The sister would be an investor and Fran would be CFO. In the deal. Lily would have a job waitressing. Along with the calculator came the cash register computer, opening further success for her in her job. Even the computer didn't solve all of the difficulties, but with a 15-minute refresher each Monday morning, Lily operated usually successfully. There wasn't a male customer who wouldn't forgive and help such an Aphrodite with a billing error. Along with the salary she would earn tips, more needn't be said, for a living that could support her with some pride, but a captivating innocence.

The growth spurt didn't miss the rest of her development, so the sister and Fran had to watch the advent of boys. Lily was a swimming pool fish since her earliest years. By her graduation, the swimming had toned her legs making her more of a danger to the male population, and her sister. She had called on that strength when Fran swooned on the pier. She side-stepped and pulled her right up. With a good friend in her boss, Fran, she was excited about joining scuba training in the pool and in shallow lakes in the region.

With Vanna up-dated, she got Lily and took her for a warm-up shallow water snorkel. Cindy urged Fran to get a suit on and dive into the surf but kept Lily nearby when Vanna excused herself.

Vanna found Trey up cleaning the leaves and branches around Fran's bungalow.

"Trey, do you know this Fran from someplace?"

"I don't recall ever seeing her before. She is a real fox and I doubt I would have forgotten that."

"Have you ever been to Mukwonago, your last three-week vacation, for example, or in an airport there, or a connector to Chicago?"

"Vanna, I am sincere about this. I have never even been to Wisconsin. It's a cold state most of the year with few lakes with visibility for diving. There is a deep lake, Lake Michigan on the east of the state, but again little visibility. Its so cold people say you can't even get comfortable in a full suit."

"Curious!"

"Vanna, I have never even seen this "Mukwonago" name before and doubt I could pronounce it correctly.

"Ok, Trey, sorry to grill you, Fran thinks she saw you in a dream as a phantom or some such."

"Vanna, at a good time I will go and introduce myself and see if she wants to put her hand through my chest. No, seriously, I will try to help her feel safe. Not crying or fainting, she's a fox, still."

CHAPTER SIXTY-TWO

Phantom Unearthed

In the ensuing twilight, Trey and Fran were over at the wall practicing gymnastics. He had approached her and, keeping his distance, introduced himself, saying they wouldn't need a pick-up line because they had the 'phantom' in common. Fran was not inclined to question after a few more glances at him, and checking he really was flesh and blood, and six-packs. Not interested in living alone forever, she chose the tiger-striped thong for a moon-light dip. She had no transparent wrap to wear before or after dipping. Trey was all eyes. Lily slept alone until late.

In this scuba-designed situation, there was potential danger so all kept an eye on lily. Fran had gotten scuba lessons for her in a pool in Mukwonago. She was excited to do it. Vanna took her by the hand and helped her warm up by snorkeling around the reef down the beach. She put the tank on and went to four meters watching her clear her ears and managing the B.C. Vanna had to swoop in to punch a demanding thump to her chest to get her to exhale when ascending.

"Lily sputtered, yes, yes, I know that. I don't want to explode."

"Then do it!"

They did it again. Then five more times. Vanna was doggedly protecting our reputation; and Lily's life.

The following day, Lily, running on 7 of her 8

cylinders, swam laps around the dock while Vanna loaded her equipment. The dive would be to the wall where good sea life and colored novice-reef were at 10-30 feet. Vanna would keep her away from the wall.

Trey and Fran were already over at the wall practicing now suggestive gymnastics.

Lily hadn't practiced entering the water from the boat but the ramps made that easy. Vanna sat beside her, balancing her, getting her regulator set; putting her hand on the BC. She was talking, encouraging her; reminding her; trying to make her relax. They both eased into the water. Vanna set her B.C. and went to check Lily's. Lily hadn't adjusted it so Vanna did. They floated along beside the boat; Vanna took her elbow and eased her down to 10 feet.

We hadn't known in advance the amount of monitoring Lily would need. Vanna had to be in hot blood to catch every unthinking mistake Lily could make. Watching Vanna fly, I considered changing some resort policies.

No decompression would be needed for this depth. They looked around at the bottom of the boat, saw Fran and Trey in the distance. From under the transom in a wash of bubbles a barracuda shot out swerving toward them and as a flash into the distance. Lily squeezed her BC, screamed bubbles out under her mask and shot up shouting and spluttering. At least the screams prevented an embolism.

Lily was in tears saying, "that's enough, take me out, there are monsters. The pool in Mukwonago doesn't have monsters. Help, help", flailing around with her tank pulling her down. Vanna leaped and had her weight belt and tank off in a flash. She put her in a lifesaving hold and got her around and up on the ramp. Fran and Trey were oblivious, but that was no fault of theirs. It was our call so Vanna got the rest of her equipment off and comforted her until the divers returned after 45 minutes.

Worried, Fran came up the ramp responding to Lily's tears. Vanna explained, Lily said she only wanted to snorkel by the little reef she had been at the day before. The next morning, Vanna coated her with sun protection and spent two rounds of snorkeling, morning and afternoon. Lily spent the rest of the week swimming around the rafts and riding the boats while others dived.

Fran and Trey continued to be diving buddies. Interesting what can be done in buoyant salt water.

The next day, Vanna and I went to happy hour. We weren't diving the next day. Cook made a super grasshopper with ice cream so we each had one on the veranda. Trey and Fran came up and talked with us for a while. I could see his discomfort, knew it well for what it was. We soon left to our cabin; in case it might be contagious. This time, as I looked over my shoulder, they were in a deep kiss on the path on the way to his cabin.

At breakfast the next morning, there were two sets of, what do they call them in Wisconsin, 'Cow eyes. I have to confess, Vanna and I sported one set.

Camp Owner Lance, I went down to open their first dives warning the firemen about too much beer and too many atmospheres. They all had used a variety of air and oxygen tanks, but few underwater. Fran had gone down deep in Lake Superior.

The camp regimen promised in our brochure was two dives per day, morning and afternoon and a night dive once per week, pending wind conditions. For the average sport diver, this is a bit stressful. These fire guys are not average anything and hit every dive. Lily was off in her 'never, never' world supervised by Vanna.

When Fran succumbed after six dives, Trey of course was 'tired', too. She went up and got her bikini. They snorkeled and tanned on the famous east end of the island. The bikini absolutely screamed description. The ink in this paragraph would cover more than the suit.

There is some thought that mid-west girls tend to be conservative. Fran was far from being a teenager; she had lost a man she really adored. She had no intention of living alone all her life. The bikini was a thong with a bra that only hinted at holding anything in check. Tiger spot designs hammered the point home.

I still had to be careful about what Vanna might notice me viewing. That may be a life sentence. A dirty look and I headed upstairs for a snack. The morning dive came in and lunch was served. The guys flopped down to power nap, but Fran and Trey didn't arrive. We could see their splashes in the distance with occasional no-splash sun bathing. No worries.

CHAPTER SIXTY-THREE

Dive and Fight

A day to decompress Lily's mind, the second dive, Lily and Vanna aboard, headed out to the North of the island where some bigger fish hung about. I stayed on the dock with a cold beer and thick sun screen applied by Vanna. After twenty minutes on each side, I moved onto the boardwalk up to the bar under the shade of some primeval trees. I had been out for two hours. First Fran and then Trey in the distance headed back, some more clothed than others. The eastern edge of Zulinda's resort, Unclad.com, that is, may have been influential.

A refreshing night in camp, Fran and I were sitting at the happy hour bar deeply engaged in sharing diving adventures around the mid-west. Trey was on the other side of Fran, and Fran was dressed for him. Dressed for him, but right next to me. She was not a Vanna, nor even a Zulinda, but she was a stocky mid-western girl well endowed. Smart, she owned her own business. Probably a Norwegian in the gene pool; warm, loving blue eyes. The stocky didn't interfere with the right curves in the right places. I wasn't enveloped in side looks at her breasts. I was focused on the diving in the Racine quarry, a dirty dive with rusted cars; no visibility. My chair was rammed in no uncertain terms away from Fran, and Vanna plunked herself in hot blood between us. With an embarrassed pause, I finished the discussion of the quarry and turned away. Fran turned back to Trey.

In honor of guys from beef states, the cook bar-b-queued racks of Angus ribs. Fresh mixed salads and baked potatoes rounded it off. Light on drinks. Vanna selected a table well away from them. Nothing was said. I would rather have her over-protective than disinterested. Vanna should remember my touch and adoration for her by now and not be so quick to attack either the object of my glance or conversation. Dangerous as a Navy Seal, maybe she was also Irish. I had proved over and over she was THE object of my affection.

We got drinks and went up to the veranda watching the moon. Trey and Fran arrived, well plastered against each other. We respected their privacy and headed up to our cabin. I looked over my shoulder and this time he had her bra in his teeth, ushering her into his bungalow. Having seen the tiger spot bikini in action, I quickly turned away. Fast enough for the eyes on me and turns out, I had been forgiven. I had behaved in a pristine manner after the dive-sharing with Fran. The A/C covered intensely delivered sparks and moans.

CHAPTER SIXTY-FOUR

Bucky Hurt

O ur comfortable bubble was interrupted. Bucky came to sleep with us occasionally. It happened after one of our skirmishes. I guess he figured there wouldn't be anything more, otherwise he would be on guard. That wasn't the case tonight. He came in with a hard limp, a heart rendering whine, and blood in the hair of his back left leg.

Vanna reacted quickly and lovingly devised a sling for the leg. She gave him some people pain relievers and I called Roberto. Woke him up. He would come over early tomorrow and take him to Alicia Maria, the vet on the coast between Ceiba and United fruit. We put him in the bed with us to keep him comfortable from the A/C. Vanna gave him another pain pill at 5:00 a.m.

It may not be typical for a big Alpha male like me to feel so close to a dog. I was there when he was born at Alicia's kennel. As soon as he was ready, we had Alicia train him to be the alarm clock of the camp if trouble was scented. He also was tutored to be a protective force if he sensed danger.

CHAPTER SIXTY-FIVE

Bucky's Secret:

Bucky healed and saved many islanders from unsuspecting Thugs. No one knows for sure how he got the injury when the ensuing Mukwonago was in camp. Up on the hill beyond the camp, he lunged at a Don J mafia Vanna had missed, saving Vanna. Vanna dispatched the thug but didn't see Bucky's injury. It took him two nights pulling his broken leg behind him to get to Vanna's cabana. Vanna used first aid and sent him to Alicia for re-training never realizing Bucky had saved her so she could dispatch her threatening feral father in law, Don J.

CHAPTER SIXTY-SIX

Saving of Lily and Wooing of Fran

Vanna and Bucky finished their circuit and checked for any lagging snorkelers. Vanna and the boat captain, who had guarded the camp yesterday, would lead the morning dives. I would sub in for Vanna in the afternoon who would work with Lily.

The firemen were used to Lily in a variety of sexy attire and ignored her. They had about as much interest as the Germans in Melissa. There were only a couple other men working. Both on the morning and afternoon dives, Trey and Fran were quickly buddies.

After dinner, Vanna and I went up on the veranda. Soon another couple appeared. Fran and Trey focused seriously on each other's eyes wandered up the back steps. We quietly and quickly said good night and headed for our cabin. Heading up to the cabin with Vanna, I turned back and saw them saying good-night with one kiss, but one of merit. They went separately to their cabins. Lily was already down.

Nothing was said. I guess I would rather have her over-protective of me than disinterested. Vanna should remember my touch and adoration for her. I told her about the battle starting out to the west.

"We should go, Lance."

"Honey, I've got Roberto, Rayban, his armory and maybe Zulinda. Brearly is also aware. If they get within

50 feet of his island, he has authorization to take them out. If they need help, we can be there in ten minutes in the Chevy. I got the radio, let's go up on the veranda and try to keep folks down here or on the beach. You can be kissing me and embarrass them back down. We can go up to the tower if we start hearing explosions. Maybe give some intel. If they move closer, we'll meet them with the Chevy."

We got drinks and went up to the veranda watching the moon. Trey and Fran appeared; they were a single person with four legs. Lily would be sleeping alone in Fran's bungalow tonight.

As they went in, I heard the first roar of several muted explosions. The RPG's. If that hadn't been enough, we didn't have many heavy munitions left. I had forgotten clearly. I realized that and relaxed. I listened for the suppressors but they were doing their job, we couldn't hear them. A few minutes, seconds really, later, the Mexican-American guy came rumbling up. He stopped next to us back on the tower. He listened for several seconds.

"Lance, you can tell these people whatever you want if they hear the explosions over there. But I know damn well that no army training drills are ever anywhere near here. I was born in Central America. There's an extended runway in Cuenca. America built it. Nobody is going to be doing a 'fucking" thing on it if a dozen trucks and helicopters with U.S. flags waving aren't there. I'll keep my mouth shut if you confirm none of these people here are going to be hurt."

"Jorge, we have protecting forces against some drug marauders in that area. The last two explosions were the end of that battle. I'll be getting a sitrep in ten to twenty minutes. All are safe here. Good evening."

Octavio came on in five minutes. "No survivors, no

escapees. We're heading out to 400 feet and will meet with you tomorrow."

"Our group will leave at noon before the winds come up. Come any time after two. But Roberto, take several of the heavy weaponry from Rayban and store them. He can get more, cheap, from Frumpland, liar of the home-grown White Supremacists."

"Roger, out."

CHAPTER SIXTY-SEVEN

Sneak Attack; Mukwonago at Camp

Next morning, moving quietly up toward our cabana, I got a radio call from Roberto. "We got a group of three smoke pots with three pirates in each. Maybe remnants of last night. I know you have a big group from the mid-west now. How do you want to handle it? We have an hour and a half."

"I could probably get away, but Vanna will scalp me if I leave her alone with this group. She's got a bombshell young woman, short a brick for a full roof, who keeps her hopping. It would be good if you can do this without me, unless an unexpected emergency requires. Do you have some armament?"

"Not much, and not enough. I only have two RPG's and two sound-suppressed rifles and one revolver. And Bucky, of course, but I'm afraid we could seriously endanger him."

"Call Octavio and see where he is. He's fully loaded. Call me back immediately with the info. I hope he's not in Sambo Creek."

"Birdcage, some luck finally today. He's leaving Zulinda. Will be back in 20 minutes. He might be able to bring Zulinda.

"Ok on Zulinda, but no pressure on her. This isn't her fight. Octavio is going to have some heavy equipment, loud equipment. Try to start the attack as far west keeping noise east of airport island. Are you ok with this, Roberto?

"After what I went through last night and I'm still here, I figure I'm ok."

"Try to box the invasion to the west. I think you should leave for the east of Roadan in 20 minutes. Good luck, be careful and call me back with a sitrep as soon as you have them neutralized. Out."

One fight we didn't personally have to face. And no injured had been mentioned. The A/C covered some intensely delivered sparks and moans. Mostly Vanna, of course.

CHAPTER SIXTY-EIGHT

Alicia and Cesarito

In the failed state where we lived, I was very cautious choosing a doctor, or a retailer, or a vet with all the cartel lackeys around. I almost didn't choose Alicia. I used a contact in the embassy to do a background check on her. She was pristine clean, but she was married to the son of one of the most infamous drug lords in the area. I contacted Juan of the Railroad Street Regulars. His knowledge of her background saved her a new client. Bucky was born two weeks after she returned from Texas A & M. That summer she taught him to be a protection dog with two weeks in being an attack dog.

Alicia Maria, was from a wealthy family well founded for generations, long before the cartel. She was academically a shining star in all her elementary and secondary English-medium education. She had 4.0 grade point average and scores at the top of the SAT I and II's. She was all over the community charity work, partly because her family was so wealthy. The family was well-prepared to handle her university costs, but she was given a full ride at Texas A&M. She even met with the admissions committee to describe her family's situation, and no need of extra help. The response was firmly, "This is not based on need, this is based on the excellence you have shown as an academic and a caring community member. We have no doubt about your potential of success and frankly, we think you may be a resource and interesting support to your classmates. We are not going to lose you to the University of Houston, nor Oklahoma State without a struggle. The die was cast and she became all she is and what they hoped for.

The Don J. Mondo had a boy at her class level. Ceasrito, a handsome youngster but naïve and only moderate in ability. He had some unusual abilities to memorize. He couldn't analyze what he knew. That wasn't enough to gain a scholarship. The Mondo extorted the teachers to give false, successful grades. Threats to family members. The Don J. Mondo also went to the gift coordinator at Oklahoma Ag. and built an addition of private practice and study rooms to the library. Ceasrito was welcomed with opened arms. He never saw or didn't realize that part of the library had his name on it.

Many undergrad classes could be passed with memorization skills; he got by. He went to a summer combined seminar for potential veterinarians including universities in western U.S. Texas A&M was there. Alicia was there. She was brilliant and beautiful and he was built and pretty. Before the end of the first date, she recognized the academic and analysis skill he didn't have. But plenty of girls choose fewer academic mates.

They lived on the north coast only forty miles apart so in summers they would be seeing each other again. After the seminar, he returned to Sula looking for summer work. There was a vet with property and horses a few miles east of the Copan Ruins. He had advertised for summer help. Ceasrito mentioned the job in the family and before he could go to interview, one of the lieutenants had visited. There would be no interview. Ceasrito would be given the job.

"Oh, look at your lovely wife and daughters. It would be terrible if any accident should happen to them." Pure, blatant extortion! Fine-tuned in the not so hallowed halls of northern neighbor's congress.

The vet had been there for years. He knew it was a land of no legal recourse. Unaware, Ceasrito reported for work. He didn't understand why he got such a cold welcome, but started, following directions and being cooperative. He loved working with horses and was kind and supportive. The vet had some hope for this boy in the short run.

The next summer, Ceasrito contacted the vet to work again. The lieutenant visited again with his not so veiled threats and Ceasrito started again. The vet quietly moved to downsize the business, or sell it, the following year. Either way there would be no need for a cartel boy to be employed. The family would probably have to move away as well. They did, to the Guatemalan border.

The senior year was a year of a platonic relationship between Alicia Marie and Ceasrito in spite of the intellectual difference. Alicia had worked again with parent support to finalize the veterinary hospital. She could graduate right into her office with the license on the wall. In fact, she did.

In March of her senior year, she learned that Ceasrito was Cartel. The relationship stalled, cooled. He was heartbroken with no realization of what the problem was.

Alicia knew of the criminal extortions of the cartel and would not be so stupid as to tell the crime boss's son why she was balking. He was so unworldly aware he might unintentionally cry to his father and get her killed or at least her business destroyed.

She stayed awake nights pondering and analyzing what could be salvaged, if anything:

1. He was kind to people and animals all.

2. He had fallen completely under her influence.

3. They could practice veterinary together with her interest in small pets and dogs and his in horses.

4. He was not schooled in the higher arts or dance. On the other hand, he was an excellent dancer. Enthralling even.

5. She had never considered buying a new pair of shoes before trying them on, so any future bed-play had to test explosive. There was time.

6. His unique memory skills would cover her friend's doubt in her choice of him.

7. To wake up each morning to the adoration in his eyes was stunning.

Refocusing on the darker aspects she would face; she was sure his father would do no harm to his son's wife. He would also not damage a veterinary office that offered his son a career that he had the mental ability to handle. She faced the discomfort she would meet in attending family parties and business discussions. In a life-threatening emergency, her own family could try to protect her.

Carrying a torch for her, Ceasrito could be influenced to give her all she wanted. She also steeled herself for the worst because any divorce would be a death penalty. With his adoration, few problems between them occurred. She wore the pants in this couple and got what she wanted.

She slowly began to accept his invitations to date again, but sleeping together was put on hold perhaps until after they were married. The increase in his hunger caused him to relent to her every whim. Every unfilled night more.

She soon learned of the boredom and disgusting activities of the cartel ladies' club and their laudatory remarks about how clever their husbands were in business extortion. They considered non-cartel families, a lower class to be taxed and taken advantage of for Cartel comforts. Shades of modern-day Re- inequality for blacks or browns.

She immediately stopped going to the lady's club despite many efforts to get her back. She went once when anyone missing would be expelled. Ceasrito did whatever she wanted in all things and everything. She left meetings as soon as she would not be missed.

CHAPTER SIXTY-NINE

No Way in Hell Will Alicia Be Trounced

The Donny J. Mondo hated her. He knew her roots and soon realized her striking intelligence. Both were a danger to him. She was a F==king woman; "Batt and I traffic that shit!"

He and the present trophy step-mother staged a war against her. Shameful slurs came at her from all sides. "Quechua bitch, Inca sucker, animal pedophile, Mayan Whore," Lessons from the North. Lackeys and wives were kissing his Don J. feet for their fear of what he and his allies could do to them. Extortion, lies and dirty money spread on the community.

Incensed, Alicia fired the love-making to hot and hard and right now and thrilling. No wait for marriage. There was no way she would be defeated in this conspiracy. Ceasrito was ever under her spell; needed her arms. He went. She responded lovingly. She gave him his deep desire and in the loving bubble afterwards, they (she) scheduled the wedding for two weeks later. She charmed him and he fought his father's distaste. She influenced and he forced the mother to plan the ceremony.

Alicia held him in deep kisses and demanded that the wedding only include immediate family. The relationship was going as she had analyzed. Her joy in his adoration grew and became the most elusive tool.

They had been married three years. She heard another bigger raid would be carried out against the Guanaja groups.

She mentioned it to Ceasrito. He said, "Yeah, my dad's going on this one. He thinks they need more motivation to win this time. They are taking some underwater diver transports."

Alicia informed Roberto that evening.

CHAPTER SEVENTY

Mondo Down, Limbo for Alicia

The cartel invasion began the following day. Cesearito had nothing to do with the cartel. He was sickened at what his father was fomenting. The distance couldn't have been further between father and son. Ceasrito was making a pair of horse shoes that afternoon.

Rayban roared into the inlet of the veterinary kennel with Bucky. The Don J. Mondo, Ceasritos' father, in his flaunted dress had been the last one off the boat near the airport. Bucky took him down so Vanna could get a safe shot. Don J. took a diver's knife swinging at Bucky's rear right leg. In a second, a double tap ended the fight and the existence of such evil. Vanna was under fire from behind so she turned and flattened, not noticing Bucky's injury. No correlation between the two incidents was ever uncovered.

I knew. I knew that Bucky had laid in the woods two days trying to lick his wound. A healing dog's tongue is not enough for a broken bone. Bucky finally came, whining and dragging his back leg to us in bed in our cabin. Roberto, who knew Alicia, the vet, from elementary school days, responded. The medical recovery required extended time and therapy. He had to be taken to his original guard dog level of response back to the attack dog level. Three months later, he was barking and excited to be back on the island with his human friends.

Three days later, no one returned from the raid. No Don J. Mondo. No correlation between Bucky's attack and Alicia's medical care for the dog that took out her hated father-in-law.

CHAPTER SEVENTY-ONE

Lives Reset

Alicia had to reset and consider what her situation might be with a strange new Don J. Mondo. She again spoke with her father. His years of experience in this sickened society provided an answer, at least short term. "No Mondo would harm a previous Mondo's son. The ugly relations among family cartel members at least didn't permit that." It was an advantage that Mondos were disappearing so often in the islands. Scheming, she would shimmer out "wet lightning" to drive Ceasrito slowly out of his mind whenever it suited her. She would make greater damage to the Cartel, sometime, someday.

CHAPTER SEVENTY-TWO

Love Confirmed

Bucky was gone with Roberto and his wife, Cindy. Early in the morning a sheepish looking Trey walked to our table and sat down. "Lance, Vanna, it would be sorely anticlimactic for me to review the fun and fright I have shared with you. I will wait for the promised two weeks, but then I have some Pizza to deliver in Mukwonago, and a sweet young girl to protect from guys like me. Maybe some fire-department training: using a tank above the water. I can pronounce the name now. It's in the lips. We all smiled and congratulated him. Every one of us knew, Fran would never let him out of her arms, or away from her lips.

Lance glances, "I could see in Trey's stance how disappointed he was, not going with them that next noon. He would have to weather another attack. Both Railroad Juan and Sarah's intel concurred. I saw the invasion size; I put him up in the Drone tower. Effective shooter and located safely, I wanted to assure he would make that dream for Fran and Lily come true.

CHAPTER SEVENTY-THREE

Last Bow for Trey, Much to Live For

"Birdcage, this is Black Bird, we've got bogies coming in from the mainland and others from Drug Island. Five diesels and a half a dozen under-water transporter. ETA, one hour. Their transporters are heading toward both resorts. I may bring in two helicopters. Over!"

Vanna replied, "This is birdcage, the help would be welcome. Standing bye."

"Lance, try to get Octavio and Roberto. I'll wake the captains and see if I can find Trey. I'll call Zulinda."

"Octavio, are you out fishing, yet?"

"Birdcage, I'm out and will be there in a half hour. Automatic weapons, rifles and two small depth charges prepared."

"Roberto, wake up. Bogies coming from shore and Drug Island. Approximately ten craft, maybe twelve. Intel says we got a Mondo. Bring the RPG's. Artificial Island is responding with two helicopters, but they need some time. We have to hold until they can get here."

Now an hour of waiting. Octavio arrived first and took station on the east end of Zulinda's beach. Vanna rousted Zulinda crawling out in her not-a-stitch body. The two got the other staff and guests herded into safety. This was the worst-case scenario when guests, who might talk to others, would not have positive things to say. Starr was lucky; we had just sent Mukwonago home.

Trey was on the drone targeting green ray, honing in on the underwater transporters coming from Drug Island. Zulinda ran down to the west end of her beach, bouncing a glorious vision, where she had a bunker with weapons such as I have never seen outside of a military weapons cache.

"Black bird, we are in place. In ten minutes, Trey will start taking out the underwater transporters nearest you. They show up clearly on his drone screen. Over."

"Negative, Bird Cage, hold fifteen and let me take the helicopters in to deliver impulsion mines. When I finish, Trey can take out what's left while I land the helicopters. Safer all around. It looks like you and Zulinda are going to get three diesels with three thugs each. I'll disembark two SWAT guys near the airport away from your dock. Three to Zulinda. Over. "

Lance responds, "Roger, thank the Force, Mukwonago is gone."

Lance re-engages, "Vanna, meet the SWAT guys at the west end near the island channel. That's where the thugs always try to sneak in. Bucky can lead that charge. Leave Trey in the tower. I'm not gonna send him home damaged goods. Take three RPG's. Shoot as soon as their boats come into site. You can call in a strike from Trey, or have SWAT launch, but we've got to neutralize those to protect our resort. Send SWAT to back-up Zulinda. She has guests and we don't so she may take an undeserved marketing hit."

Lance orders, "Boat captains, watch for submersibles. Both SWAT and we have drone finders to locate them. Call me if you see one that is not already burning. I'll have Trey clear it. We've got to keep the pier and the resort free from any sign of conflict."

Bodie, boat captain growls, "They'll enter here over our dead bodies. Concentrate on your major assault and rest assured we will handle with dispatch anything that comes our way."

"Bodie, above and beyond your call of duty, but sincere thanks", Lance tense voice.

Octavio, they will soon be coming right at you. You will have two or three diesels and the same number of submersibles if Brearly's helicopters and Trey's green waiting laser don't sink them. Sorry, I know that is a hand full. Watch for survivors and neutralize. Octavio, if the diesels come, try to lead them and drop the mines where their bows will slam onto the beach. If you miss, head on to the west end of the beach and see if Zulinda needs back-up. If not, hurry back and rake the diesels with automatic fire. Don't shoot any naked people. That should be plenty to sink them. Same treatment for survivors. Continue patrolling back and forth until I tell you to stand down."

Roger that, Octavio, out.

"Vanna, sitrep?"

"Birdcage, one submersible tried to slip by. Trey hit it with green. I am 'shooting gallery' the others. One other diesel has a thug ducking and screaming. A suicide runs to our beach. Out of Trey's site-lines. Over."

"Vanna, you've got to stop him. Have the boat captain nail him with the other RPG. Follow in case he surfaces. Put Trey on your shooting gallery when he can get them in site.

Vanna barks, "Black Bird, do you see the suicide boat heading toward our dock?" Support please."

"Black Bird, on it. Now you see them, green laser, now you don't. Birdcage, some clean-up will be needed before your next clients hit the beach in the morning. Mukwonago left in time. Octavio has decimated any floating object near Zulinda. You can have your boat captains stand down but remain wary. Watch for stragglers.

'Thank you, Black Bird, much obliged". Out.

"Zulinda, Sitrep."

"Lance, all but one down. One got away into the woods, coming your way. God, could I use Bucky!"

Lance neutralizes the stray, then, "Vanna, could you get Trey down from the tower and our Boat Captain to help you get the bodies into the thug boats. Trey's unharmed, right? If you need more room, use our security boat. Tow them around the corner and north while we clean up here. We have so many, and a Don J. Mondo. They have an endless swamp of these treasonous bastards, as obsequious as our local thugs, sliming their way to the Autocratic top. We'll cover Octavio's deck for blood with a canvass for the Davy Jones Trip."

CHAPTER SEVENTY-FOUR

Starr's Loss, Fran's Future

Vanna updates "Trey's fine, looking sweaty and good enough to eat."

"Lover, save your appetite for me, I'm marinated."

Lance summarizes, "Black Bird, it's done with no injuries on our staff except Roberto with an embedded thorn. Cindy is at our resort and will be all over him.

We have a full Valhalla load going soon. Any donations? Over"

"Birdcage, one of our guys got a 30-06 in the arm. He's patched up and will be fine. If I have extra refuse, my helicopter will follow your boat to the deep. Get some sleep now. Out"

CHAPTER SEVENTY-FIVE

Pedro Jet coasted to the end of the gravel runway of Guanaja. He turned into the wind, braked and jumped out of the pilot seat. He loaded the meager amount of passenger gear; circled around opening the passenger door. He pulled straps tight and went back to buckle himself in. Good wind, he raced.

As the wheels came up, Trey looked back, waved once at the staff waiting in the trees, turned ahead, and never looked back. This chapter, so beautiful, frightful, and maturing, was over. Next stop, Mukwonago, the Place of the Bear, pure joy.

END BOOK ONE

Follow the ensuing pleasures and horrors of Lance and Vanna with now Alicia and Laxmi, the Nepali security guard. Look for Guanaja Defense TWO and then move to Croatia in Book Guanaja, The Final Chapter.

GUANAJA BOOK TWO

Modern Day War for the Bay Islands

BY LANCE STARR

PROFESSIONAL Caribbean Scuba
The Starr Resort. Guanaja

CHAPTER ONE

Sites of Passion and Intrigue

The weather surrounding the owner's bungalow on Guanaja in the Caribbean was not hot although seriously warm with never ending humidity. A/C was quietly humming inside. Down the hill in the kitchen/restaurant on the path to the dive ramp boats, the cook and assistant were trying to organize breakfast without waking the boss, me. I had awakened to the sound of the lapping surf and the light breath of my Vanna at my shoulder. We didn't have a dive group until tomorrow, so no need to rise early.

I rolled over to doze for a while longer and my hand flowed gently down her side. Her blond hair shivered around her breasts. My touch raised a single bump; she didn't wake. Her lovely closed green eyes hid the constant energy she evinced every waking moment. She and I were co-owners of the resort, seconded as needed by Roberto Fernandez, a Honduran I had first met in the University Dorm. I had gone to Honduras with him for Spring break while others went to Miami. He'd had enough beer with me and my room-mate to know my dreams, and I his. On this trip with his father supervising, he bought a reef shrimp farm and dolphin riding show. To be developed after graduation and a trip across Europe, he didn't get past Spain.

They also had scouted this island, Guanaja, for the Lance Starr Resort for advanced Scuba Diving. A foreigner buying land in a country faces a momentous challenge. In a country fighting daily against several drug cartels with fingers polluting all levels of government, it was torture. The fact Roberto's Dad had been in government service for years before the cartels, gave me the good luck to buy it at all. Roberto had power of attorney for any window dressing in the ownership documents. It was not the operating understanding of the enterprise. He was a diver, shrimp, not tourists. He backed me in short term emergency, or when I had to go to Frankfurt for Mercedes. It was the genius of my college room-mate, Greg, along with my degree in metals and plastics allowing me to develop the resort. A patent pay-out from Mercedes for a futuristic dash board saved me from bankrupting my parents. Greg imagined, I designed.

I quietly watched Vanna sleep, "my cup" in Jim Neighbors words, "overflowing with love". She was as lovely with them closed as she was fiery and caring with them blazing.

We avoided any nostalgia for her horrors faced in saving my life four times in skirmishes with the Cartel. I had returned the favor, but the speed, judgment and accuracy were hers.

As she was flickering, I slipped away. She'd make no negative response to a morning kiss. Given the chance, I'd lead with something minty and sweet.

At seventeen, I dated three girls: One Return to School Dance, one Homecoming, and finally, Prom. The second told me on her doorstep my kiss was a candy cane. Oh, so foolish and naïve, I invited someone else to the third dance. The following year the girl who had complemented my kiss had moved and I never saw her again. Until this day I never prepare to go on a date, I think of her. I seldom fail to 'mint up'.

In our little cabana, there was no reason to hurry. I had to cool because the sheet, the only covering we needed, was pretty much nowhere to be seen over her. I heard a humble moan and a slap as she tried to locate me in the bed.

"Where are you?"

"Cleaning up"

"Lance, I wish I could make feeling you the first thing I do in the morning, come back!"

"Be careful what you wish for."

"Get back here and I will show you what I wish for."

Dressed in the minimum for an excited guy, I emerged from the doorway, satisfied her instincts, and left with a sweet wisp of mint.

It was sweet; not simple. Vanna is a woman five inches shorter than me. She has flowing blond hair and deadly green eyes speaking tons, wherever. As I sit on the edge of the bed, she moves in and I wrap my arms around her hips, erotic flicks where she is pleasantly shaven. Delightful, exploring her thighs drives new sensations. Along those miles, she is soft, warm, and slippery. Squeeze, and you find a firm, iron-like underpinning. She is a diver, a lifesaver, and honed as a Navy Seal. To have such a woman wishing for me in the morning, stops my breath. Frivolous with me as I splash, usually too soon, roaring two, three, four, more times sharing her OWN, is my heaven on earth.

CHAPTER TWO

The Conflict

After the mauled wardrobe, we went down to the bar/restaurant. The local scuba ramp boat captains were there with Josh, a new professional diver/businessman. He replaced Trey. Trey fell in love with the owner of a pizza restaurant who brought her volunteer fire department for ten days of diving. After giving the two week contractual notice and fighting his final Cartel skirmish, he went back to her.

Bacon served up hot, as forks raised, the camp sea-band radio crackled. The window identified radio call name: Octavio. Rayban Hernandez, captain and owner of the Octavio, a combo commercial fisherman and deep sea fishing tour cruiser, responded.

This could be good news or very bad news. Food back in the oven, we hurried to the top of the resort where radar, sensors and a drone were always minutes from activation.

The usual marauders were radicalized Cartel drug minions, occasionally a White Supremacist trying to refill the treasury of which the previous club officers had absconded. Today, we located Octavio; no other bogies.

"Birdcage, this is Octavio, over. Do you read me, Birdcage?"

We had been involved for some time with Octavio being attacked by these same pirates, sometimes to beat him up, and sometimes to steal his catch and take it in their boats up to Gulfport wholesale markets. There was a four hour trip usually involved for Octavio. Unfortunately it had to pass west in attack range of the pirate rats located on Roaban. This, the largest, infested of the Bay Islands.

With the support of Captain Brearly of the huge, mobile island neighborhood moored on Roaban, we had ridden shotgun for Rayban. We reduced pirate attack success, often with much thug life lost, or sunk.

Our protection took the form of the Blue-Coats in the Revolutionary War. Large cartels with radicalized thugs, and the country's army controlled by the Cartel against the few of us. This was the only way we could protect our livelihoods.

We look for weaknesses and capitalize on them. At the same time, leave no evidence of our operations; including all implements and, oh so ugly, remains of killers.

Roberto and his father were having trouble with the shrimp farm. They went to the local police for help; laughed out of their offices. The Cartel was paying officials at all levels. Son and Dad went to country mainland courts with no success. To the highest levels in the country, paid off. Rumored with money shared for campaigns of Southern Senators of the U.S.

There was no law enforcement nor court order to bring justice to this sick organizational collapse. On the other hand, I had several hundreds of thousands invested in a life/business here. Roberto did as well. The mobile Island was affected occasionally. If their extremely wealthy board of directors lost patience, the response was thunder personified.

CHAPTER THREE

Neighbors

Rayban, call name Octavio, a single operator of a business here had to depend on friends and neighbors for assistance. We provided!

"Octavio, we have you 5X5. Are you ok, what's happening?"

"Birdcage, we are fine and making good headway. I wondered if you would check your long-ranging radar to see if any threats are developing."

Lance responded, "Octavio, I checked all sources including the drone on your call. Nothing developing at the moment. Now we know you are on the waves, we'll keep an eye out. Run flank speed for two hours and I will check again. If things are clear, I will tuck in against Vanna and you can back off to three bells. If not, I will call. Good sailing, Birdcage out."

We returned to breakfast, a mourner for desert, and down to the dock to clean and prepare for the next day.

Octavio had a mom and younger brother living in a village called Sambo Creek on the north coast. Most of the inhabitants were the offspring of the slave boats coming from Africa. Decades before they blew south and foundered on the reefs of the Caribbean. He was coming up on thirty years old with one of the most lucrative businesses on the coast. He wasn't married, nor even dating much. Friends kidded him and chided him. Nothing developing.

The thugs too frequently frustrated him launched from Roaban Island heading north-east where he was running northwest toward Gulfport. They'd celebrate if they ever could rob him and push him into the Atlantic.

Octavio was going to dock, wholesale flounder this time, east of the bayous of the south coast. There was a good number of outlaws in there I worried might someday join up with the Mafia Don. J Mondo.

CHAPTER FOUR

Vanna and Zulinda: Sparks!

With the new tourists in mind, I asked Vanna to call Zulinda, owner of the "Unclad. Com" resort south on the island. Before Vanna arrived at the resort and became my love and co-operator, Zulinda and I had joined forces against cartel pirates sinking or stealing our supplies from Cuenca. We needed a joint supply run.

Zulinda modeled the behavior she expected of her clients, and wore nothing. No thong, nothing! We sent two boats, or one, with two guys running shotgun and the problem was resolved. The woman was a 6' 5" grey/blue eyed wonder. I had seen her in the distance when we were building Starr. I had never gone over, knowing reactions come forth quite expectedly.

Zulinda had been running her camp three years before I began to build mine. Eventually, we talked about our similar business problems once per month. I, fully dressed; she thread-less. Business and survival on the island occupied our minds and the relationship smoothed out to be warm, supportive, but platonic.

Vanna came and she and I bonded, fiercely. Vanna knew the timeline of camp development and on the day Zulinda first arrived, in the nothing-at-all, Vanna reflected on my hunger for herself. She assumed what I could be with her, I'd be with the striking beauty Zulinda.

Assumed! I was not without a woman several times building camp, not Zulinda. The Fifth Amendment on any others, but Vanna went to the changing room of the cabana, undressed and chose to compete nude to nude. Vanna went after Zulinda with burning eyes. Verbal, but viscous. I moved aside. Eventually it ended. Zulinda tried to heal the feelings, Things were only on hold.

Zulinda shamed Vanna for her assumptions and pointed out which man she was actually concerned about in the upcoming self-defense raid: Rayban Hernandez.

Zulinda left and I took Vanna to the bedroom to sooth her feelings.

It was cool for the night. Vanna settled and morning was hot. Almost delayed the trip. We hurried off together to prepare our counter-attack if endangered.

If inter-camp meetings were needed or joint supply trips, or any little, tiny thing developed between camps, I sent Vanna exclusively.

CHAPTER FIVE

A turn-around on the way back

The dive clubs came in on the six-seater Cessnas from Cuenca to a gravel airport on a nearby island. It served Unclad.com and the Starr Professional Diving Camp. We had the two ramp diving boats and another security high speed coast guard type craft. We took four trips to get clients to the pier and belongings to ramp boats, or cabanas. The group had one woman. I had specifically searched for a woman camp co-operator and was glad to have Vanna here. Temporary for now but apt to contracted in the near future. Of course, more for other reasons. There were 28 total guests so we used both ramp boats and boat captains.

After dinner, I spoke with all guests reminding them of underwater hand-signing and camp response to any damage to the reef. "Take only pictures and leave only bubbles." They had a morning and afternoon dive available daily and a night dive on Wednesdays depending on weather. Northerners, our signature storm typically developed at sun-down, full force before we knew it.

The next morning, we decided to send Vanna in the boat with the other woman, and our diver/administrator Josh with the other men and captain.

With Octavio in Gulfport, which we expected to be two nights, I went with a boat captain and one of Zulinda's staff, dressed and well-armed, to Cuenca for supplies. Depending on weather we might get the two,

two-hour trips in one day. Northerners concerned us. On this day, while loading supplies, one hit the coast. We had to unload and get into a hotel. Anticipating the camp arrivals, we left very early the following day and had the cook re-stocked and bubbling well before the third and final flight.

I scanned to locate Octavio on his way following the storm. There was no Octavio anywhere. I was hopeful he had found a date to last overnight for a change. I went to my now lonely bungalow and lay for a snooze. No sooner had I closed my eyes, the camp sea radio ramped off.

Rayban finally had a date, overnight, with a sharp girl. Returning to the port, two cartel thug boats were stalking him. He headed for the east exit of Gulfport and they'd followed. West they'd followed again.

Lance with sleep in his eyes, "This is Birdcage, what's wrong Octavio?" Lance paused to listen. "Ok, Octavio. Go back among the yachts. If you know anybody there, stay and chat with them. At least don't get out of the breakwater. Hold on, Octavio."

Lance radios, "Roberto, where are you?

"I encouraged some shrimp relationship building and Cindy had a better idea. Why are you interrupting me?"

"Roberto, I'm sorry, my shame to Cindy. Listen to this conversation with Octavio in Gulfport:

From Lance, "How many thug boats are hunting you? Is there something they want on the boat, or will they steal the boat? Do you have the cash on board from the flounder sales? Do you have armament? Good, Octavio, keep it absolutely out of sight. If cops there see a big black guy with an RPG, I'll be hunting for bail money. Better, get a sound suppressed rifle with regular ammo. One sec., I've got Roberto."

"Guys, I put all cash in a safe deposit in Gulfport for my lawyer Felipe to deal with. They are going to take my boat only over my dead body. I can out-run them. I got 23 knots to their seven."

"Octavio, at ease! Songbird, the U.S. Drone base told me he saw them cruising at 18 knots with an empty boat. Roberto is on his way to me. We (Birdcage) will come part of the way for you. Don't run until I tell you we are in position! Only then do you make a run for us. I will call the timing. Understood? Only if they make a move to come inside the breakwater do you start shooting and running. Clear?"

"Well, you've always been right before. Put your boat in overdrive on hot. I am sweating it here! Octavio, out"

CHAPTER SIX

Pirates Don

"Octavio, Roberto should be here in a half hour. Remember, my security craft can run over 33 knots. Octavio, don't depend on the U.S. Coast Guard. They will have to request orders from up a chain where these Texas congress' payoffs may already be in the bank. Their response, among others, bartered by mafia, Don J: to lie and screw with you. By the time help arrives, if at all, you'd be destroyed. Don't trust even a black cop if he is decked out in gold chains. He'll be on somebodies payroll. I may sound a disloyal, chagrinned American but in the last five years, the worst has always become reality from the hog to the complicit Re-s.

"Vanna, where are you in the dive, over?"

"Birdcage, only the pros have more than five minutes air left. We're boarding over half of the clients. What can I do, over?"

"Vanna, we don't want to spook the divers. Get the pros early if you can. Take a slow turn back to the dock and floor it. I need you there quickly to get the drone up, green laser. Get us on radar. Call when you are set, over."

Vanna, "Roger, out!"

"Octavio, be there soon. Put your suppressed arms close at hand, out of sight. If you actually need to shoot, use them so authorities or crooks can't locate the source.

I see Roberto In the distance, Birdcage Out."

An hour later with Lance's big Chevy inboard whining, the distance had been closed only to half. Lance radioed Captain Brearly on the mobile island. He had his big drone, Black Bird, up too far away. There are no dependable U.S. rules of engagement here. We needed to get the meeting outside of U.S. waters and away from any Coast Guard 'authorized' involvement. Their Rules of Engagement would kill us.

"Flank speed, NOW, Octavio", barked Vanna. Octavio hammered his cruiser out of the East breakwater heading west of south. The thugs were surprised, maneuvered after him losing a minute and a half. They were up to 18 knots with Octavio at 23, he was not making needed separation. Armament from the thugs could cover the distance.

With Roberto, I had my Chevy screaming and was, with wind direction, heading North-West to Rayban at 35 knots. If Vanna's calculations and sea currents cooperated, Roberto and I could thread the needle between the rogues and Octavio with the distance of 200 meters each side.

Roberto slipped below and brought out the armament. Three sound suppressed rifles with the first volleys dark, and the second two with tracers. Two RPG's and four subsurface torpedoes.

Octavio had even more lethal weapons; but in choppy waters had trouble shooting accurately.

Lance orders, "Octavio, we're between you and your attackers. You have no assistant. Get low, full speed, and let us do the shooting."

"Birdcage, Vanna said, I'm here. Fully locked and loaded. Orders?"

"Vanna, Roberto has two torpedoes in the water,

port and starboard of us. Get them on your drone scope. Bring some fire immediately on the port boat since their rifles are getting awfully close to me. You can use the yellow lens. I'll stall the starboard rifle fire. If Roberto misses either thug boat, green lens either or both until it sinks. Anything left, I will take out with the Holland and Holland with four power scope. Copy?"

Octavio stutters, "Birdcage, I've got a bazooka. Let me defend my boat! Out!"

"Octavio, come back, stay down. Roberto is arming the torpedoes. If he doesn't take both boilers out in the next minute, Vanna will laze them out. If that fails, you can pop your head and use whatever you have aboard. Do not use the bazooka unless it is absolutely the last option to save your boat. The thunder and flash will be unmistakable even from Gulfport. Do you copy?"

"Copy birdcage, my stop watch is running."

"Roberto, send a torpedo each way. If you sense a miss, go hard with double taps. The rogues are not hiding below their gunwales. Shoot bogies or the bottom of their boilers to the port side.

Roberto's torpedo hit the port thug boat solid in the boiler. Two flailing bodies rocketed up and away. With his tracers, he hit them both before they hit to drown if they weren't already gone.

Vanna quickly switched to the starboard thugs where I had been suppressing fire and it was not sinking. She green-lazed the flame hoses on the boiler and it whammed all parts and all thugs to decimation. We inspected the area for any remnants of our action. It was clear Octavio would get home safely tonight.

CHAPTER SEVEN

Breather

We escorted Octavio south until we saw Guanaja on the starboard side. He continued to Sambo under the eyes of our radar and drone.

It was after midnight with full moon as we moored the security craft to our dock. Camp lights were on generator as normal and all tent lights were out. Some interesting snoring. Our luck was holding; we had been able to deal with the Cartel without worrying our important guests, our best "word of mouth" advertising. Josh and another boat captain took both daytime dives the next day.

CHAPTER EIGHT

Discussion with brearly and work trip to Frankfurt

After our day of purported rest, we both took the group morning dive trips. Divers had viewed the wall a mile off the north coast and today would explore the shallower, more colorful reef to the east of the island. Vanna and I were now taking pressure off the captains because in two weeks we'd be going to Frankfurt for two or more months. It was still more busy hours for the full time captains. We took the Wednesday night dives as well. Our itineraries for divers were intense, and not for novices unless booked in advance with accompanied trainers. Diving the whole itinerary seldom happened for all visitors. The recent exception had been the Mukwonago Volunteer Fire Dept. team of twelve, who ultimately absconded with Trey. Or Fran did! They didn't miss a breath of any dive day or night.

CHAPTER NINE

Familiarization

Vanna and I made a point of taking the night dives for three weeks before any travel. Again, she was a delightful exception to any rules. She'd do Monday and Tuesday, both dives and the Wednesday night without missing a beat. When I wasn't expecting it, she was apt to do me any given Wednesday night after the dive. This week was not the exception but we were taking the first Thursday dive.

A choppy surf vibrated stiff knees for me while Vanna was making "poor, poor boy faces" at me from the other ramp boat. Stiff or not, it was a joy to see her teasing the seduction.

We knew our flora and fauna very well. Everybody got as close as they could to the moray eel. They saw only the sand in the water behind the ray who slept here. We had visitors under the pier as well. Two squid flashed to deep water every day, and a rock fish hung around. Step on the thorn of one of these and worse than an allergy, you'd be down for days or more.

CHAPTER TEN

Brearly's concerns after Octavio's curious attack

We did the two morning dives the following Thursday because Captain Brearly had asked us to a late lunch. There was no doubt in my mind about the discussion. We took the security boat for the 20 minute ride, depending on wind, to the huge neighborhood he led. Big smiles Maria, on a luscious Mrs. Brearly body welcomed us on the dock. She was a bronze tanned woman with roots a couple of generations back in Costa Rica. We'd heard the story of the Captain's capture of this university grad-beauty a few years ago. Educated women around these islands were few in number. The Cartel ignored any law and killed any enforcement for the trafficked.

Maria stored her 300 Weatherby with the security captain. She escorted us to the six block Captain's tower and quarters. Time for a drink imported to the island, not available even at my upscale resort. The invited minute lunch, more a dinner, was served.

Brearly was in his dress whites, clear why Maria let him catch her. His face showed some concern, nothing other than our Germany and his desire for a leave with Maria to his home culture, came up. A double Bailys was desert and Maria called in the housekeeper to clear. Vanna got a peck from Maria who floated off somewhere. Brearly, front and center, would give her a full debriefing on her pillow tonight. She was intellectually much more than a north coast bed-warmer.

He said, "I heard some noticeable popping and

banging the other night. Sound travels fast from Gulfport over the water. I saw you escorting Octavio later. Is he ok, any damage to his lovely cruiser?

Vanna quickly answered, summarizing the actions.

Brearly, with an endearing smile for Vanna, said,

"Lance, something here is wrong. We have cooperatively defended some lives and property. Every skirmish has initiated from the North Coast near SPS or the other side of Orilla Island. What generated something on the doorway of the Gulfport Marina?"

"Vanna recounted what happened. I added we kept the skirmish well off-shore to avoid any blowback from a harbormaster.

Lance continued, "But, why, stumps me. I was hoping your board might have something. The only anomaly other than theft is the common thread of trying to force Octavio toward the east. If we have a west wind pushing him closer to the north of you, or Orilla, their efforts are more nefarious to push him east. The drone picked up that slight deviation. I missed it completely. Octavio had nothing of value on the craft other than the craft itself. His cash goes in a bank downtown Gulfport and his lawyer keeps track of how he can reduce taxes, and avoid most of them from this scam government. Even his assistant wasn't there. That, he may want to re-think."

CHAPTER ELEVEN

Reconnaissance

Brearly ponders, "Lance, my corporation has been snooping around very gingerly to see what we are facing, the core center group or individual sending out these raids. I expect knowledge by the end of the year, possibly U.S. Senatorial elections driven. I can't promise it will be actionable information. If you volunteer, you might escort well, and very well, Octavio, to the port north of SPS. Go secretly, heavily armed in your two fastest boats. Take Vanna! Do nothing if you can avoid it; observe as long as you can. I know I've interfered with hours of sleep in your mind, but I can't say more.

Brearly and two armed securty escorted us to our security boat at which point he left us and the security people drove along in a boat accompanying us back to our dock.

We monitored Octavio's trips to Gulfport for two additional weeks. There were no anomalies and I had to get back to Frankfurt. As always, Roberto hovered about Starr Resort and skyped weekly.

CHAPTER TWELVE

Frankfurt

The first month in Germany was hurried with the design and construction of various Mercedes components. I did reverse-engineering training and forward training with new ideas Greg kept rolling down his pike. Vanna kept herself busy with shopping, every night meeting me with devil's eyes. Finally I gave up on guessing. The runway upon eventual return to Guanja would be breathtaking.

After the intense month on the continent, I had a three week break before receiving parts tied up in the Suez Canal. We had talked our last trip of visiting Austria. We had time and the climate was tolerable. We trained to Munich, borrowed Greg's Mercedes and headed for Salzburg. It was only a half day from Munich through humungous mountain passes. I was glad we had passed on our idea earlier because a snow-slide could wipe us out.

Heavy wooden planks and dirndl wall hangings put us directly in the culture. The room with bed and couch was floating with soft comforters and carved erotic ceilings.

We were full; did a pre-bubble. Thanks to Brearly, I was nightly trying to project what problem his people were pursuing in SPS. We were scanning the Caribbean from west to east, checking out coastlines, any other shipping, any danger to the banana industry, a giant there. From Western Florida on through southern Texas, control of behavior regarding guns, attitudes toward federal government, and healthcare were torture on the sick or elderly. They even had their own electric grid which couldn't be attached to the national in case of local outages. Pay their own costs rather than taxes and be responsible for their own maintenance. Recent outages had brought the inadequacy to country-wide recognition. One of their southern Senators was so indifferent he went on vacation while the people who were continually fools to vote for him suffered cold, heat, and water access. Speculation among world-aware people were he was personally receiving illegal campaign money. Older citizens paid with deaths. We could go around and around on this but spied a bottle of Kirshwasser on the mini-bar. Two shots each, and under the thick comforters we basked in local "lieben". Very culturally sensitive!

CHAPTER THIRTEEN

Pacho Mantanya

GUATAMALTECO father, Pacho was born in Managua, Nicaragua. There his name was Montanya, or mountain. He was brightest of three siblings, street smart. Eventually under the tutorship of Cartel recruiters, he became the epitome of Evil Street smart. The second echelon of the Mondo in the country met him and knew what they could do with him. They avoided giving him any idea of history.

In the ten years following, he moved up the ladder through training in fighting, shooting, water boarding and beheading. They had him watch the right TV and he became a slippery, "buddy, buddy", guy of the worst villains. He experienced directly the use of his grisly skills. He could sell ice cubes to Eskimos.

At sixteen, they bought him a wife and in three years they had three children. At 20, they bought him a green card. They moved him to a Spanish Speaking manufacturing neighborhood in Texas. Time for pay back!

CHAPTER FOURTEEN

Bloody Reset

Ceasrito's Mafia brute father had been dead for over a year and a half. Alicia had now seen two further "Don J. "Mondos" deflowered with no ramifications to her, husband Ceasrito, or their veterinary business. She watched Ceasrito carefully, closely and from afar. Their marriage was going as she drove it. She was magnetic and Ceasrito was in awe of her beauty. She controlled him as women have the armament to do. He was a guy with terrific memory but no analytical skills. She had it all. What he also had was a body of ripple and eyes entranced by her completely. His loving was intense and to see his eyes adoring her each morning was a priceless start to the day.

The reason she watched him closely was he had been son of the dead mafia Don J who had estranged him from the family. Forcing him to do disgusting Cartel tasks was relieved by four years of university. Perhaps low analysis skills contribute to an innocent mind. Home, He was a different person and soon Alicia was guiding his morals and values. They lived together for a while as Alicia tried on her new shoes before buying them.

The lightning of degenerate Mafia filth hit when a lieutenant of the Mondo took Ceasrito from his home and forced him fighting to an arena in the center of the town.

Don J barked, "Now I will make you a man who

contributes to this organization. Bring in the insolent lout who teases me nights on TV and demeans my leadership."

Ceasrito tried to shake off the lieutenant and another joined in pinning him to the wall. The corpulent Mondo strutted to the center of the arena, raised his arm, looked to the wooden door and walked to the edge of the seats. A man in chains was dragged out, pulled to a log in the center of the ring, head thrust down, rolled right to Ceasrito who saw the moving grimaces.

Ceasrito ripped his arms from the lieutenants and ran to the nearest bathroom completely losing it. He ran out of the arena down to the beach and ran from vomit to vomit until he was empty. He didn't want to involve or describe any of this to Alicia but couldn't stop from seeking her solace. She took him in empathy soon offering his deepest desire.

CHAPTER FIFTTEEN

Marriage Preferred Sans Step-Anything

Ceasrito removed himself from any other Cartel horrors. She decided the marriage was due. Alicia wondered to her father, well-grounded of the horrors here, whether she could safely stay in this marriage. Speaking with his years of observation he said, "The Cartel will not attack the son of a Mondo, or immediate family, nor destroy the only business where the boy has the horsepower to succeed."

"Do I need a security guard?"

"At the moment, no. I will check sources over time if my opinion changes. Take him for a healing honeymoon over to Guatamala to dusty Antigua. Behind the clay walls, you will find quality local entertainment. Somewhere at least away from here."

I took him and with ecstasy rebuilt him for intense loyalty. He passed some exhilarating tests. I informed him to start a baby. With his dad and evil paid trophy wife gone, we could safely have a baby. We pulled into the home driveway; I took him right down. I knew him intently as a male, and myself as a veterinary. The machinery was there; no question.

Seeing the social cruelties toward women, I decided to have a boy. Sounds a bit presupposing. With lightly acid baths, vinegar pads and by controlling C's frequency and speed, I slightly increased the overall probability of effective Y sperms. Abstaining for thirteen days caused much wailing. Completely ignored, I hit pay sperm the second month.

I am built perfectly for baking babies. I wasn't certain if I want one here. We didn't peek and my recipe charmed out an 8 pound, 8 ounce bruiser. After one loving day, my heart was no longer my own. No cartel thug unless over my dead body would touch his mind or body. For the first time my emotions ignored my father's advice. I called my Asian Language teacher at A&M. I got the contact info for the Nepali guest lecturer I had evocatively befriended before I saw the fervor in Ceasrito's eyes: LAXMAN SHRESTA

CHAPTER SIXTEEN

Into U.S. Corruption

Pacho was not slated to be a lowly drug runner. The Cartel's radicalizers capitalized on his elusive evil to get him into office first at the community level with Republican monies into State Government in Texas where he now had residency. They continued to groom him using Cartel money to get him a large Villa where elected betrayers of a democracy could plan their obstruction and subversion of the U.S. Government. He had a budget deep enough to take representatives and wives to Caribbean Resorts. He needed no more.

CHAPTER SEVENTEEN

Long Lasting Love?

Our small group of few against the evil-many monitored each other routinely. Octavio didn't return from Gulfport in three days, I radioed. I heard music in the background, waiting for him to get outside. I listened for a few minutes, signed off, turned, and sent Vanna into paraxioms of joy: "Nerven".

Octavio pulled up to a "preparation for offloading" dock on each arrival to Gulfport. It was one hundred meters from the conveyor. Rayban moved the Octavio to the required ramp position, noted the line-up growing to the main port fish conveyor, and decided not to face the melee. He pulled away, went down, showered and dressed for a beer on the dock closer to the shore.

On the left side on the way down, he saw a woman laying back on a sun couch with a big hat over her head. He couldn't see her face. The remainder of the view was worthwhile. He slowed, she apparently didn't notice, and he walked on. He had an imported beer and headed back. He got back on his boat and with a glance back, caught a glance in return. He moved over to the conveyor, unloaded, and headed back to Sambo.

When deep sea fishing tours are out of season, he makes usually three trips to Gulfport each week.

Big Hat was back tanning the never ending thighs as he passed up for a beer. This time they had a civil, shallow conversation in passing. He took his beer back to the cruiser and went to unload, heading back south. He checked; there were continued flash glances. He docked next to our ramp boat in Guanaja, said hello, and took Vanna firmly by the hand and hurried her up to an intense conversation. Half skipping to his boat, he left full flank back south.

After dinner and a particularly flashing bed desert, I closed bubble and asked "Vanna, what was the secret conversation with Rayban today?

"Lance, let's keep it secret, as I promised, for a while?"

Dive groups came and went with no interruption from the Cartel. It had been so long I began to wonder. I remembered Blearly's encouragement to reconnoiter the SPS north port area.

Octavio's trips to Gulfport were lengthening with me watching to be sure he wasn't in danger. Back in the bubble, Vanna showed no concern. I wondered if maybe it was some kind of relationship I'd missed. I dozed finishing my beloved voluntary chores.

Brearly's rough voice woke me. "Birdcage, this is Black Bird. Copy?"

"Roger, I copy but a sweet dream interrupted. What's up?"

"I'm afraid you'll have to shift to nightmare. Octavio is headed north and has picked up a tail of two boats. Octavio has Junior now. You better get them up to speed. Out!"

CHAPTER EIGHTEEN

Fought With New Beginnings

I launched the drone and lit off the radar.

"Octavio, this is Birdcage. Are you aware of what I'm calling about? Over"

"Yes birdcage I have them on sea radar. I'm well-armed, with Junior by my side, and probably can outrun them. However, I have a special package to take to Sambo on the way back. Fragile! I'm concerned about the return trip. If they shadow me again, I absolutely cannot gamble. I return on day three from now. I need to have the trip go as quietly as possible. I may need to have you escort me from the breakwater up there. Will you be around? Over"

"Ok, Octavio, any changes, we'll know before you do and light off the Chevy to join you. Call me early on the day you want to create your 'Phantom Parade'. Standing bye, Birdcage."

"Octavio, out!"

It was morning nap, dunk and bubble after breakfast. "I think I know the mentoring you are giving Rayban. There's a woman enjoying his rippled shoulders and other bubblable attentions. We need to plan if his heart is set on bringing her to mama in the next week. Tell me the truth."

"Yes, Lance, it's a woman, tall he says with the other

accoutrements. With abundance of shy, he hinted they are involved from top to bottom. His age, I think."

"Vanna, you should radio him the day after tomorrow and have him say the things he needs to say to prepare, but not scare her. Be sure she has a passport and any virus tests required. We will meet him up there with the security boat and all armaments and Roberto. It should go without incident. Difficult conditions, but I don't want him to lose a "keeper" due to mistakes on our part. "Vanna, use "Birdcage Drone".

CHAPTER NINETEEN

Body Guard

Ten thousand Nepalis apply to be Gurka's. Four hundred are chosen by British recruiters after grueling activities and competitions. Applicants need a working ability in English because this is the British Gurhka Division. They are trained beyond some's endurance, but are one of the most feared fighting cadres in the world.

The traditional fighting weapon is a short curved blade sword which is called the 'Gurkha'. Modern weapons have now been added to the armory. The Gurkha is worn on every belt. Candidates must be from 17 ½ to 21 to try out. The normal term of service is 15 years with all pension and health for soldier and immediate family. The pension provides a quality salary after exchange rate, ad infinitim.

The war between the British and Argentinians raged on the Falklands; the mercenary British Gurkha unit was called up. They fight quietly in the night and shadows. Their enemies, looking at first alive, melt. The Argentinian soldiers quickly retired from the slashes in the night. Laxmi Shresta was a veteran of this conflict and others nearer Asia.

Laxmi was of the Shresta caste in Nepal. Ask any policeman his last name; it's Shresta. At the minimum age, 17 ½, he went another way. He could, in fifteen years earn a lifetime of security for his family. He already was a mountain of a man. He went among the 10,000; a

British recruiter saw the look in his eye. He was a medaled soldier never losing in the 15 year life plan.

At 33, he was retired, bilingual, financially sufficient for his family, and free to seek a new life. His first goal was to renovate his family home into this century with modern appliances and ornaments. Soon, he looked further.

The suburb of Bhaktapur was a half days walk from downtown Kathmandu. Ancient monuments and statues adorned streets and central squares. Having a knowledge of both the East and the West, he saw the monument the most visited. The depth of the stones steps worn off made it clear.

There were a half dozen women with their daughters viewing; discussing seriously the meaning of the carvings. Playboy and the "Art of Loving" were not seen in this culture. The carvings were accurate and included everything a young girl of arranged marriage needed to be a good wife. In this culture, birth control methods were included. And more.

As a single man, he kept his distance and showed respect between him and the participants.

Typical at these things, foreigners not knowing the customs moved right up between him and the families. He heard English, German, French, and some oriental girls speaking something he didn't know. People's dress shouted: 'Peace Corps.'

He had seen those people and knew they tried to help people out in the villages. In town they were always interested and friendly. There was however a set of horizon blue eyes under long brown hair flashing at his. A smile, brief. There was wonderment on both sides if this could be something. Blue eyes was clearly a little older and leader of the group. She locked eyes back again as she led her group away. His eyes fired. He turned away.

He wandered around the cobblestones with one thing he couldn't delete from his mind. They were gone. He didn't know anything really in depth about them, Tracking, however, had been one of his military skills. He could surely find them.

He did find them at Casey's, one of the few places you could order a water buffalo steak with no worms nor amoebas included. He walked to her and introduced himself. She smiled and responded. They closed the place down.

Two days later he was kitted out far more cleverly than the others to find out exactly what Peace Corps people do. He had some doubts about it and Connie challenged him to come along and see for himself. He was beholden to the British instructors who drilled his English. He focused his British accent on Connie.

There were hours debating about how to deal with cross cultural parents and families. The biggest challenge of all: Connie had been appointed head of the Peace Corps in Central American/Caribbean operations. Marrying was tough enough, taking him away was rivers of tears. They were off to the small city of Cuenca where the office for Central America was located.

CHAPTER TWENTY

Is she a Trouper; can she tolerate life-off shore?

Vanna called Octavio the next morning to brief him on emotions he might have forgotten or hadn't had to face. She laid out a sample of the speech he should give Nerven about special conditions of our Caribe. Was she babying him? Absolutely.

Apologetically, Octavio called us from Gulfport very early the next day, the departure. "Birdcage, we are being stalked. They are hanging to the west of us. They want to drive us East, or attack. We need your help. I'm trying to make this a vacation fun-trip for Nerven. I think she gets some vibs. She's very careful to do immediately what I ask. I can't give her a Rueger without knowing how she'll handle the emotional trauma.

"Octavio, Birdcage back to you. I agree with your Rueger judgement. Keep her as far out of it as you can. Secondly, don't leave safe harbor until you see the lights of my eyes. I have armament on board for this theater of operations. I have Roberto. Vanna already has you on the drone. Her call is "Birdcage Drone". I don't see how they could ever successfully attack you. I read your questions about pushing you east and shared with Brearly. He only hints he may have info at the end of the year."

Octavio breaks in, "What is so important about Orillo Key and the west?

Lance, "Octavio, we're not going to be asking them. If they attack, I will decimate them. If I don't succeed, Vanna will light them both up. Then you and I will sweep. Come to the lip of the break-water in 1½ one hours. Hold there until you see me. I can't let them get you between me and a cross fire with the boat docks. Don't start any firing. Wait till I wave to move out to deeper water. Birdcage, Out!"

CHAPTER TWENTY ONE

Round Trip Desecration

The largest city on the Texas coast had been hammered by a huge hurricane. To be hygienic, large parts had to be rebuilt. Garbage transportation dykes had to be rebuilt, as New Orleans had done. The large corporations balked; they didn't want to pay the taxes. Even with new Re's legislation unfairly putting the burden on the general middle class and immigrant community, their greed ran rampant, SICK! Don J., Southwest Mafia head was called. He called Pacho.

Riding high in his Rolls Royce, Pacho scanned a map and developed a plan. Nobody in government wanted to improve the plan. Nobody wanted to be associated with him in any way. He was the hitman. Eventually, he became dangerous excess baggage.

He boated down to the largest port and charted a flight to follow the coast of Mexico, past Cuba, and Merida. Destination: the southern tail of Mexico, and on to San Pedro Sula, one of the most dangerous drug centers in the world.

He contacted Border control to avoid the obvious chance of being shot down as a drug transport. "Ah, how is my old friend, Don J. Mondo doing these days?" An envelope changed hands along with an evil smile. No flight plan nor flight problems. He went and returned to the U.S. port, went to a strip club and spent the night. The following morning he flew the Texas coast over to the Mississippi. He followed the river north a short way and saw a group of rusting barges and noted the name of the company. He flew back to the port and had his Rolls take him home.

He had dispatched his trafficked wife and kids to cheaper lodgings and had his latest waiting for him in his hot tub. He rested most of the evening and slept well late the next day. He proceeded to study some maps and much of Delores.

He called his "friend" in the port asking him to locate, rent or buy, three, thirty five foot trawlers, war surplus with gun placements. Look for some rusted on the outside; reclaimable and stable on the inside. He visited a well-known illegal arms dealer. "Ah, how is my old friend, Don J?"

He got on the internet and located the web site of the Mississippi barge dealer. There was none. Better yet. He called information and got the land line. Ah, there was Cartel stink in the air. Orange roses to him. He agreed to rent six months in advance, paid in full by courier coming in two days. "Clean up three, not noticeable. "I tow them with Coronado's. Include chain connections. Drivers next Wednesday.

He needed a large crew, automatic with the Asst. Capo in Alamo Heights. Anybody loyal to Capo had work. He flew to San Jose, Costa Rica and got lost in the striking love pits.

CHAPTER TWENTY TWO

To become expats again

Connie and Laxmi flew to Montana where there was an American consulate not overcome by Central Americans running literally for their lives. Even married to an American, it took the better part of a year for a green card visa. Several more years needed for citizenship. He had a pension well above what they needed, Connie had savings. She wanted to get back to work, excited about her new leadership role and as a matter of feminine pride. Laxmi had been in many cultures, he faced no culture shock. What was shocking, in Honduras, they got citizenship in less than a month.

He recalled at the end of his service, his Brahmin friend Devi at Texas A&M had invited him, a veteran Gurkha as a guest speaker. He also remembered the Honduran girl there whose eyes trapped his. Never to be as he had to leave her for Nepal immediately. He did knew her dreams and had met the guy in the running for the +1. If her dream came true, she was a veterinary somewhere in Honduras. They had parted on good terms. There was no rancor when, "surprise" Connie brought Alicia home from work one day. That they already knew each other knocked the socks off Connie. A blush on Alicia. Her professor, the Brahmin, was connected. Laxmi was the one shocked to an embarrassed silence. Of course he remembered the eyes, but there had been much more. Typically shy in temperament, he spoke little. They talked about Cesarito and the new baby, clearing the air for everybody about anybody. Laxmi relaxed and warmed up.

They worked together to prepare, uphill, for Moon Mountain. Alone, they camped; he showed his outdoor skills. He pitched the mosquito net. They shared some indoor skills! The next day they arrived by sundown. He went for first introductions. They met Connie's team. She sat them down to outline their mission.

CHAPTER TWENTY THREE

Welcome Procession to Sambo

Trying to act relaxed with Nerven, Octavio was relieved to see Lance's Chevy evolve in the distance. Lance waived him out of the breakwater and flew toward his starboard side. Rayban headed Octavio southwest, the thugs hard after him. Trying some experiments, Octavio changed to due west. Birdcage copied him. The thugs were screaming their limited vocabulary, cutting back and forth to force him south or east.

"Octavio, this is Birdcage. Now try to head due south and see what happens. We'll need distance from the breakwater if there is noise. How is Nerven doing?"

"She's downstairs, dozing I hope."

"Stay at full flank and I will parallel you."

"Octavio, do you notice any change in their actions? "

"Birdcage, they have maneuvered to my west and are going south losing a little separation. Stand by!"

"Birdcage, they're staying in rifle range, which spooks me. I have my suppressed rifle. I may lose this volley if I don't shoot very soon, now!"

"Octavio, wait one, dodge west again. Birdcage Drone, are you with us?"

"I'm about 150 yards behind them out of sight."

"Octavio is with me on-line. He's going to veer west. Their previous actions indicate they may attack. Octavio, patience, let us handle this so Nerven doesn't get waken and scared. Roberto has a torpedo in the water. It may be too slow. If they fire anything at Octavio, Vanna, take them out. We'll use the torpedo on the second boiler, be ready to back us up if we miss or don't seriously disable it."

Birdcage Drone, "Standing by."

Octavio, "Veer west, NOW!"

Lance with steel determination to protect the new girl, "Birdcage Drone, there's a tracer at Octavio. End it!"

"Roberto, what's yours doing?"

"They're not firing at Octavio, they're firing at us. I released two torpedoes."

"Too slow!"

"Birdcage Drone, we have sniper fire. Green laze the second boat."

"Roberto, use tracers to keep their heads down while the torpedo tracks."

"Birdcage Drone, if the first boat is sufficiently disabled, cover Roberto and me with the laze now.

"Roger, I've saved your ass before and will gladly do so again."

It takes a Seal to find humor in a firefight.

"Octavio, what's the situation with the first boat?"

"Dam it, Birdcage, I'm still waiting for the torpedo. Ah, excuse me Vanna, and Roberto. It's here. Wait one."

Roberto, "Birdcage, I've been raking them with fire; they keep popping up. "Whack-A-mole." I think Vanna hit only the boiler and they're still functioning."

"Roberto, get down out of line of fire immediately!"

Lance, "Vanna, you got some cleaning up to do!"

"Roger, anything for the step brother-in–law. Out!"

"Roberto here, both laser and torpedo collided at the same time. Only oil on the water."

"Octavio, sitrep?"

"Birdcage, my heart started beating again. There is clean-up; will you handle it for both boats. Nerven is stirring. She doesn't need to see whatever there may be."

"Octavio, understood and agreed. Don't go far. Go out two hundred yards south and circle. I've got you this far, I'm not going to lose you to any anomaly following us."

Lance, "Roberto, take us first to the oil spot."

"Nothing but oil and gas, no implements. It's 400 feet deep here."

"Roberto, flank toward the other boat; drop a flare here."

"Roger?"

"Octavio, can you talk down Nerven for five more minutes. There'll be a flare I don't want her to see forcing you to lie." Up north they do enough lying for the whole world.

"A pleasure. She has dressing moves needing more than five. Circling, Out!"

"Roberto, we need to brick two or three things nobody should see to Davy Jones. When Octavio's bow shoots away, drop another flare."

We caught up with Octavio and escorted him unmolested into the break water at Sambo Creek.

Nerven had the right smile.

"Roberto, I think we hit a raw spot with our jinks to the west. Time for a visit to the north SPS docks."

CHAPTER TWENTY FOUR

PACHO'S EVIL SITS AND SPINS

"**I** stayed and paid. See you sometime, whores!"

Pacho jumped out of the bordello in a decrepit taxi and headed off to TACA's direct flight to Houston. The Rolls took him back to San Antonio. Even a three hour flight demands a whole day. He showered in his Villa, Delores professionally soothed, and he hit the sack.

South-west Don J. Mondo had acted. Pacho selected his garbage scow crews. Nine for trawlers with one on each barge. A rotation having one loading in Texas, one en route south, one sleeping in SPS and finally heading to Texas north-west of Orilla ripping the reef. Within two months, the garbage didn't sink fast enough and the already pollution-challenged Orilla had more ringing the island. Little used pristine reef was choking in excrement. In return, U.S.waste management was in action benefitting corporations with 70% less costs. Re' repression passed the other 30% onto local citizen's taxes. The Senator crowing!

The environment was dying, the corporations flourishing. Nobody knew, or wanted to know their Cartel poster-boy benefactor. He had his purchased pleasure women and wealth in homes throughout tax shelters in the region. Wallowing in his greed, he had another idea. Don J. smiled. Maybe it could take down the Federal Department of Justice, too.

CHAPTER TWENTY FIVE

THE SHADOW MISSION

Laxmi hovered protectively over the start-up of every new Peace Corps. Project. Connie returned every month; it was honeymoon all over. He often visited her on site with every intention of getting out of site. He was a product of the outdoors and grew up on a subsistence farm. He knew every nick and cranny of forests around his clay home in the region. He knew every animal and healing plants. He was a loner by nature and lived happily with the occasional visits. The Gurkha regiment turned everything upside down.

Fifteen years later in retirement, he had found comfort, a woman's devotion, and forests to explore. He could be out for days, but never miss honeymoons. Few others knew him, he was a wraith.

From their nights at A&M, Biblically and personally Alicia Marie knew his core. She was waiting for the right moment to launch him on the trail the Brahmin had plotted with her.

You could find him visiting the Veterinary and helping with the operations. He was drawn to large animals of unique jungle heritage. His options always for horses. If there were a complicated life-threatening injury with a smaller animal, Alicia Maria was quick to consult.

It was on a warm, rainy day Laxmi was sheltering in the clinic while Ceasrito was purchasing supplies in Cuenca.

Alicia sat him down for a serious talk. She reviewed the animal's people called the Cartel. He had recognized them long before, in other countries, too, but was quiet. She explained Ceasrito's background and desertion from the local gang. She spoke vaguely of information gained from her father. She spoke of the torture. With tears in her eyes, she recounted her struggle and fear for bringing a child innocent to this desperate pit.

"Laxmi, I need to speak honestly from the start. I met you at A&M and after some memorable love, surprisingly, forgot you. I feel embarrassed about that. When the baby came, I again thought of you. You can enjoy that train of thought. I flew up to see your Brahmin with my fears. We pondered for days. Ultimately, I was sure a man of your character and background was the safest, best answer. It wasn't completely an accident you are here now.

My father has been in the Honduran government previous to the Cartel and still has a few ties. Your friend, Devi, is strongly respected by the U.S. State Department. That government has lost values, ethics, and decency. I checked non-governmental sources. I have a two-year old boy who's going to survive in a very dangerous environment. He is going to face pure evil and will have to go through it here. I can't take Ceasrito to the U.S. and hope to have him considered for any kind of visa. They know who his father was.

There is resentment in right-wing circles here: Ceasrito, and me, as well, should be punished for abandoning their terror gangs. There have been two half-hearted attempts to attack or burn. Ceasrito is good of heart and I love him, but, only my gumption and shrieking caused us to survive, saved us. I am sure you understand where this is going. Please stay with me for two other things. First, Connie's involvement in all this was neither anticipated nor expected. She was a university friend. I have never spoken of this. Your meeting in Nepal was a surprise. Perhaps I had some influence on her transfer to Central America. I'm fooling myself. These things are decided at Devi's level or above.

You and Devi are the only people who know. Ceasrito is innocent and naïve, he could inadvertently destroy me and my boy. One mistake is terminal. The other thing concerns me is were you hurt or emotionally damaged in your wars and couldn't endure any further stress. This is the most hurtful thing I have ever considered. You must protect Connie by not telling her. From Ceasrito's occasional reactions, I know how this coud hurt.

Laxmi, in soothing British tones, "Alicia, I have had free will in arriving here. I had no idea you were here. I was the one who ghosted from A&M. We spoke of Karma. It led me to Connie. It has continued for you with Ceasrito.

I learned much more about you than love, western style. Your intelligence and ability to survive in dangerous surroundings are laudable. I've been in the swilling back rooms, know the emptiness of distorted minds. There is no way to heal the harrowing radicalization tortured into these creatures.

Shiva was our devil and hell in Nepal. The legends of his demonism don't hold a candle to this. I don't relish but realize death will have to be part of this life if I want Connie. I will face every risk."

CHAPTER TWENTY SIX

NERVEN FACES THE CHALLENGES

Vanna may have had a hint. I was not anticipating the stunning woman Rayban found, and won. She was a couple of shades more bronze than he and his brother. Made hazel eyes glow even brighter. She didn't have ancestry in the North Coast Culture. He had to be a veritable crooner. The other surprise was her being a diver. A connect with Vanna for sure.

You might hear me as the strident leader in a fire fight, but here I was all eyes. Buxom wetsuit required. No wetsuit tonight. I looked. Vanna knew Octavio even medically in depth. Thus, my respect for Nerven didn't get me a boxing of ears. I did have to make a comment about her huge hat.

CHAPTER TWENTY SEVEN

A DEAL BREAKER?

As the dinner waned, Rayban and Nerven wandered away to visit the Manatee nests. She had enhanced his pride meeting with his friends. He was confident now he could describe the realities of life with him. He told her about the struggle over protecting the Manatees from the Cartel teenagers. She stopped him.

"Honey, you know my dad owns the bar. I didn't know your or that you were involved in these activities. You may not know the exploits of your hidden environmental actions have traveled to bars beyond the Pan Handle. Now I am getting the un-embellished account, I couldn't be more proud of you and to be your fiancé. I should probably be more welcoming to Lance."

"Nerven, true, Good Samaritan Behavior. There are more, seriously dangerous things going on. I fear to tell you. Distraught to lose you, I can't live with myself if something happened to you because I didn't prepare you with the truth. No criticism if you left me right now. I'm certain you will re-evaluate Lance, and Vanna, and Roberto, although you don't know him as well."

"Rayban, I may not have the second ring, but I'm going no place without you. I don't fear. We know each other well, certainly well enough to predict a successful marriage and family."

Nerven continues, "There is more related directly to what we are discussing. I have worked in the bar since I wasn't old enough legally. These cruel chauvinists daily shamed me. Of course, under present circumstances, you, I welcome. They individually get their come-uppances. Every one of them has since, paid a hurtful price. They get viscous responses from me and I don't avoid sensitive parts. Drunk, they walk home; I can strike and leave scars. This is a constant battle. I tone down one uncivil guy via a world of pain, a new thug shows up and I have to start over again. We do have a pistol behind the bar. Dad says use could lose customers who aren't even aware of my injuries. He can mix a debilitating drink. I am very accurate with a pistol or rifle. Am I glad to be here with you where I can be a sexy woman and not be sleeping with painful bruises?"

"I'm sorry you've faced such disgusting behavior", Rayban with venom. I'm glad to have you here where such things are not tolerated even in excited loving. I cannot bare to give any pain in love."

"There are deadlier conflicts here with the cartel, effectively life and death, and much death. This is way beyond bar harassment. I don't relish, but am involved for self-defense and now I depend on the others."

"This Cartel depravity pre-dates me. Protection of my business has put me vulnerable. There is no way this will stop anytime soon. I can't maintain a business without joining the resort owners and the Captain of the Floating Suburb. Can you still, seriously deal with this?"

"I haven't had the life and love you offer, Nerven whispers, nor have I ever anticipated it was close, until you. Risks I will gladly take; outliving this ugly inhumanity with you.

"Fine, let me tell you something positive. Sambo Creek is a close community. I have special relationships because my business brings thousands of dollars to town. We have faced the Cartel occasionally in the past. We unite and protect each other. I can guarantee your safety here in sexy clothes or not. Dealing with the Cartel out on the island or on the water is another thing. I should tell you more.

"Rayban, you can go on telling me grueling stories; at some point "diminishing returns" set in. This problem will go on for a long time? How many years did I have to fight off depraved drunk men? It continues!"

Nerven having had enough, "Finally, the Cartel. I know their ilk. They're often the most disgusting at the bar. Have I not heard the braggadocio of their drink in the fights they supposedly fought? Their recounting of the legend of the Manatee is a hoot. Black phantoms in the night who can't speak. I count the numbers increasing as their fantasy war goes on? Some get so drunk they forget they told the story and repeat it again. Can I not recognize these animals have no direction in their radicalized life other than destruction?

"Rayban, I ask because I do."

Nerven firmly, "listen one minute more and let this rest. Do you believe I was quietly dozing in the bedroom of your cruiser with radio chatter so intense, rifle fire so obvious, detonations so close, and some flickering of a green ray or something? I wasn't dozing or anything of the kind. I see the love in your eyes, but I am not an innocent unaware woman in a cocoon that you may be imagining. I was tense and praying I'd never hear your pain hit by a projectile. My blood pressure was spiking because I could do nothing to protect you. You tried to calm me in sensitive ways. I was writhing inside with fear for you, and for me without you. I don't want to face such a situation, ever, where I can't actively be involved. It's hard to internalize as nice as your family and friends are, I am here uniquely and only for you. If you are gone, I have nothing. I willingly put all my eggs in your basket and we will have joy. If it ends, I want to go, standing by your side. None of this is a "deal breaker!"

"Rayban, maybe if I am pregnant someday I will relent. In the meantime, face my heart break if you don't depend on me. If you have some specialty military offense or defense to teach me tonight, go on. Otherwise, with your family home and friends on the cruiser, there is a flat area of soft grass inland of the Manatee nest. We belong there!"

CHAPTER TWENTY EIGHT

JOB DESCRIPTION

Connie was back from the wilds with bells on, so Alicia Marie stepped back to give Laxmi a chance to whisk her away to some continued honeymoon. She was not certain he could keep such an intense responsibility to himself.

Besides the prime importance of the baby, she spoke of her vow to help merchants fight the Cartel, starting with her friend, Roberto's, tricky shrimp situation.

All eyes were big and wet the next morning. There was disbelief and surprise cloaking them. He asked if they could go out to Southwest Key for a long weekend before she went back to the Moon. My proof of secrecy had held. Connie's eyes would have shied away.

"Better yet, I'll get you a ride".

Octavio, dually manned and womaned swerved into the bay ten minutes later. They were off.

Alicia had tossed the coin and decided to take the risk or never get the "stones" to do it at all. She needed Railroad Juan and his eyes and ears. It could be death to depend on Ceasrito for any of this. Ceasrito knew Laxmi only as a fellow horse aficionado. She pondered if Juan and Laxmi should ever formally meet. Or if she should maintain the task of cross path communication. She decided to keep them apart to start.

CHAPTER TWENTY NINE

JUAN AND THE RAILROAD STREET REGULARS: THE TEAM IN THE MIST

Juan had, over several years, encountered orphaned boys and some little girls, parents executed. In his 20's, he had seen what life had been before the Cartel. He remembered in his adolescence, he'd sworn to do something to stop it. Great plans in adolescence often fall by the wayside. The horrors and extortions he saw built him deliberate. He couldn't do it alone. It required local waifs who knew the reasons, and could dissolve in the night. Most had lost partial or full families. They could never get caught. Most action happened in the misty shadows of the night.

A fireplug of a guy, his five foot five stature didn't cause younger guys or girls to shy away. His knowledge of every alley and path in and around Cuenca amazed his initial group of twelve. They quickly learned to vanish.

Growing trust with his Railroad Street Regulars, his projects were moving from ignored to angrily cussed by the lieutenants. Three years of sniping in the night led to a stark opportunity to join another group fighting the same Cartel.

The Starr Scuba Resort opened and boats went from Cuenca to Guanaja. They were hijacked by the Cartel in front of his very eyes; food supplies and equipment stolen or deep-sixed.

Zulinda, owner of Unclad.com on south Guanaja, met with Lance to develop defense. Juan was known to Zulinda because he had helped build Unclad three years earlier. She brought his name up in their first discussion. They devised a defense and didn't see each other more than once a month thereafter.

Lance spent some time at the American Bar in Cuenca and came to some of the week-end long dances. Indirectly, Zulinda arranged for Juan to meet him. Stand-offish, wary, leery, they got to know each other. Snipped attacks began at this time in the resort's life. On several occasions, Juan got on his sea-based radio and warned Lance of impending attacks. Lance remained shy. Juan warned correctly the third time. Lance headed flank in the security craft to research this guy's bonafides. Obviously he wasn't a Cartel guy. Juan recognized Lance immediately and motioned him to meet in a shadow. Noisy young kids were running around.

After some fencing and testing, Lance said "We need to speak more." He took Juan down to the bar at the edge of town. It consisted of a dozen empty cable rolls flipped on their side. Self-service was the only service. They had their privacy, except for those same street urchins running around in circles.

Juan expressed his feelings recounting some missions he had completed against the Cartel. Lance burrowed seeking why Juan knew so much of what was going on, or going down before it did. Why could he know and warn the resort?

"Lance, I told you uptown my motivation feels a career. What is bad for the Cartel is my reward. You are facing them with comparatively limited resources. I could be your ally. As for the forewarning information, I don't have someone inside the Cartel so far. That event is clearly doubtful. I do have the Railroad Street Regulars as trained scouts. With the thug's liquor consumption and Regulars' sharp ears, several cross-checked threats find me every night. You have expressed some distress about these boys and girls running around us here tonight. Watch! One whistle.

The sand flipped up footprints and every child ran for Juan's side, warning in their eyes. They formed a circle, a group hard to attack.

With respected stance, Juan quieted them. "No se preoccupe, este hombre es nuestro amigo contra los ladrones. Mano a mano vamos a molestar.

Ahora, que vaya a su propio bar con orejas abiertas!

These kids have assigned bars and know every street and every alley. We have completed some very debilitating action against high level Don J.'s."

Lance replies, "Notable! We don't sign contracts at the resort. Agreements are signified by a handshake. I offer and ask what we owe for the information you've shared? Oh, and Juan, Roberto says Alicia wishes to see you in the next two weeks."

Juan responded, "Ok to Alicia. Lance, we're not some form of mercenaries. We're in this to clean our country. These kids have watched and experienced horrid things done to their friends and families. They have seen what no child should ever see. Their bodies are small; their hearts are scarred. They couldn't be more serious. We have resources to feed and equip all the troop. If I needed more, I'd not have too much pride to ask. For now, your team with shared goals is a worthy asset. Don't underestimate Zulinda as a resource. We need to dissolve now to avoid the Cartel linking us with the Regulars. "

Lance turned and the fireplug was nowhere to be seen.

CHAPTER THIRTY

EMINENT CORPORATE GREED:
Collateral Damage

Pacho summarized the inefficiency of the garbage deliveries. He proposed a solution to the Southwestern Don J. The Mondo said, "Great", and beat it from the Villa post haste. As vile as the Donny J was, he was reluctant to be seen with brain-washed Pacho. His greed was worthy of a position on the defeated outgoing Federal administration; his evil, the idol they followed.

The barges went south with the garbage, dumped it, east towards SPS. Reversed, slept three hours, and peppered the waters with M-80's, firecrackers and small sticks of dynamite to limit explosions back to Orilla. Every living form of life was ripped from the reef and floated to the surface. Fish, octopus, flounder, and squid were netted from the large welded screen into boxes owned by the peons. The less valuable items in a market were left to die on the surface.

Now the corporations didn't want to see Pacho. They lied and let him tear away. He could skim and still pay an additional $1000 per boat to the Mondo for the thug Corps. Located out of SPS, some of the north coast Cartel guys approached Pacho to cash in on a percentage for port fees. Some of the north coast cartel boys were "lost at sea."

CHAPTER THIRTY ONE

THE LONG TERM PROPOSITION

Laxmi and Connie thumbed a ride back with Octavio the following Tuesday. By the look in their eyes, Alicia knew if Connie wasn't on the pill, she'd be five days gone. Woman to woman, she knew she was on.

Heart beating for the next honeymoon, Laxmi waved from the clinic as Connie left to her moon.

Wasting no time, Alicia put ice tea on the wooden picnic table, and hoped he was at least refreshed enough for the long term protection mission.

"Alicia, I didn't discuss this mission with Connie. I did need to know what she thought might be our timeline here. If we're going to be here for a year or two, I couldn't leave your child without protection. Once bonded, my responsibility lives on, according to my culture. A dependable replacement would remain on my mind with occasional, personal monitoring required.

Laxmi continues, "Honduras itself has scores of villages to profit. The Peace Corps head office continues to exist here, and with her international record she takes over the whole region. Maybe a couple of decades. I'd be here for some of the most difficult years you speak of, so I can say "yes".

"Laxmi, I am relieved. The next step is to agree on a contract. This will be a salaried position. For cover you can work along with us as assistant veterinarian, previous experience in Nepal valuable. You live in your house with lunch and dinner together. According to your senses of the forest, or informants, you decide what your hours should be day and night. Salary remains in force no matter if there are safe times. I know what your Gurkha retirement is. I don't want an argument from you because you are retired; your culture does not permit additional salary. If you have a cultural issue, understand you are here to protect us, and if you didn't have a salary, someone in the government sniffs. The salary will protect me."

With a smile, Laxmi responds, "I guess you're a difficult boss to argue with. I have, however, argued with the Scottish. Don't push me into their mode.

Alicia closes, "Here, we shake hands on these things".

CHAPTER THIRTY TWO

INVESTIGATION BEGINS IN SPS

As the U.S. government fell prey, D.J. Mondo, an ideologue with an incomparably stupid grasp of foreign policy, pursued a tantrum of insult toward allies. Before that, there was a drone reconnaissance base near Cuenca. Its call sign was Songbird and the officer in charge had been on the ground and among the people and knew the challenges of the brutal Cartel and running a business in a failed country. We could trust him and timely information.

The D.C. swamp swarmed into a cess pool and DaLJoy of the slimy suit was assigned here, intending to shut it down. Not a word of Spanish. The Re. group now calls the shots. No help offered anywhere, the resort was investigated for protecting the environment. Any communication followed the book and only the antiquated book. For three years, we avoided communication or request for assistance.

On a Monday with Octavio returning Nerven from a fish delivery and family visit, the military-band radio sounded off. Problems for sure. Lieutenant John Clark's voice boomed over." The Force had answered.

"Birdcage, Songbird here, letting friends know I'm back in the neighborhood. My replacement who didn't speak highly of your operation is gone and that we can discuss over dinner. I'm back from Costa Rica. Over and out for now."

Without delay, Nerven and honorary 'Mama' put out a Sunday feast. The "Suit" in tandem with typical present government behavior had been convicted for child sexual molestation, and female trafficking. Those eyes of a lying rejecter of subpoenas won't see a palm tree again. How I hope! (Surely he was a "great guy." I appointed him.) A loyal Regulars had scores of photos at Pimp a Largo. He slipped through the cracks and didn't get a pardon.

Having Songbird back as a friendly resource, we invited Rayban, Nerven, Roberto with Cindy, Vanna, and I to the resort to discuss options. We invited Octavio Junior who was a strapping teen-ager now.

Brearly had spooked me with comments about something going on in the west. I was reluctant to even venture into those waters. Comments, vague from Songbird egged me on. I had enough strife going on in and around the Bay islands. Brearly was pleased we were going. A promise the black helicopters would be at ready if we got jumped.

We picked a rainy day in spite of the poorer signaling of the drones. Brearly had his up and Songbird was up very high. Maybe too high. My plan was to focus on what the water in the port might tell. Camouflaged, our boats easily lost in the rain. We took our security boat and a deeply hidden Octavio, canvass draped all over.

We ran hard, four bells for both boats until Vanna warned us off. We backed down to burble speed to enter the hidden marsh. There were enough tall cat-tails with acres of brush. We could see but not easily be seen.

Hidden, we arrived an hour before dawn to deadly quiet. Eyes made radar scans in every direction. I checked Roberto and Vanna in our boat: human radars. Rayban, pegged to Nerven scanned from his cruiser with a smile.

Movement finally. A ragged haired, long dirty black beard stepped out of the square building. He carried a slop bucket and emptied it half way out next to the pier. Fish were flashing away from the area as he hawked his acid reflux onto the water. Our Guanaja boats shared faces of disgust.

Another hour passed. I knew my crews were beginning to savor heading back. I held a stone face. The smoke of what they would be swilling down turned our stomachs. Three joined the line, with the first slop-carrier behind.

In ten minutes, two stumped out to set the twenty footer free from the pier. Shoulder bags dripping white, riding on the edges of the gunwale. Money offered a flaunt of drug laws. Not our prey today.

Three more groups of two detached their twenty footers. One came our way and we ducked. Headed south, he missed us. The other two left using the north wind-break. Heavy exhales, we settled back down, adrenaline dissipating.

The sun grew reflecting off the hills behind the port. It was reducing our stealth. I turned to the electric motor. Vanna moved to pull. Viewing her feminine form, my eyes swept up over the transom. I pointed. Our jaws dropped.

I swerved to Rayban, signing to stop engine ignition. Nerven was in the stairwell. He didn't see me. She did. She catapulted out of the well, pushed his wrist from the throttle; hugged him to the pilot's room floor, turned his eyes to the north entrance. She noted his understanding, and lovingly helped him up.

CHAPTER THIRTY THREE

PROTECTING ROBERTO'S SHRIMP FARM
FROM BANKRUPTCY

Roberto and Alicia had been classmates in the K-12 English medium school in Cuenca. They were good friends. He went to Midwest University and she to Texas A&M. Summers, they might see each other at the beach or the best quality restaurant. The friendship endured, but remained platonic. Alicia came home after graduation with a handsome admirer who lived 40 minutes along the north coast. They had been dating at school until she learned his father was the head Don J. of the brutal Cartel on the north coast. Relationship went to stutter-stop.

He was heart-broken and innocent enough not to be aware of his father's involvement. He learned later. She was magnetic in her beauty and top of the class in her intelligence. He was the male mirror image of her beauty. She was controlling and he was complacent and willing. There were few disagreements. She created a resounding 'night with her' and her plan was accepted the next morning.

Now she had the baby; she also had Laxmi as lab assistant and more importantly, as security for the boy from the cartel.

Roberto graduated a year before Alicia. He had bought a shrimp farm and "Swim with the Dolphin" pool on the very south-west Peninsula of Roaban Island. His dad agreed he could have the fancy-free year to travel Europe;

fine-tuning his native Spanish with the Spain 'th' in Madrid. He didn't get past Spain; returned alone. He had met Cindy, a Peruvian woman. They had been deep in a relationship in Madrid and around Spain. When he had to go, heartbreaks were physically painful. They struggled on "What's App" and lasted for six months. She flew back to Lima and he met her, her family, married and exported her to Roaban.

They met the others and settled successfully into Dolphins and Shrimp. Successfully until the cartel extorted the restaurants with threats to families, his market. A new Mondo mafia boss decided to take the Dolphin Concession. Roberto with his father sought legal protection. All levels of law enforcement and related government offices were on the Cartel's payroll. He struggled on for a couple of years, but on a moment of weakness, he told Lance and Vanna about his situation. They had been facing the same and sometimes petitioning Roberto for help. Three months later, the Guanaja Island group struck back.

The shrimp business improved for a year and the Cartel struck back again. Alicia had been listening.

Roberto introduced Cindy to Alicia and Cesarito at Jorje's quality restaurant. Brearly was there and introduced his Maria. Alicia Marie learned for the first time what her estranged father in law had done to her old friend, Jorje. She quietly swore to fight back at the right moment with the required resources.

CHAPTER THIRTY FOUR

GROUND-MAPPING IN SPS

Nerven kept Rayban's head down as a Vietnam War era river gun-boat ground in to the dock, and ground as a stinking barge followed. The gunboat reversed and swerved to bring the barge up to its side putting both boat and barge prow-out next to the dock.

Ragged food-sticking beards swarmed from the rectangular building with barrels and boxes soon chained to the barge

I motioned to Vanna and Roberto to look over the gunwale slowly and briefly. Nerven moved Rayban craning over a similar position on his cruiser. Peeking occasionally, we waited for three hours. I heard a hawked cough; a lashed out response of invective. Somebody was sleeping, or trying and bleary drunk. The sun was approaching late morning. After approximately three hours, the commanders emerged shouting the peons into submission to depart. Engines cranking, voices swearing and long handled nets slapped into position. The gunboat growled back north the way it had come, metal reef rippers waiting to desecrate thousands of years of growth.

Three hours noted, this was our cue and we went to full "burble" sneaking around east and north of the breakwater. We succeeded in getting Vanna's signature-mile north. We reached flank-three east to their west; all hell broke loose. Baby blasts forewarned a miniature war. I was listening for a mortar to whistle by. A fire fight right where the gunboat had headed. Suddenly it was, at our distance, completely quiet. I had an idea; the drone to confirm.

CHAPTER THIRTY FIVE

ALICIA, LAXMI, VANNA, AND JUAN RAILROAD REGULARS: FOUR AGAINST EXTORTION.

A certain tension existed. Alicia couldn't countenance the direct introduction of Laxmi to Juan. She and Laxmi had scouted the layout of the first restaurant east of the clinic.

Juan Railroad complains, "Alicia, we are on the same team here. Why the secretive voodoo about your other partner? Oh, we do know about him and have since he arrived with Connie. He's a clever forester. We tracked him to Moon village the first time he went with Connie. Moonlight displayed how sweetly the marriage is proceeding. Nepali, his English accent and movements in the dark confirm a Gurkha. His name is Laxmi and is a loner, polite if addressed. You know the skill of our group and we have never failed you. Why?

"Juan, now listen carefully. There is no offense intended. This behavior on my part is not some kind of serendipity. Listen well because of my respect for you and your group. You have saved my whole family on various occasions. I couldn't be more beholden to you. You are part of my ability to do what I am doing"

"The efforts of your large group of Regulars are the only shining lights in this sick society. You, I can't risk. You know the general plans for returning self-choice to owners. You know how complicated and dangerous parts of it will be. Laxmi knows it well. You know what has been going on in the night from his protective processes. You know it better than me. You have protected me in the night and showed you are effective. I have Laxmi here for several reasons. I try to avoid ever putting him in the same place with you. For the safety of your group, you need to avoid him. The decent people can't afford to lose your support if you are ever caught linked to him. I will continue to be the go-between avoiding the worst. I hope you can accept it and stay with me. I will never insert myself between you and your Regulars. Independently, please continue to do the helpful things you do so well."

Alicia continues, "We did reconnoiter the first restaurant last night. These people have had their families threatened so will be more than skittish. Using whatever respect I have as a known veterinary, I will quietly begin by meeting with them. I will start tonight. Both you and Laxmi can be in the environs although I expect no push back in the short run. I will occasionally give a progress report to Roberto but don't want him anywhere around. No discussion with Cesarito. The restaurant tonight is in the trees. If I can be convincing, it will be a good place to start.

CHAPTER THIRTY SIX

NO LOOSE ENDS

A way from the explosions, returning from the SPS observations, I contacted Brearly saying, "Up-date in the morning." He expressed relief we were all ok. I had expected him to be more exuberant.

I wasted no time in getting the drone up to validate my predictions. I waited an hour to see the gunboat leave the gutted Orilla area south of the island heading north-east. The water around the boat was littered with the colored wrappings of M-80 fire bombs, short sticks of dynamite, and a field of dying reef life. The north-east tack took it south of Orilla to avoid the garbage ripper coming south from Texas.

Rogue lights glimmered constantly when Octavio got north and west of Roaban. He was no farther north nor west than the windward tail of the floating suburb.

CHAPTER THIRTY SEVEN

HEARTBREAK AND FRUSTRATION

Maria and her Weatherby escorted us well before wind interference. She was unusually quiet. Brearly was morose in his big captain's chair. We were excited to report but settled down sensing dismay. He said, "Go ahead, Vanna first."

I finished with the distant explosions off Orilla to our stern.

He thought forever; weakly thanked us for putting together the final pieces of the puzzle. His demeanor sickly with loss of self-confidence. This was way out of his parameters. I confronted him about his attitude and particularly his health. If it's serious and we are involved, we need to know.

"Lance, I need a nap now.

Maria escorted us back to a much anticipated interlude and a prelude in the bubble. The extreme stress and danger left Vanna in rivulets of relief. We could make no sense, so we de-stressed, wrapped up and napped.

Brearly rebuffed business until all was eaten with the Maria': "cherries jubilee". The chromosomes were surely from a French conquistador. It was obvious she knew his delicacies and the cherries were especially for him.

He took two generous shooters of Southern Comfort. We had never seen such behavior from him. We couldn't relax. How bad could this be?

"Lance, Vanna, this began to be obvious the trip before Octavio brought Nerven. It had been in operation. If we hadn't had the D.C. swamp slime in Songbird, we'd have known long before. The western movements of Octavio stirred a bee's nest on the shorelines between the Island Suburb and Orilla."

Brearly got the hint; launched Black Bird to the southern coast of Texas. Returning, a slow monitor skirting Orilla, opened the evil box. The disdain, greed and corruption immediately bare, sickly exposed.

I didn't say anything to you because I heard rumors the U.S. government or its self-appointed congressmen were involved. You are much more exposed than our Floating Suburb. These owners can fight the outgoing filth dollar for corrupt dollar.

Brearly continued, "They had some crook named Pacho Mountanya, Cartel trained, corporation and Re-funded, and directing corruption for large corporations near the damaging storms. He started out transporting garbage from the affected companies to an area southwest of Orilla. He decided since his barges were returning empty, to dynamite the reefs and scoop whatever came to the top. On return, he delivered to wholesale dealers in the bayous. The conspiracy between him and the corporations along with seed money from the Cartel made him rich.

Brearly continued, I learned the whole story, I went to the authorities in Texas. I received the same response you got from the cartel front in Tegucigalpa. I was shocked the cartel had gotten enmeshed with U.S. authorities. I went higher and got nowhere. I went to once trusted fellow military officers and got nothing. I was near to tears. There was no law, nor enforcement under this train wreck corrupt government. I was broken. I returned to

Maria who nursed and encouraged me in another attempt to protect.

I tried hiring mercenaries with catamaran boats to harass or even sink the war vessels. Gunships blew them out of the water. I met with our corporation board and they permitted use of the black helicopters. They had enough success the routes to the bayous got too dangerous to be profitable. We focused on the Texas garbage trade. On our second attack, two fighter jets strafed our helicopters. What cartel girl is in bed with a U.S. Air Force major? Whoever, he had a role-model leader right at the top.

We reset and concentrated on short attacks from protected copter bases. We could be out and back before the jets could get there. It was a fight of a mouse with an elephant. We began to feel some success. The following morning, six fighter/bombers emasculated all our bases.

Maria entered, "Brearly wasn't injured, but came home in tears. His pride in the government he had fought for, was broken".

Brearly, "And dammit, I see no way to stop this. It will affect us and surely your diving."

Vanna shifted, "I have some ideas you might consider. Let Lance and I kick this around.

CHAPTER THIRTY EIGHT

EXTORTION: CLEANSING IN BABY STEPS

Alicia talked, encouraged, and calmed frightened restaurant owners. It took several weeks to get a man with no family to risk the new push-back.

The Cartel trawler approached the dock in front of the restaurant. The owner came to the dock. I was hidden in the trees. The owner, Pedro, refused the delivery.

"Pedro my friend, you better get your attitude adjusted or you will be selling whatever you may salvage from a horse cart. We'll give you one night to reconsider. Any spoiled shrimp will be on your bill."

They left; I stepped out. "Pedro, you were brave in your response. As I promised, I will take it from here. Get a good night's sleep tonight. You may be disturbed for a few minutes tomorrow night."

"Alicia, I won't be sleeping at all for a while. I'm risking my business on your honesty and strength of character.

"I'm not the only resource you are depending on. I'll stop by if there are any revisions to our plan. You can trust in some noise, mostly a full night's sleep."

CHAPTER THIRTY NINE

POTENTIAL FINAL HEARTBREAK

After delivery by Maria, walking up the resort path, Lance deftly headed Vanna off, "Blearly may not be lucid enough to read you. I know what you seals would do in this instance. I know exactly what you are thinking. And my heart is in my mouth. We have never put you or ourselves in such danger. I'm torn. Is the Western Caribbean worth the risk you will take? If the worst happens, how will I weigh this against living alone for the rest of my life?"

"Lance, we've made no commitment. The tension was thick over there I couldn't analyze an option to a logical outcome. It's critical to do, and have your devil's advocacy for my safety. You may need to come with me. I think we need to get some unofficial commitment from Songbird. Blearly will surely be with us. There is much more I haven't even touched on in my thoughts.

It's already too much for today. Let's take a quick shower"

Our quick shower never was nor ever will be "quick". The intensity of our vulnerability to each other and these killers rang in my mind. I know Vanna as deeply as a man can know a woman and she was stone tense. I'm now at a mental stress point.

I stepped behind her as she reached down for the shampoo. I raised her and feinted. She eased back turning only her neck to look into my eyes. Firing, she fixed me and didn't relax. I was destroyed as never before.

"Lance, look at us, right this instant. You have raised me off the floor as though I was light as a regulator. I can lift you only through adrenalin charged great stress. Women always want to say they are as strong as any man. I am strong but not stupid. As this unfolds in my mind, I can see I will need your stature as well as your mind."

"Vanna, you know......"

"Lance, yes, I know, and I trust. Now, I only need to trust your nature. Call it healing, or mental first aide. Call it anything, but I can't talk or think or wait anymore. Come on!"

I held her tight while she fought off the demons and I fought for endurance. She was afraid more than I had ever seen. I tried to repress, losing in the end. Her stress grew and fear washed off her, mauling me trying to get her relief through some diffusion from my skin. I forced myself to give what she really needed until too tired to be tense.

Weakly she whispered, "Lance, if ever there is a time we should do this together, it is now. I need your warmth."

I released the endurance fight; pressed her at her cliffs, and energized her with romantic friction. The warmth arrived; she was asleep.

CHAPTER FORTY

PACHO HANGS ON

With the loss of the helicopters, he could ramp up the garbage end of the transport shutting down the Mississippi routes. There was some reduction of graft monies from the Re. Corporations. He simply reduced commissions to various outliers working indirectly. There was an auditor with the Cartel who quickly noted the reduction of money to the evil coffers of greed.

He soon got a visit at Alamo heights. Donny J Mondo was the Mafioso this time to question. A great choice, he had never run a successful corporation in his life. Look at his bankruptcies. Look at his personal greed. The absolute stellar choice.

The discussion uncomfortably bounced around the costs versus the number of villas Pacho was supporting and country club memberships he was providing. Donny J suggested while profits were down, he reduce some of this lobbying. Pride immaculate in itself, Pacho countered with wild dreams of bombing in the Pacific and bringing the catch into the Caribbean for wholesale. The repartee nonexistent, phrases stuttered, awkward responses.

Finally, Donny, frustrated, said, "Ok, try your ideas. The bottom line is net profit. Deaths be damned!" I urge you to off-load all the villas west of Roaban.

Pacho's final response, selling iceboxes to Eskimos, "No, no. I don't need to lose Deloris. The Pacific will cover us.

CHAPTER FORTY ONE

SHIFTING TEMPERMENT OF EXTORTION

This was the first attempt to drive shrimp suppliers from Cartel back to Roberto. Alicia knew this could be a do or die. She spoke individually to Laxmi and Juan Railroad, reviewing the odds and in Juan's case, requesting more boots on the ground. Other shop owners were watching like hawks.

CHAPTER FORTY TWO

OCTAVIO'S STRUGGLE

A college sophomore, Octavio Junior was going to be the first ever of the family to graduate with a university degree. The family and even the community looked at him as a bubble floating over the fields, fearing something sharp fly by and pop it. Rayban with record of several years of intense efforts, and successes could easily be mayor of Sambo Creek.

Once offered, "Sure, you want me to be a politician. Look to the North to see what a Politician who is not a statesman can destroy. If I'm doing well here, my self-esteem from you couldn't make me prouder. It's time to concentrate on Octavio Junior."

Junior came home two summers and stayed for extra curriculum credits for two. He felt the need to help his father, who was paying ultra-tuition. Rayban would have none of it. To smooth the waters, he let him join with Nerven for a group of three. He also monitored the absolute safest routes. He loved to have him home, was relieved the day he had to return for classes in the slightly safer, but still racist U.S. He could afford to send him to Europe or even New Zealand. Despite the atrocious behavior of the right wingers, up to the moment the U.S. program was strong and flexible opening more paths to graduate studies. Two more years could signal the collapse of that U.S. Curriculum. He would have his diploma by then.

With the concentrated activity around Orilla, there was less pressure on Octavio's trips to Gulfport. Unfortunately, the smaller boats had enough radicalized animals to mount occasional dangerous forays.

Octavio analyzed and decided the Wednesday trip should draw least attention. He and Nerven welcomed Octavio Jr. aboard at sunrise. Being abundantly cautious, he contacted Birdcage for notice of any blockage. At the moment there were none. He pushed off and ran at three bells. Conditions permitting, increase to four passing Guanaja.

Passing the island, he got a demanding notice that a fast Cartel boat was launching from Roberto's shrimp operations pier.

Lance barked, "Octavio, reduce your speed. There is trouble and I need time to re-boot. Steer east north-east at two, no three bells. Maybe if you are moving away, they'll break off. They are streaming some tug block with a few less knots than my Chevy. They may explode. Hold on, check your sea radar, I see a smaller diesel way behind in their wake. I'm pushing off.

"Josh, can you man the drone tower for a while."

"Glad to, this excel program is crossing my eyes. What do you need?"

"Josh, I have never ordered you into a firefight such as this. You listen carefully and do whatever Vanna or I command. If the worst should happen to us, you automatically green-ray decimate all Cartel boats and crews, save Octavio and wait for anything from him."

"Octavio, I know Junior is with you. Everything I use will have him in mind. If you think I am missing a viewpoint you see, do whatever is best for him."

"Vanna, there is something off about this attack. There's some player we're missing. Contact Juan and see if he can fill in the blanks.

"I will contact Juan, remember, he is supporting the "extortion reduction" mission."

Lance resets, "Dicy, if Juan is tied up, tell Roberto to fast track up here. Give him our location. Contact Songbird and see what he can offer."

Vanna quietly adds, "Roger, Remember who wants to live with you forever and make your decisions accordingly."

"Roger, out, sweetheart."

Blackbird growls onto the radio. "Birdcage, go to camp radio. No other ears need hear. You're trying to analyze what's different here from other attacks. I believe I know. I respect your character and success, I need to call this one."

"Excuse me, Songbird here. Do you read?"

"Five by five, Songbird. Blackbird, we can discuss my involvement. Please shut down for a minute. I have something coming in from Songbird."

"I'll stand bye but this is not a happy camper over here. From me, come your helicopters. Out!"

"Back to you Songbird, what have you got?"

"Birdcage, you and Octavio are being pursued by a big discontinued block shaped boat. Narrow bow, a barge. Further away there is a smaller diesel which I don't think will play any roll."

"Roger, I have those on radar."

"Birdcage, I know you're concerned about the barge. It's big, its optics emerge faster to you. You and Octavio are pulling away in good measure. I think I know the slime pilot there. I urge you not to engage him in the present area. You are heading to Gulfport harbor, correct?"

"Yes".

"Focus on that, forget about the lumbering barge; get in the harbor of the breakwater. He will break off. Songbird, Out!"

Lance relays, "Octavio, did you follow?"

"Roger, I wish I trusted the U.S. government like I used to, even Songbird, when my boy's and partner's lives are involved. Over."

"Understood, I also have non-governmental information coming from Blackbird who is fuming waiting for me to get back to him. Listen with me on camp radio. Let your crew listen too."

"Birdcage back, apologies. I think I have other information for you. Octavio is on-line."

Blearly frustrated retorts, "Oof, finally. Bottom line, Cage, I not only want, but demand to lead against this motley bunch! I know of the garbage crook, and he is on your tail right now. I know you are soon for Gulfport. I will call and you will not get into any fight which you might even win up there."

"Blackbird, help me direct personal care for my close allies by being more specific."

Blearly pants with disgust, "This little dong whose mouth wouldn't digest pig shit was personally responsible for the downing of three helicopters and the lives of four men. Additionally Greenpeace lost a woman. Collateral damage to humans and reef in the Caribbean goes on and on. My mental attitude toward the country I once served is washed up. Enough"?

Lance softens, "I'm sorry. You do outrank anybody in the trenches here. I'll tell them to follow your lead."

"Thank you. Now, no engagement before or during your time in Gulfport. We will be there a few days. There are other anti-Cartel projects going on which if planned carefully can jointly bring results. Octavio, slow down and transfer Nerven to Birdcage and keep Octavio Jr." Black bird, out!

Lance follows, "Pull your boats together, and avoid using a radio. The four of you go to ground immediately. You have to hide or camouflage the boats. Nerven, since you grew up there, you may have some options?"

"Yes, I know the port area because my Dad's bar is there. Do you want to discuss these now, or let us do it shortly before we get there?"

"The only thing I know about the city is the entertainment I partook of before Maria. If it's still there, it'd be dangerous. This thug would be there. Avoid.

Go ahead at your own discretion. Get back up to speed to increase separation with the goons. Black Bird, Over and Out!"

CHAPTER FORTY THREE

GONE TO GROUND IN GULFPORT

Nerven quickly responds, "Using what I know, you can fine-tune. I'm a diver, not seasoned. Between my Dad's bar and the seafront is a huge warehouse. It's used to store boats in the winter. It's empty by now. Upon arrival, Octavio and Junior alone go to deliver the fish. We'll quietly move the Chevy up to the door, and hold. When Octavio and Junior finish, we open the door, once, and move the boats in, prow out. We need to organize a canvass or suitcase to carry things we will need in a hotel. With separation, we will go up, staying behind displays, and exit the bar. I'll tell my Dad so he doesn't jump me for joy as though Rayban isn't doing enough.

There is a B&B owned by a work-friend of my mother. I'll call from the boat here to be sure there are three rooms. While there, we will go out individually, not as a group until we depart. Returning through the bar concerns me. The thug could well be there. Comments?"

Lance looks at Vanna, "Any thoughts?"

She ponders, "I think we'll have to order in food, not to be out in restaurants for any extended time. I share your concern about the bar. We should take re-breathers from the boat here in emergency. We need to close radios to only specific times we hear from the Captain."

Vanna continues, "I think we have to put duct tape on

all running and emergency lights. Junior, we need you to do this after we are moored inside. Find an entrance to the water and go under the planks inside. One of us will monitor from the distance. Nerven pops in, "There was a ramp next to the bar."

Vanna back, "Check as a possible entrance for you and exit for all of us as we depart. Nerven, you could even call and ask your Dad to close the curtains for a few days."

CHAPTER FORTY FOUR

JUNIOR STEPS UP

Wearing the wet suit and some burned cork on his mother's bequeathed bronze skin, Junior crept down the street to the ramp adjacent to the bar. From a place you never consider, "Commercial Loving" his Dad watched his every move. He noted the bar curtains were closed and relaxed. Junior slid smoothly into the water. He inhaled not exhaling through the breather until two meters under the surface. Now Dad had to wait.

With only the dim blue light from his cell phone, fish and jellyfish swarmed and wrapped around him causing his movements to be awkward. A stone fish threatened and a squid exploded to the darkness. He jumped over the stone fish and reached the bottom of the sliding ladder. A deep breath. Paused, he realized the fish didn't make him awkward. He was frightened and shivering. He moved under the ladder without raising it and was next to the Octavio with the running lights automatically on. For the moment he could see shadows. He climbed the short ladder firmly and grabbed the duct tape left in place for him.

To get this over as soon as possible, he raced to tape all lenses. He finished the Octavio and couldn't be patient enough to walk up and down the ladders to the Chevy. He leaped ahead to the Chevy, water resisted, he missed every step and hung on the outboard wrenching his shoulder in attempt to avoid a splash. He soon let go and floated to the cement floor. It took several breaths to get him back upright. In pain he reached over to the Chevy ladder and acted appropriately this time. As a now disabled person, he gently worked his left arm to cover the lenses. Now only his cell was glowing as he ducked to the door. He moved tenderly under and came out noticing how much light was reflecting from the bar. Reminded to avoid making waves, he took a breath and held it till he was well below the surface. Surprising how much noise was escaping from the bar. He knew his Dad would be analyzing his every wiggle. He maintained silent, consistent movement every water-impeded step of the way. Now on the silent traipse to the B&B., he had to pretend he didn't have a pulled muscle.

Vanna met him at the door and helped him out of the wetsuit. Seeing his grimace, she gently massaged his shoulder as he moved toward the shower. The big question mark glowed on her face.

"Please don't tell him about this?"

"Please don't tell him about what?"

CHAPTER FORTY FIVE

COLLATERAL DAMAGE OF THE THIRD KIND

Pacho was not street stupid; pure evil and dumb. The day after Donny J. West left, he packed. He knew what "damaged baggage" gains in a Cartel departure. He left Delores with an uncomfortable red booty and stormed out the door. He could be home free, or at least in Honduras, in a day. He headed for the dock where the barge was loading.

Deloris called two of her girlfriends and gutted the house. Bye slime!

CHAPTER FORTY SIX

THE WAY DOWN, KICKING AND SCREAMING, RESULT; QUIET

He was still the owner; the gunboat command accepted he be left in his own room with meals delivered. When the gunboat reversed mooring and the dynamite was loaded, the dock was still. He dissipated into the woods of SPS. From a duck blind of branches, Juan Railroad watched him go. Now, Brearly knew he was near.

CHAPTER FORTY SEVEN

NEW PICKINGS

They knew he was Cartel; not much more. With silver tongue he worked to ingratiate himself with the leadership. Don J. again. No matter how many Don J.s you kill, another "Capo" loyalist rises from the swamp.

He waited for another assignment and waited and waited. Finally, he groused so all could hear. Don J. called him to his office. "And now, what the hell is your problem?"

"I am trained years beyond any of these gooks. I ran a multi-million dollar mission in the Western Caribbean. I'm sitting here twiddling my thumbs. What?"

Mr Mantanya, you ran a multi-million dollar project into the ground. You were cautioned and warned. You knew you were running down here where you thought we wouldn't know of you. I gave you a second chance and a big boat and sent you to interdict the Guanaja group. You lost them in Gulfport and wasted time until I called you back. What the hell else could you screw up?

CHAPTER FORTY EIGHT

BREARLY SHARES COMMAND

At the exact programmed moment, Black Bird crackled through. "Are you all well?"

Lance responded for the group. "What's up?"

"Can you leave Gulfport unnoticed?"

"We'll leave partially under water."

"Ok, the crook is still in Gulfport. You must be pristine prepared to leave in the early hours, two-thirty recommended. Get out of the harbor on electric motor. At one mile off, squeeze every horsepower your beasts can deliver. You'll be able to take twenty minutes to get necessities at Starr. At high speed run over inside the Floating Island's boat storage. Get everything out of sight. We can plan further."

Three nights ago, Octavio Junior had stealthily slipped down the ramp and taped the lights. His elbow is now healing. Rayban had watched everything in the seedy neighborhood looking for potential dangers. Nothing. The group decided to use the same escape.

Well after midnight they set out with a spring in their step glad to get out of the cooped up B&B. Two widths of hedges and a copse of old trees were left to maneuver to get to the side of the bar. They managed quietly the first. Rayban pushed his head out the second, and "What the hell?" he ducked back again. "The whole bar is outside wading, splashing water on the ramp."

Vanna edged forward, focusing and retreating. "They are having a freaking wet t-shirt party in the middle of the night over under and around the ramp. The only way we'll get through there is if Nerven and I take it all off. Now what?"

"Lance follows, "We have to go tonight. No option. There is no way a white nude and a bronze nude are going to go unseen. We'll have to go back to the unloading ramp and make our way underwater. You have your rebreathers.

Moving back two shrub densities, they trekked the fifty yards to maneuver under water. Junior familiarized them with underwater fauna they need to avoid.

They slipped down the fishy smelling ramp easing themselves into the water. The local girl, Nerven led the group forward. She shooed off two barracuda drawn by Vanna's white skin. She dovetailed and turned creating a path devoid of 'man of wars", bone fish and red fire coral. The docks looming above, Lance slipped up, hit his head and came down shaking the blow off.

Everybody got the message and the rest of the trip re-learned to exhale the breather. It had taken forty minutes to cover fifty yards. They carefully eased their heads out of the water catching each other's eyes. Absolutely still, not a wave.

Frustrated, Junior whispered, "I guess all the girls are wet to full exposure and went inside." Rayban's face was smiling with chauvinistic pride. He had few chances to see what his young man was thinking.

Lance reset the group. "Things have changed a bit; we can revise. We need to open the door, but not wait to close it. Junior, get on the front deck and reach over, get a grip and open it quickly. Don't worry about noise.

The rest of you, start your electric propellers; you hear the door, fire out, not on top of each other. Head directly south to Guanaja. You get one mile out, light off four bell horsepower and keep your heads down to avoid drag.

Josh had stayed up late. Brearly, now comfortable again in command, had him on drone night scope shadowing the group. When they hit the full mile, Josh painted them with the drone radar. There was no other shipping in the channel. He didn't want to tip an enemy off. He didn't radio.

It took two and a half hours at 4 bells before they pulled against their Guanaja dock. Everyone scrambled to get needed belongings for an unknown amount of time. The Suburb would provide meals, Maria in her element.

Once again in their fast boats, they flew under the covered docks of the 'Island.'

CHAPTER FORTY NINE

SHRIMP PRODUCT DENIED

The restaurateurs maintained hopeful patience. The first rejection of product had caused a virulent mouthful of filth. Threats, warnings, vile you have never heard before. Vocabulary training in the putrid ditches had been limited.

One night later, it descended. Two heavily armed thugs went through the woods above the restaurant. They vanished never to be seen again.

Alicia took one careful step further. Seeing the success, the next owner agreed to cooperate with her. She in the trees and the owner facing some danger on the dock, product was rejected. Vitriol again spread.

A day and night passed with no confrontations. Unsettling.

The second morning, Juan reassembled in her operating room and said five were coming on the next raid. "Should we back-up Laxmi?"

"The right idea, I need to get his idea. Are they coming through the trees again? Could you come over again this afternoon, around four?"

"Ok. I don't have confirmed times. There'll be light for a couple hours after four. They'll wait till dark. You are calling the shots to this point, Alicia."

"Juan, thank you for your patience. Protective mothers are obviously difficult to deal with. Have you any idea why they didn't hit us right back last night, as before?"

Juan responds, "I've seen some things to which I can't give context. There may be some new fighter, or leader they're grooming. I'll let you know when I do." He left back to Cuenca.

Laxmi emerged as a phantom of the windbreak. Alicia warns, "Laxmi, I have intel the response will be tonight through the trees again with five cut-throats. I can get some back-up if you wish. Wouldn't it make sense with five to one?"

"With extra planks, prepare your burial boat."

CHAPTER FIFTY

ONE AFTER THE OTHER

Lance and Vanna were rested, on the same track, smoothly breathing, and blush fading when Maria picked them up with her big gun.

Post haste, Maria escorted them up to the dining room behind the pilot house. She quickly put out some breakfast snacks as Brearly settled into his command seat.

We had decided Vanna should start because she had developed a very close relationship. Where he might rebuff me, he would never her. From our many previous experiences together, you might anticipate a jealousy issue here. Not a hint.

Vanna jumped right in. She spoke of our reconnaissance about the boats and barges.....and he stopped her right there.

"I don't mean to be rude. I'm sure you've got this planned beyond my ken. I mentioned on the boat there's another mission on-going. A major battle to provide continuing health to Roberto's shrimp farm. He's already lost the dolphins and only a joint push-back will keep him in business. In the long run it still may not be enough. We have you and your staff and your contact on the railroad, probably the largest and most prepared we could be. It's basically now or never and hope for the long run. First, we connect you with Alicia, the Vet. I think she healed your dog a couple of times. It's a complicated, even dangerous story. Better you hear it directly from her. She's an old friend of Roberto, who, as you would expect, is aware of what's going on.

"No-one must be aware of your meeting." Brearly finishes.

Lance adds, "We'll get Juan to connect us with Alicia. Soon without delay, we need to start on the damage to the reefs and overflow of garbage the sea can't absorb."

Brearly, "Get the shrimp farm out of danger. Finally go ahead with your reef project. I doubt you need anything from me."

Vanna quickly reacts, stress between her eyes, "Captain, you need to hear the plan because you're a critical player."

"Fine, get back to me later.

CHAPTER FIFTY ONE

MINISCULE EVILS' DEMISE, PREPARED COLLATERAL DAMAGE

"Vanna, Octavio has closer relations with Juan Railroad. We'll go camp radio and see if he can get a meet; his boat a good locale for privacy. Alicia will determine how she will attend. Both Brearly and Roberto trust her. I guess we can. I need to hear a whole lot more detail before I put us in harm's way."

It was a week and a half before Octavio could get all the players together. We met on his cruiser behind South West Key. The meeting lasted the night and Vanna and I learned of another player from Nepal. I was amazed at the risk Alicia had been taking, first to protect her child, then to right Cartel wrongs and hurt them secretly as we did. She surely had a big set of "intestinal fortitude." Cesarito was never involved in any of these actions. There was concern about his naivety getting everybody killed. She was sending him, under duress to continuing horrid cartel pow-wows where he inadvertently gathered useful information. She never let on how his information was used. "Just to protect our little boy." Alicia had many other plans. I was amazed and firmly in her camp by the end of the evening.

We set up communication channels between Alicia, Octavio, and Juan-Railroad. Alicia privately planned with Laxmi.

Something in the wind, Juan knew first. Ceasrito

would accidentally say something helpful with no idea of the total puzzle. Laxmi through Alicia was very insightful of danger, guiding in strategy.

Alicia had now drowned thugs out of two restaurants where the cartel had threatened families. The number of cartel responding to their rebuff was growing. Five thugs had come to the second skirmish. No sign in the woods except the tracks of the bodies being dragged to the funeral boat.

Seeing Alicia's promises kept, other restaurateurs agreed to take the risk. Alicia hidden, the owners would meet boats at the dock and refuse their product. Roberto's wholesale market was slowly improving, Risk meandered in the mists. Extortion was hard to kill.

Alicia in the trees, Ricardo, owner of a leading restaurant, faced off with a fourth crass boat of pirates. Same refusal, same vitriol. Two days to mount the punishing attack. Juan immediately called us on Guanaja and Rayban on Octavio. In the darkest of night, Octavio picked us up, quiet running engines. We unloaded our people and our armory downwind of the anticipated attack. Juan kept to the woods, informing us there was a big square barge-boat loading thugs. Three of us set up in locations where we wouldn't get caught in our own cross fire. General Alicia was hunkered down in logs where she could dispatch a few from behind. I didn't see a Nepali, nor did I ever.

In the square boat's pilot house was the renowned Nicaraguan poster boy of the cartel. At the time we were unaware of Pacho's falling out with the cartel. He was trying to regain his stripes. His eyes were black hate; an American-made automatic with an over-the-shoulder ammunition vest. A gift from Texas Oil.

Yellow on the inside as the leadership of these blood-loving animals were, he waited to dismount until many of the others entered the melee. He leaped to the ground and dived over to take Rayban with a scuba knife. Rayban fought him off. Now confident, Pacho pulled his automatic to get distance to raise it and down him. We were all fighting two or more marauders. I looked over feeling sick at what was developing for my dear friend. Our general Alicia didn't have a sight line to the poster-boy scum. I was fighting for my life, trying to disengage, and the FORCE was with us. Vanna's double tap I had learned to love hit his neck; a curved knife landed dividing his lungs. I looked around and saw Vanna, but no one with a knife. Octavio could thank the phantom. She saw where I had lost advantage. Swinging back from saving Octavio and piercing Pacho to his last rest, she glanced behind me; another signature-double.

Scuffles continued with three of Juan's teenage Regulars. My rifle locked but Vanna backed me up. Thugs disappeared, Railroad Regulars ln shock.

Octavio, at 6' 5" was knife to knife. Brains empty as chaff, they fell off him, ripe walnuts in a north wind. As a herd, they saw the fate of Pacho and jumped to the barge. Others headed up to the woods; came out prone. I scanned the battlefield. The curved knife gone, Pacho's body slithered to the ground.

We helped fill the funeral cruise, then got aboard Octavio and headed back to Guanaja. There had to be ten dead, five not being permitted to heal and attack again, and five on their barge, running, collapsing as Vanna was following the protocol of no survivors. Their barge finally went out of control and slammed an empty dock exploding the illegal armaments bringing ugly flares to the night.

In the meantime: the other owners followed suit and merchandizing returned to fair. New "animals" hatched from rotten eggs and were brainwashed rapidly. Alicia had to have some plan. I certainly didn't!

We had claimed territory back from criminals. For a long time, Laxmi held and appreciation began among the owners. Vanna and I were asked twice more when Juan Railroad predicted something bigger. Life of never being able to let down and relax, except in Germany, was wearing on us.

CHAPTER FIFTY TWO

A POSSIBLE SURVIVAL FUTURE

Privately, after years of strife, in our bubble our thoughts were beginning to wander to an island in the Adriatic. Rab sat off the new, wealthy country of Croatia, created from the break-up of Yugoslavia. Approximately thirty miles in diameter, I had dived there alone twenty years before. There were four dive resorts equidistant from each other. An ad for a resort for sale crossed our joint worldwide scuba website.

We moved the boats and equipment back to the resort from Brearly's basement. After going to ground in Gulfport and the fire fight for the sea food restaurants right on top of each other, we wrapped up and slept. We lustily re-connected the next day, but the bubble now included thoughts of a long range future. The boat captains had not been involved in either skirmish. We lolled around in the bungalow and kitchen for another day.

As battle after skirmish dragged on, we became more impatient in our bubble. In general things were not going well. Alicia's rebellion against the cartel, even with the power of Laxmi, was waning. The thugs on Roaban constantly feinting attack on the wired fence. Unclad. Com and Starr resort were fighting battles at night keeping guests unaware and unharmed. The odds were turning against us. Brearly was supporting us. His island was impregnable; the only good news.

The constant U.S. government minions allying themselves with murdering Cartels for illegal campaign funds had empowered them into running battles against all of us. Sick empowerment from the top affects unknown millions of people, national and international, directly and indirectly. Voters need to check carefully. Regular is the dangerous choice.

CHAPTER FIFTY THREE

Northerner

The weather had been shiftless. The East Troy group got out early morning before the wind. We had had another night chord from the thug congregation but they didn't get close enough for us to take them out. It was another damper on the joy of running the fine Starr resort. For other loads of ignorance the thugs sported, they knew the weather.

I hurriedly slid the drone into the shed with the attached guy poles and cables. I disconnected the electric line trip wires and secured the CCTV. Down on the dock both captains knew the weather and were frantically re-cabling and moving the ramp boats away from the normal dock-side hook-ups. They moved out to connect them with thick titanium cable to tons of ballast off-loaded by a tanker years ago on the verge of leakage and sinking. The three captains were wearing orange life vests planning to swim from the new anchor site back to the dock. The wind was thundering. There was no way. Vanna saw them while trying to get the security boat to a vertical angle up on the beach. She gunned the engine in reverse and threaded the boat through the new cables to pick them up. The waves were tossing them as they helped each other with vice-burly wrists onto the slippery gunwale. Vanna backed the security boat off and ran it right up onto the sand beach. Only the inboard's propellers were left out over the water. The captains sprinted east where their families were hunkering down in bungalows set back in the forest.

Vanna came running up the hill giving me a high five as she went around the north side of the bungalow tightening the lag bolts as she went. I met her at the East end and we anchored the center pole to a weathered pine. It had weathered eons of Northerner's.

Flying into the door, we flopped down winded as crackling and whining took over the sea band radio. It was Octavio on his cruiser running hard for the airport island for Guanaja.

He had two fat-cat wealthy fisherman. Even with all his stabilizers, two hours back to Sambo Creek was not an option. He was yelling on the radio to Pedro Jet warming up to enjoy the strong wind, a boon to him for take-off from rough Guanaja runway.

Octavio hollered, "Pedro, I have two customers who are doubting their swimming abilities. Let me pull up to the dock and get them and their tackle onto the plane. Get them to a hotel in Cuenca for tonight. I'll take care of them in the morning or when this Northerner clears off."

The wind whipped the client's long pea coats teetering them off the fall to shallow rocky water. A heart attack could this be. Octavio with rippling arms stood them straight to attention; escorting them the rest of the way. They ran to the plane.

Pedro shouted over the wind, "Roger, Octavio, I'll send you the bill for dinner and drinks at Janet's."

"Accepted. I owe you at least one. Now Go!"

As Octavio re-boarded his cruiser, Vanna radioed to see he was ok. He was only 100 yards from the edge of our resort. She said he shouldn't try to run back to

Sambo tonight. He could bunk in one of our now empty bungalows.

Octavio, relaxing with a smile in his voice, responded, "Thank you very much guys. I see a light on at Zulinda's. Soft mattresses for sure over there but this time I will be true to Zeren. Out!

CHAPTER FIFTY FOUR

FORBIDDING CARIB SEA DESTRUCTION SUNK

The virulent Pacho was gone, but filthy garbage barges continued. Kill one crook, hire another. We had seen the SPS port and determined the mission they had for the corporations in Texas. Vanna had been spinning her wheels and bouncing ideas off me. We finally went to face Brearly.

He was a new man. He had been excited by how the shrimp thieves were decimated. He looked back in command with a wink in his eye, never seen by us before. Bathing in pride his efforts made this happen. I brought up the barge mission, he stiffened.

We remembered very well how the thieves and U.S. government corruption had brought him to tears. Clear again, Vanna outlined the plan: a huge exercise needing timing and cooperation of people not closely related. I was hopeful, but fearful. Brearly felt he could easily perform his far-ranging part. A sigh of relief from me.

Vanna and I went back to our resort, an armory now. Zulinda had promised back-up if needed. Vanna, happy I had requested nothing from her, was designated to go to shore to sweet talk Songbird for his drone.

There were always hesitations in working with the big self-aggrandized buffoons above him. He was with us in spirit and needed us to ignore any actions we didn't understand that could come to pass in his support. They did come to pass, and we did ignore.

CHAPTER FIFTY FIVE

PAYBACK

I was cog number three and never let her out of my sight. Troubling; she was under the barge several times for distant fin strokes. For port waters, there was decent visibility.

Brearly, Songbird, Vanna, and I, with drones, daily scanned the weather and the behavior of the barges and gunboats. The timings of departure of the three caravans were hard to read. They came clear. They steamed as to have one leaving the Texas port while another was dropping filth on the waters north of Orilla. The other was resting in SPS. The SPS gunboat steamed southwest to rip and dynamite huge swaths of life south and west of Orilla. Reversing north north-east it avoided the one coming into Orilla waters east from Texas. The third, having polluted Orilla had coordinated its rest time with the one in SPS. When the ripping started they'd cast off and follow the last to leave now being an hour north-east. When it came into sight east of Orilla, it decimated a swath parallel to the previous and headed straight north to a Texas corporation for a new pre-paid load.

While Brearly was registering thug trips, he came upon a constant, a period of time the Mekong River gunboats were repeating.

With fewer reconnaissance instruments to divert our thoughts, Vanna and I were doing more planning on What's App for an R&R in Munich. The map also showed the relatively short distances from Munich to Croatia's island of Rab. By Zoom, Cheryl warned: "It looks close now; any day after August twenty, you'll be driving through a mountain snowstorm worried to find a log resort to batten down for the night. Carry extra blankets, power bars and liquid."

Playing it down a little bit, Lance returned, "If and when anything happens, we'll keep it in mind. We have perhaps one of our most dangerous missions coming in a day or two. Birdcage out for now."

CHAPTER FIFTY SIX

DIRECT CONTACT

The first stage with possible direct contact was the most dangerous. We headed Octavio's boat, camouflaged, with Rayban and Zeren, to the SPS port. We left at 1:30 a.m. with no moon.

We anchored in the cat-tails and Vanna quickly took a satchel of limpet mines, other explosives and in plastic, a pistol with suppressor. She slipped under the water. I missed the wake of her rebreather. The Viet Nam gunboat command was asleep.

In the early morning wave-reflected sunlight, I couldn't see her for a nerve-stressing time. Suddenly she popped at the stern of the trawler, beckoning urgently to me. Warning Octavio, I slipped gently under the chop and swam hard underwater until I bumped her with my right hand.

She stayed in the water and pulled my ear close. "Lance, I'm sorry, I can't do this alone. Both the gunboat and the barge are too long for me to arm in one trip. I can do the gunboat and one on the barge. I need you to mount two more on the barge. I never meant to put you in this much danger. You'll have to swim with me, fix one of the limpets under the water line of the bow and another under the belly. I'll be longer; wait for me at the stern. Be careful not to float into me. I'll have the final mine for this group.

I affixed front limpet and reached to affix another. I couldn't reach the midpoint. I had to swim two quiet strokes over; quick back. I now understood what her difficulty had been.

I moved to the stern and tried to spot her, fending off any danger if it arose. I could see her struggling trying to reach with her arm to avoid breaking the surface. I thrust my hardened right elbow. She pushed off lunging to affix her third. She pounded, fins submerged to get back to me and out before trouble arrived. They could wake at any time. She tugged my hand dragging me three strokes until I got up to speed. We returned our escape under water, dampening any loud inhalation after our distance with no snorkel.

Sweating taking her mask off, it was not ocean water.

Tense, we heard the wailing and grinding of the two-some, gunboat and barge leaving. We burbled back toward Guanaja; at midpoint cranked to loud and fast.

Thirty per cent done. We placed the remote charges during the first rotation of the rusted craft, waiting. We had only five hours of sleep and had to go back. She gave me additional training. In a flash, I placed two on the front and middle of the barge again. She was right there with the third as I finished.

Brearly was going to have the Black suits with helicopters standing bye up on the Panhandle. Songbird had been cooperating. I'd be operating the drone with the third remote from Guanaja on the tower.

CHAPTER FIFTY SEVEN

PERSONAL DANGER

The personal danger was not over for Vanna, nor me. We relaxed and slept, so to speak, for two days. Dealing with danger is a major aphrodisiac. Our strong stress sweetly relieved, we slept.

Brearly stationed the black suits outside the Texas port. A day later, he hurriedly radioed, "This is the time. They're in normal traveling format."

Adrenaline surged again and I asked Vanna to inform Songbird. He said he could operate only within a mile of the shore. Officially! I wished those stinking Re's were sitting on the filthy barges.

We had to wait till twilight again for the third convoy to arrive. We had the drill down and were fast-in, but... not out. Limpets set, pounding away, I heard a muffled scream below the surface and blood was flowing from her left shoulder. I returned to assist and was hit in the calf, more blood. We grasped each other with the undamaged limbs wallowing to the boat. Now we had to depend on friends.

They were camouflaged. Rayban lifted Vanna effortlessly, a butterfly, and struggled with my straining wrists pulling me aboard. Zeren floored the Octavio to overdrive and headed north away from the port and west to the island suburb.

Bridge handed to Octavio, Zeren spun to deal with

the bleeding. Octavio kept looking over his shoulder to see if there were any fast boats in pursuit. A thirty-five horse aluminum poked its prow out of the fronds, no hope.

Vanna had no shrapnel inside her. Zeren quickly grasped my calf hurling a howl from me. She felt metal and grabbed the first aid kit for a forceps. I screamed again and it was out. She stayed with me temporarily tightening a tourniquet to stop the bleeding. She sprayed local anesthetic, the damage was not only on the outside. She turned back spraying, coating the drying blood on Vanna's back. She put antibiotic cream on Vanna causing her to freeze with a viscous growl. An angry huff as the bandage went on.

Zeren with command, "Sorry to you both, I know what I'm doing."

It took me a few minutes to snap out of shock. I remembered the other major actions under way. I struggled with the pain until I could move the leg and right myself. Zeren slammed me back down. I ignored her and asked, "Vanna, what's your sitrep?"

Dealing with a Seal, I got, "The spray anesthetic was the worst of it. I can move and don't think I'm bleeding much. It must have been a glancing blow off a rib. Zeren, I'm not bleeding much, right?"

Zeren, "Not much I can see under a tight bandage. I'm not going to dig it up to find out. Nobody is going to be ballet dancing off this boat tonight."

"Vanna, the injury is on your back, can you walk?"

"Lance, I can walk pretty well and know what you are trying to do. I agree to do it and can do it. You'll not be involved. Stay sensible! I know your piece of the puzzle, can walk to the drone, not carrying you, and coordinate with the other guys. Assuming the thugs haven't discovered our third set of limpets in SPS, we'll succeed with this.

Zeren blubbers at Vanna who says, "Zeren, I am beholden for your capable care. You know I am a Seal and therefore I know my limits. I'm not stupid as to invite failure or serious additional injury. With a hole in his leg, Lance is in danger if he tries to fight his way up there. Tie him down if you have to. I will be leaving with no essence of ballet. I'll be in touch every step of the way."

CHAPTER FIFTY EIGHT

COORDINATED REPRISAL

No congressional derelicts counted on the hit they would take from the impending loss of dark campaign money. They would laugh off the pain I anticipated to endure. My back burn was within my pain tolerance. No feeling of bleeding. I took Lance's Orilla track. Brearly was on the Island. His troops hidden on the Texas coast.

We had set watches according to the three time zones. A single touch of a remote by each of us;.....down before they could talk to each other or anyone else.

Brearly made the call that shook the Island. I responded in tandem. Time dragging on for me, I heard Songbird.

Brearly had eyes on the sea outside the Texas harbor. Mission: nobody lives to tell the tale. His drone saw little left from the limpets. Blew another hole in each craft to guarantee rapid sinking.

I pushed off on my cell phone and looked to the drone picture. Orilla was in the background, the reef ripper was imploding taking the barge gasping down with it. A thug roused at the front of the barge. A piece of metal from the ripper down with the wreck. A far quicker death than he deserved after the continuous torture he had caused. The water was three hundred feet deep. The location was far from swimmable to Orilla. Their total loss.

Songbird was last to push his remote device. I guess he was waiting to see if we would really do this. On the other hand, he had extended his mentioned wavelength and took the third rusted crafts a mile off the SPS coast. A floating inferno of fire.

Afterwards, and with a few pain-killer Southern Comforts, Lance and Vanna mused, "Few decent humans in the world would be aware of a caravan of cartel thugs annihilated near Central America. The bribed congressmen from Texas surely did. No garbage Don J. Mondo was ever held accountable. They would lose their big election cartel campaign monies. This time! (Lempiras)

They could damage my career and ability to personally manage my life's investment, the Starr Resort. Not In a court dealing with the truth. There was no evidence; no corpus delecti. However, they owned the courts.

CHAPTER FIFTY NINE

FINALLY INEVITABLE

Vanna was down for only ten days. With a hole in the leg not hitting bone, I moved little and slow for three weeks. Both Zeren and Vanna were my doctors. I didn't have to gamble with a Cartel one on the coast or an ungodly expensive one in the U.S. A bullet wound raises other unanswerable questions. I was tight-rope pushing in opposition, travel to Canada was significant.

CHAPTER SIXTY

ON RAB AGAIN AFTER TWENTY YEARS

With Vanna strong and me reduced to a slight limp, we headed to Munich and points beyond. We had deep conversations with Cheryl along with unexpectedly precise advice from Greg. We borrowed their Mercedes and drove on to Croatia and the ferry to Rab.

The island, part of Croatia, was thirty miles in diameter. Several dive operations were in existence. We had corresponded with the one on the market, but visited several others. Pricing a foreigner was a joy because we were moving into a culture where over-charging innocents was the way of doing business. I had been there twenty years before and that would not be part of a culture that would change any time soon. Not unaware! Beyond that, we learned snippets of important local marketing information. The two most important snippets were the clientele were from Southern Europe with some from Croatia and the countries no longer called Yugoslavia. The other fact was the diving was not much for rich reefs. Wrecks from the late 1800's through the Second World War were the fascination. Man-made reefs were in process in the area. In the cold water they'd take longer than any developer would live.

We were now prepared to begin dealing with the seller of the listed resort. An old guy who could be a brother of Brearly met us. Same rough weathered skin and eyes with no nonsense attitude. Borna, afraid of nothing, much less foreigners, was welcoming but distant. His wife, Anika was and had been the relationship builder keeping friend and strangers at ease. Borna was in his middle sixties fit with rippled shoulders, but weakness beginning to show the awful crush of aging. Anika was ten years younger, still in her prime, still his young love. Both gifted with such life. Down on the boat dock were two young bucks manhandling the dive boats and tanks.

Borna started, "Lance, and Donya Vanna, if I may, welcome to the resort, Horvats's History. It was an active resort forty years ago in our youth. It has continued to be profitable except for the years of the downturn of the destruction and division of the Yugoslavian Peninsula.

It's back now, even better. The only reason I've tentatively put it on the market is the increased help I need from the two you see on the dock. I'm fighting age the best I can. I'm aware. Anika, mine, doesn't make a peep.

I'm not decrepit and still need, for emotional balance, some labor within my comfort zone. At this age, things could change unexpectedly. Therefore, I sell the resort with the understanding you will technically be the owners. I will work within my limits and consult when years of experience put me in the know. My salary expectations will continue. As I will retire with social security pensions, they won't be high. You will soon find my salary in the gross costs will not hinder other operations or development.

His requests were clearly understood and although we were on the verge of entering the middle years, with those young guys on the dock, we could easily handle the operations for several years longer.

With the mentioned priorities on the table, we discussed an offer related to the sale of Starr Resort to Roberto.

CHAPTER SIXTY ONE

HEART-FELT PARTINGS

Arriving back in Guanaja, we had set a path. The complicated changes, soul-searching and heartbreak hit each of us.

The deepest pain for me was leaving a business I had built from the very jungle floor. What I had seen for sale in Rab, there was a future in my field, with Vanna's share consistent. We were out of the clutches of the worst corruption in the U.S. We paid U.S. taxes only on monies above the $80,000 per person per year overseas deduction. Uncommitted up to $160,000, we had American Passports which gave us the background to settle most anywhere in the West. The passport no longer had the power and unblemished respect it had before Trump. Some foreigners had approached me to say they were sorry for what I, as an American, had now. Sentiments of several people in several countries identical.

Nobody else in our group could easily go and get a work permit in another country. Deep family issues boded. An overwhelming concern for Vanna and I was the idea of going and leaving two defensive positions open.

Roberto was Honduran and Cindy held a work permit for Honduras, a Peruvian Passport. They had family and business issues nor did they want to walk north and face the Trump Stockade at the border. The bright spot was they didn't have to pay U.S. taxes.

At the same time, Alicia was losing her grip keeping the cartel from again threatening restaurant owners and their families. The rows and ditches of Central America were festering scores, hundreds of these mind-altered thugs. An army would be hard pressed to bring back any order. Vanna had had to save my life many times and I hers. if we wanted to survive, and odds were against it, it couldn't be here.

CHAPTER SIXTY TWO

UNIMPEDED WARNINGS

Vanna and I were analyzing what our most empathetic actions needed be with Roberto. As an original part owner, the future of the resort ultimately fell to him and Cindy.

Sea rescue radio blared, Blearly hoarsely reported, "The thugs on my island here, which is yours, Roberto, are gathering between you and Half Moon Bay Resort. I only see Cindy there holding the onslaught on the barbed wire fence. You better get there stat, set up the new armory you got from Zulinda and get between her and danger. She only has an automatic. It won't carry a breath in this windstorm. I'll have a few of my security snipe them from a distance, you need the Gatling."

We jumped out of our bungalow and Roberto raced for his inboard. Vanna and I grabbed weapons and ammo as much as we could carry. Vanna called Zulinda to locate Octavio and Zeren. I called a boat captain to volunteer help. Rayban had an argument about Zeren coming and immediately lost it. They roared to the west end of Zulinda's beach and gathered more weapons and ammo. Zulinda, panting and womanly bouncing to the stash said, "Lance, while you were in Germany, we had some trouble here. As a result, and due to his shrimp farm's small barbed wire fence, I gave Roberto a Gatling gun to protect Cindy. He has it camouflaged on his back porch, You need to bring packs and packs of ammunition. I'll help load. Octavio, awash with armory, Vanna on the front deck shifted weight ahead to bring the bow down lifting the engine up to secure the plane-off. Speed enhanced our 23 knots by seven.

Roberto ran his whole cruiser up his sand beach leaping off with two submachine guns racing to find Cindy and get her behind him. She was on one knee firmly and deliberately knocking down thugs on the fence. If it weren't dangerous it could be a shooting gallery in a carnival. Bodies piling up.

Roberto hugged her back to the porch where they had practiced mounting the gun. They had burrowed slits in the bottom of the wall to insert the legs. The recoil didn't knock them up against the house. In the delay for set-up, several thugs got into the yard. Cindy rammed in the first magazine; Roberto cleared the yard of crawling demons. They appear like cockroaches. He focused again on the fence.

The whole group of Starr Resort protectors initially had discussed trying to defend; not use offensive procedures. Our civilized attempts at rules of engagement soon ended with a shot fired or some another attack obvious and looming. Yard clear, Roberto paused, letting the creatures decide their fate. A roar of filth erupted from a lieutenant in the forest behind the sniveling mob. A rush for the fence with explosions and fire, the bodies now fell on the opposite side of the fence.

Cindy shouted, "We only have a half dozen clips left."

Roberto, "Listen honey, Octavio will be here before we run out. Can't you hear his cruiser coming in planed-off?"

Cindy, anxious, "We didn't get earplugs for this monster, I can't even hear my heartbeat, and believe me, it's racing."

Lance, loaded with arms and ammunition swerved around the left corner to the porch. Vanna on his right protecting him, firing accurately; a new cleansing of the fence. Zeren couldn't get in front of Rayban, no way, and came loping behind him while he unloaded scores of clips next to Cindy. Bido, the boat captain was the last to arrive his machine gun on full report. Two women and three men left scores of bodies on both sides of the fence. The fighting paused, the boat captain fired off a final fuselage hitting three interlopers, and the rest whined into the woods with the lieutenant screaming trying to force them back. An ugly quiet fell on the yard. Octavio and the boat captain surged ahead to dispose of the bodies to the other side of the fence.

CHAPTER SIXTY THREE

THE SORRY DISMANTLING

The team pulled chairs inside up to the door. Roberto, still on the Gatling, could hear.

Lance immediately took lead. "Roberto, I'm sorry, you are not selling enough shrimp to risk your two lives here. They will burn you out in a matter of days. As we discussed, as part owner of Starr, we will sell it to you at approximately half of actual value. We need the other to set up shop on Rab. You will remain very financially viable. I don't know what to say to Alicia. You'll have to decide according to your agreement. Vanna and I have already talked to Blearly and Maria. They aren't going anywhere. It's in their interest to have a pro scuba diving resort located near their island. With them, you know it isn't only about money. They'll bend the rules of their board to protect you."

From the porch, Roberto jumped in, "Octavio, Starr will continue our protection for your Caribbean businesses. United we'll stand".

Lance hurries, "We have to absolutely, immediately, get you and Cindy out of here. Give me the Gatling and you two and Vanna get your belongings packed with waterproof wrapping where possible. Boat captain, "Bido, we can't leave these people alone after dark. Take the security boat back, get the other captains and bring all boats including the ramps back. Go quickly, run it as fast as you can handle it. It'll churn 35 knots without damage."

The house became quiet with the sounds of packing and quiet tears when a treasure had to be abandoned. Lance concentrated on the fence at setting sun. Vanna helped with packing, mostly standing near him pegged to the Gatling. When they are in danger, they are invariably back to back, eyes burning with radar precision. Looking sadly into the distance Lance called Roberto and Cindy over to his perch.

Lance, quietly, "it's going to feel forever waiting for the ramp boats. We need to take a minute to decide how we handle Starr. I can't avoid all heart break. I will run a plan by you, accept changes at any time. We'll be ready to organize upon arrival. Vanna and I will need a day to pack and clear our stuff out of what will become your bungalow if you wish. Tonight, you and Cindy take one of the full service bungalows. We'll leave the household goods on the boats."

"Octavio, could you and Zeren either come up and sleep in a bungalow or sleep on your cruiser tonight. I'm leery about what these louts might dream up after losing scores of their underlings. I want to be as close to full defense mode as we can.

"Vanna, do you think Phil, in banana operations is still there at this time?"

"They have a train every day at dark. He'll be there for a couple hours at least."

"Ok, see how soon he can get a skiff out. We'll pay all, and take our house-hold goods and security boat to the next banana boat going empty to Europe. Ask the help of two pickers but keep it as confidential as possible. I don't want Donny J. to get wind of this and seek sickly advantage. Tell him there will be two automatic weapons and ammunition."

At exactly sunset, two misshapen animalistic faces jumped up on the fence to test for another attack. As they jumped, they were blown back onto the Half-Moon bay resort impaled on a fence post. No movement. Lance didn't even look down at Vanna reloading her rifle.

The waiting dragged on and it was one in the morning the ramp boats rumbled in. Loading with minimum lights, they rolled out again at 3 a.m.

It took two days to get the skiff pick-up. We had our last loving and bubbles in the Caribbean. "Well, let's review, said Lance. For Starr, Roberto brought his cousin full time as diver and island defense. They need one more. He has not had time to request the FBI clearances. He and Cindy also had dinner with Brearly and Maria to confirm further support and any prohibitions. Soon there will be a journey to United Fruit area veterinary to plan a future with Alicia. Josh is now handling the drone in coordination with Blearly's Black Bird and Octavio's trips north. Juan and the Railroad Street Regulars have shifted their protective services to Roberto. Bucky came back to Guanaja living with Roberto and Cindy.

Schedules conflicted and we needed to wait another day to fly to Frankfurt and on to Croatia.

We took snorkels down to the East end on the sand. We experienced some of the elation Trey and Fran felt as they fell in love there. Vanna was a woman with whom I could repeatedly fall in love, and did!

CHAPTER SIXTY FOUR

RAB, THE REST FROM STRESS?

Roberto, my friend since university dorm days had been supportive, self-effacing. From money, not a hint of braggadocio, fearless in defense of the resort and protective of all. Self-confidence varied. He endured bravely to support his now wife, Cindy, through a disease she got in Nepal. No doctor, at least in Spain, could identify or treat. On the other hand, he left feeling shame when Vanna had taken all four cartel goons down in the camp Mondo attack and he had not gotten a shot off.

Shy, yet sophisticatedly proper, you'd never guess Roberto came from a serious financial family in Honduras. He was staying in the most luxurious dorm room in our building. His hall could house three double units. He had two of those renovated into one with more chairs, beds, and desks. He was generous if Greg or I had a beauty we wanted to impress. He took most of a spring break searching for a site for my scuba resort and at the same time bought a shrimp farm and dolphin riding concession. His father agreed he could take a year off after graduation to do the famous backpacking trip across Europe. As recounted in Book I, Cindy short-circuited the trip in Spain.

He developed close friendships with Greg and I and the guy who was living in what was the remaining one third of his hallway. From Croatia, he was the furthest from home in our complex. Surprisingly, Marko was also the best basketball player. Greg and I double-dated and at times Marko and Roberto shared a view of their lovelies. He was here due to the reputation of the school in Marine studies. After graduation Marko and Roberto maintained their acquaintance via skype and Zoom. With Roberto frequenting the development of the Starr Professional Diving Resort, I often joined in the repartee and learned more about Croatia and specifically Rab. Marko had never been to Rab, although he was a certified, infrequent diver. I had been there before the horrible clash in and around Serbia. Marko and I had that connection and he was surprised and pleased we were going to take over a diving resort. Roberto kept him informed about the terrible fate of Hondurans and the serious affect it had had on his shrimp farm and Dolphin riding concession. He recounted his now new ownership of Starr Resort.

CHAPTER SIXTY FIVE

RAB, THE INEXPLICABLE INTRODUCTIONS

Marko was there at Rijeka Airport to pick us up and escort us through Istria and onto the Rab Ferry to the island. It was about 25 kilometers by Ferry. I planned to buy a car once there. Marko would lead us by the hand through the red tape of buying a local car. It needed to happen soon. With an exchange of 15 local currency, Kuna, to a dollar and the generous proceeds from the sale of the resort, we quickly bought high power, low gas. Frankly, I bought formidable, not quite a tank, because if Vanna ever got into a collision, I wanted her to have as much metal as possible between her and the intruder. We also anticipated some transport of divers. We knew of the 2023 change to the Euro, which would make our purchase in dollars, much more expensive.

Marko took his car onto the ferry to the island of the resort. At the ferry, we were early going for the fresh breezes from the Adriatic. I saw in dreadful slow motion something I had seen once in Greece and expected never to see again in this lifetime. The boat was full except the last car row. There was a metal plate affixed to the dock and a similar plate on the back of the boat. While docked, the two plates overlapped so cars could drive on and at the destination back off. While underway the boat's ramp was raised. The one on the dock was delayed in closing a few seconds each time to raise a more structural steel barricade. The ferry was raising steam for the path across to the island. Both the ramps were still down. A guy in a Lada sedan came barreling over the small ridge which marked the parking area for the ferry. I couldn't imagine what part of his brain was fomenting this absolute stupidity. He didn't slow and hit the shore ramp before it had raised. The boat's ramp was still down, had pulled away a few feet from the shore. He floored it to jump the distance, ramp still down; then brake. Front wheel drive, weight in the front, the nose plunged causing the two front tires to slam the ramp steel now rising. They exploded leaving the metal wheels to bear the brunt of the front bumper of the car and then the radiator. Up in the air soared the front body of the car causing a perfect rear summersault. It landed on its roof and pressure inside the car exploded throwing the driver out. After his shock, his eyes flared, he couldn't swim. If you ever see the eyes of a drowning person, you have no doubt. Flailing, the guy was delirious. I am more than a professional life guard and absolutely would not to get close to a guy in this condition. I grabbed one of the boat's yellow floating rings, threw it back to Marko at the rear and he threw it on to the man. The guy wasn't lucid and didn't even see it or know it was there. Marko quickly retrieved the ring and this time threw it right at his head. The guy flailed again and touched it, hugging it closely to his chest. Marko reeled the guy in and before he could stand him up, the Captain throttled him by the neck, dragging him up to the pilot house. I heard the engines pause, a dingy was floated out from the lower stern deck. The First Mate man-handled Mr. Russian, late owner of one Lada, into it and rowed him back to the dock. Leaving the lawyers to fight the obvious, the captain hit full flank throttle, not looking back. The Police were there. I looked at Vanna. We shook our heads.

CHAPTER SIXTY SIX

A CIVIL CHALLENGE

Rab had developed rapidly during the twenty years I
had been away. Where there had been sheep-filled
rocky fields, buildings and high rise hotels lined the
beaches. One of the dive resorts got such an offer for
their beach front, they retired and closed. Three were left,
mine and two others.

The little Bed and Breakfast where only brackish water
had been available, salty coffee had been a non-starter.
The hosts were so uncomfortable, they gave me Slivovitz
as my liquid to start the day. It was a high start. The folks
had been well beyond retirement and now, the old house
was no longer there.

Borna and Anika were out to meet us, surly and sweet.
Marko had never met them. There was a few minutes of
Croatian give and take. Dead tired from jet lag, I urged
all hands to get our suitcases. We sent Marko on his way
with a promise to join him and his fiancé for dinner
within a week. I corrected the timing to wait one day for
every hour we gained in lag.

After four days, we woke and christened our new, and
safer, love nest. There were two temporarily heated heart
beats and back to doze until evening and full sleep again.
We woke the next day to hunger.

Two more days getting time arranged to local zones
and we swam off the dock. Evidently, Marko was counting

the days and called in with the dinner invite. I responded, ok, but let's look for a truck for Vanna before the Kuna evolves into the Euro. Marko came alone; took us to the dealership with the largest selection. I asked about bargaining. He said, "Absolutely, let me do it. They take tourists for a ride."

I was satisfied with a 20% reduction and we drove in tandem back to Horvatz, my resort. Maybe we need to think about another name.

We took Marko down to the dock to discuss the quality of the equipment and found Borna hadn't skimped. Marko agreed to join us for an introductory dive on the weekend.

Dinner day, we went up and dressed. Vanna was going eye-hunting. The visions she provided me, purchased in Frankfurt, surely granted permission. She should be illegal, but the restaurant was ritzy and romantic. We had seen pictures of the fiancé and an eye duel was possible. Thirty seconds after Petra met Vanna it could be ruled out. Here was a younger version of the welcoming personality of Anika.

Chemistry was sweet and accepting both ways. The only ogle eyes were mine. I need to hide carefully or wear very dark glasses at all times. I was careful and can professionally say, "Petra looked good enough to eat without sauce."

There was no dearth of things to talk about. Notably Petra was more of a diver than Marko, to which he embarrassingly agreed. The other surprise, and I shouldn't have been, was the wedding was booked for five weeks away. We were invited, of course, but the court was and should be composed of their friends who had been with them for scores of years.

The most stressful event happened when a well-oiled local in the restaurant fell for Vanna. He was to my left and Vanna's right. He started moving our way and I could read the vodka and lust in his eyes. Vanna read mine and turned shoulders square to his. The bouncer had seen the eyes. Two steps and he took him hard to the floor knocking his wind out avoiding any close call to Vanna.

Only I realized how close to impending death this guy would be if he got close to her. There would be broken chairs and bones in five seconds. She wouldn't even be breathing heavily.

Neither Marko nor Petra reacted, nor realized; they didn't know she was a Seal. Our table hadn't been compromised so I quickly ordered another round of drinks and shifted back to the wedding. Nuptials to be thirty feet under water near the vertical cliffs of the Adriatic beside Kvarnar Bay.

Smiling, Marko put us in the picture, or whatever picture he had heard painted from a guide when he was ten.

"The main attraction is the sand beach. South-east past the peninsula stand the vertical cliffs which extend underwater to walls, caves and caverns. They have been here for eons and their protrusion provides a seafloor meandering out to a hundred fifty feet, thirty to fifty feet deep. It drops off fast visibility literally goes black. At a depth of 300 feet hangs the hulk of a boat dating back to the Greeks. Sport diving is limited to 120 feet. Little is known of whatever crumbling may be left. Local "bar-flies" and colorful guides spin most interesting tales of the provenance of the ships in the area. With many areas to choose, we decided to be conservative and locate the ceremony where the water was about thirty feet deep. Tank time necessary would put the tanked diving guests in no danger of "the bends" or "nitrogen narcosis".

A sparkling story to end our first date on Rab. Vanna drove us home in her tank offering to present various activities she also enjoyed done at thirty feet.

The date marked the end of "jet lag". We eagerly awaited Borna's tour to create our illusion as knowledgeable locals. To a novice, grueling, between the myths and tall tales he recounted, he stopped and put us through shallow dives.

With a subtle and infrequent sense of humor, his seriousness resounded that his resort maintain its quality reputation. Thus we did an additional two days of introductory ten foot dives learning the whole area. Finally, with caution in his voice, he took us down to 180 feet for ten minutes. On a regular tank, you only stay at 100 feet for ten minutes. No decompression at 10 feet required. He had chosen his newest tanks and loaded them with 3,500 psi rather than 3,000. He was going to decide if we were what we said we were. He would soon find I wasn't a novice.

For Vanna, this was way below her expertise. She had been diving frequently, so deep she had to decompress three times for extended waits. Fifteen minutes at 60 feet and 10 minutes at ten feet, was no chore for her. I didn't have the hours of experience she had. When I first opened the Starr Resort, I quickly learned the dangers of the area and ventured down to 200 feet in several locations. I was prepared for any hot-shots trying to push the sport-diver limits. The future of my investment assured, I was more than ready.

We dawdled around ten minutes with Borna and I called the surface warning. We surfaced no faster than our bubbles and Vanna called the decompression at sixty feet. We stayed fifteen minutes. At ten feet, I stopped us for another ten. We surfaced with no pain nor pressure. I had the feeling of two hot pokers ramming my back as Borna's eyes analyzed my every move. I saw him judge

Vanna, quickly realizing what he had here. We left the water shedding our tanks. Borna was looking ugly at us and broke into a seldom seen smile. I passed and she more than passed.

In tandem, Vanna and I went three times on every dive trip to every used location. We did three separated between ramp boats with a muscled boy watching. We were ready to handle any dive and to assign the muscle boys where we wanted them, no whining.

CHAPTER SIXTY SEVEN

OUR PERSONAL SELF-ORIENTATION

Satisfied with our skill and people relations, Borna stepped back and as promised, only came out to answer questions not obvious in a new resort and culture. If we had a sick bruiser, he'd cover for him for the day.

Soon after we had been receiving a good number of divers, more than covering the costs, Anika came out with an unanticipated spark in her eye.

Smiling, she continued, "I know you are coming from the Caribbean with lots of experiences probably with South American Cultures and many U.S. divers. Not many Europeans, I guess."

Vanna answered, "A few. I've seen from marketing efforts, you target mostly southern Europe. A problem?"

Anika continues, "No problem. Maybe we've been here so long we don't notice. From diving pictures on the internet and other sources, most everybody in the Caribbean wears a suit or a wet suit. The comparative word here is liberal, the majority of women wear nothing or only a bottom. The water here is more salty and, at depth, cooler than the Caribbean. Wet suits are needed by most all divers. The wet suit comes off; there is seldom anything left. Maybe you come from a more conservative background or haven't seen much of this over there. Maybe it will be a problem for you. I need to make sure you understand this dress is ingrained in the European and

363

Eastern Block cultures we serve. If you should criticize or insult anyone, man or woman or child about this, they will be shocked, angered and never repeat a vacation with us. Such a failure will be big news and we'll be in trouble, probably bankrupt in one year."

"Anika, Vanna answers, we appreciate the "heads-up". Far away as we are, conservative mores in the U.S., are not followed by a majority. Thongs that wouldn't cover a 2 Euro coin compete. We saw a variety.

At the same time, and I appreciate it if you keep this between us, I am a retired Navy Seal and have served in a myriad of cultures. I entered the Seal Organization when women were first accepted. The colleagues I associated with were close to all men. I took more showers in the presence of men than not. I am not inhibited nor is Lance. If proper, we could well be out on the boat or the beach attired, or "not attired" as you see. We really appreciate your care in informing us. If this should be the biggest problem having a resort here, how happy we will be."

Lance continues, "Anika, this'll not be a problem with us. However, there are surely values and mores in your culture more subtle. Don't hesitate to keep us informed as we go along."

CHAPTER SIXTY EIGHT

BUSINESS ONCE USUAL, NIGHTS FREE OF THREATS

For a while, we carried idling stress with us. Sometimes a dream. The resort was well-marketed and the two Hercules males warmed up and respectful relationships developed. The hellish memories faded. We added a new cook losing the experienced one to a Michelin Five Star on the mainland. A mixed drink person to boot. Croatia, once part of Yugoslavia divided into the wealthiest of splinter states. Tourism was twenty per cent of the export national income. Here we were right in the middle.

The Adriatic is salty making it possible for even lead-footed swimmers to float. On the other hand, it is the coolest finger off the Mediterranean. A lot of Alps-driven melts find their way and keep the water cool even in the height of summer. The large number of sunny days year-round create a mix of cool water temperatures most of the year. Wet suits are frequent even above the thermo-clime.

The comparatively bitter cold of Europe drives people south even in winter months. Wet suits with this group are only suggested. Look out across the sand on a comparatively cool or rainy day and listen for the language of the group whooping it up. Eight of ten times it will be German.

Spring came early and the bus tours and cars flowed in from the North. As forewarned, the beaches swarmed with women in small or no attire. Only the diver women wore wet suits, femininely cut, one-quarter inch thick. Curves kept warm.

365

Vanna is strikingly beautiful and had no competition, but for self-protection, I kept my head down when busts appeared........ When she was watching!

CHAPTER SIXTY NINE

SOCIETY'S LIBERAL WEDDINGS AT 30 FEET

Weather cooperated up to the Big Week; the decision was made thirty feet down, no wave affect. Along with the wedding group, several couples including Vanna and I dove to the depth of the vows.

In the environment, surely a cultural thing, I laughed out bubbles. The wedding party men had wet suits with trappings of a tuxedo in decals affixed in correct location all over the black insulating texture; including cumber bun and bow-tie. Formal underwater apparel. Amusement was mild, then, breathtaking:

Down came the bridesmaids, wet-suit cleavages exposed over remnants of material on long flowing dresses. Not a bloomer culture. They frolicked and spun sending sheets of color out and up around their Victoria Secret carved waists. A repeating flurry of booty color. A phosphorescent sunrise of emigrating multi-colored jelly fish surging to sandy beaches?

We are in nude beach international. 'Default' nude. Not nude, except…One eighth inch wetsuit material Victoria Secret cut. Garter belts and lingerie some opaque, some less, a few bikinis. Stocking tops. Many not in the wedding party were less attired, much less, providing cleavages with no wet suit, stimulation too much for any male to ignore Closed, for descending, the dresses were wrapped by small velcro straps holding them to thighs to enter the water. Once the legs were flexed, Velcro slipped under the dress belt to be tucked into the arm-sleeves.

After exactly three minutes of manic panorama, velcro re-fit; colors muted, Petra, with scheduled delay, began her descent above Marko. Velcro refused. A most seductive cultural tradition. As the bride descended, her dress floated up around her presenting the most alluring vision uniquely for him. The bride, most captivating of all. Her day, his capture! Absolutely fitting!

As the diver minister moved to be flanked by Marko and Petra, women closed, only Petra's color remained. The words were heard on ear-buds under-water rescue radios and names were signed on a sharpie tablet.

CHAPTER SEVENTY

CATASTROPHE

As a few people began to ascend, a blast of huge proportions thundered out from the wall. People flying in all directions, many in fetal lock. The surge of water pushed me back. The bubbles in the water pelting every inch of my body. I saw the power of the surge and Vanna forced herself around and in front of me to buffer the turmoil. A personal flak jacket. Her fingers vice-gripped my underarms pulling herself up against me. The blast ended. The water displaced threw us over spinning, bowling pins, left and right, down hard. Yards. The shock hammered me. Suddenly I couldn't breathe. With eyes of a drowning victim, I searched for Vanna. My regulator torn from my mouth was no longer connected to my tank. I lost lucidity. As Vanna was thrown toward concussion, she took her regulator and put it in my mouth. Huge breath, I weakly pushed it back. Every dive instructor in every scuba course pounds buddy-breathing until it becomes a habit. Breaking waves threw us uncontrolled to a spot on a black beach. Where had the sunny thirty feet gone? Vanna still gripped and between breaths forced us toward the black. It was not a beach. It was the entrance to a sunless cavern. She lost me for a heartbeat and I hit my head on granite. My life went black.

Trudging with lightning strikes in her head, Vanna dragged Lance foot by foot toward the line in the cave wall showing the highest level of surf. She fought sleep. She knew she had a concussion; knew what to do. Her bleary eyes stopped her motion trying to put her to sleep. She fought and rolled on her back pulling Lance's head up onto her midriff. He was motionless. She turned herself 90 degrees to him. She laid her head on his chest. The heartbeat was weak. She moved her arms up under his head, put the left under the neck and the right above the eyes. She moved her lips down to check his breathing. There was none. Thus the slowing heart function. She raised back, forgetting to check his airway, and brought her thumb and finger down to close his nose. Suddenly realized, in her fog, she hadn't checked for blockage. She released his nose and kept his neck up, checking his mouth. There was something. Keeping the neck back, she moved two fingers in to grasp whatever was there. The rough spiraling stem of an ancient reef plant, lodged deep. She closed her thumb and first finger. In her painful hurry, broke it off somewhere at his epiglottis. She went back with fingers on both hands, located the bristly thing and ever consistently removed it. Forever long. It had gone down either the esophagus or the throat. Lack of breathing suggested the former. As quickly as she could stretch her screaming muscles, she returned the block to his nose, and her breath to rescue breathing. Her brain was showing mist and trying to put her to sleep. She couldn't succumb. Her lips met his. He lurched, throwing his head hard left and right. She got out of the way. The ocean left him.

Flashing micro-seconds, thinking cleared: was this a lost sea mine from WWII, something vengeful against Marko, an explosive from the break-up of Yugoslavia, or some sick cartel lieutenant coming half way across the world to wreak vengeance on him? Comatose, he fell to her midriff. She slipped backwards, losing focus on raging bubbles, unable to fight sleep any longer, sliding into unwelcome darkness.

End Guanaja Defense Book Two

GUANAJA CHRONICLES

LAST RESORT

BY LANCE STARR

BOOK THREE

CHAPTER ONE

Setting: Rab Island, Croatia and Pacific Coast, Ecuador

Vanna didn't move, stiff. She could hear more than see. She could hear her heart beating and a normal breathing pattern. Now she could feel more than she could see. The weight on her midriff solid, unmoving to her senses. She shook her head now knowing, and the shake put her into dizziness again. She laid back waiting for it to pass; she realized she couldn't wait. She struggled around to get Lance's chest under her ear. World's alive, the breathing was equal to what she had listened for in the thousand hours he slept and she was awake, loving each inhale. She focused remembering a bleary dream of slow pulse and weak breath. It wasn't a dream and she hurried her ear up to his lips, his neck. No impediments, heartbeat pounding. The wave passed over her and she could do no more. Her head fell to his rippled chest.

She awoke again with all signs of his life continuing. She was lucid. He was sleeping, and shouldn't be. She called to him softly with no response. She panicked and increased the volume bouncing echoes in the cave, He blubbered, turned his head, and was gone again. Her military battle experience kicked in and she relaxed. A concussion may have provoked it, but at the moment he was deeply sleeping. She laid her head on his shoulder and dozed, not letting herself sleep.

All time-pieces on tanks or BCs were either smashed

or consigned by the surf to the deep. She counted 1001, 1002,1003,....until she reached 1,500. Stiffness still hampering her, she moved her lips to his, re-confirming breath. She could feel the beating in his wrist. She loved this man, had to relinquish that, force a reaction, and a reawakening. Sometime earlier, who knows when he had had microseconds of clear eyes as he left gargling, Vanna tuned something about Guanaja, bombs, Yugoslavia. He faded as she fell prey to the devil bubbles.

Chipping a shard off her heart, she patted him on the cheek, calling his name. Nothing, a demanding slap, and volume. A shake of the head. She man-handled him around until she got his feet up-beach and his body raised over her breasts. She tried not to be hurtful but kept worrying his head keeping him awake. No counting now, a close observation she'd done for hours on end in the bowels of battleships. He began to fight back and confirmed hope. She cushioned his head firmly between his breasts and midriff. In this position, she could use a cross-chest carry to fight him off if it looked like he was going to get in front of her and give himself another concussion. She fought him and held tight until he went tired but awake.

"Lance, can you hear me, it's Vanna".

"Yes, I can hear you better than see you. Your voice is impacted deep in my heart. What are you doing here?"

"Lance, that's enough for the moment. Spend some time taking deep breaths. Remember, I am in my specialty area here. I know what I am doing. You WILL do what I say. Stay relaxed. I have done what I need to do for myself, now I need to get you ambulatory"

She reached over to his backpack and pulled out a white t-shirt. It was wet. She looked up and saw the missile silo-shaped cave vertical entrance. Water was dripping from the foliage on its edges. Better muddy or sweaty water than none at all. She wrung out the shirt, checked the taste, and squeezed it over his lips. He licked, trying to get as much water as his dry mouth cried out for.

"Lance, I'll get some more. Try to control your stress."

Vanna went sopping the shirt against the dripping green leaves. She squeezed it out removing some of the least tasty bits and sopped again. She returned with a full shirt and squeezed a more generous trickle to his lips and into his mouth. She wet the dry end of his tongue.

"Lance, stay still and wait again." She did ten more trips and gave herself three.

"Lance, roll to your left side. Don't try to rise. Go to your side, stop! Maintain consistent breathing. I'm counting the time."

"Now, ease to your back, similar breathing. Relax and move toward your right side. I will count again; this time, sit up slowly. If you don't feel dizzy, get to your feet; keep one hand on the wall to secure your balance. Stand with the support for a minute or two, then we'll walk normally.

"I'm up.

"Stop, do you feel dizzy or lack lucidity or feel nauseous?"

"I have a little residual headache; it's within my pain tolerance. What the hell are we doing here, and where is here?"

"Easy Lance, get your stress down. I'll tell you what I can, it isn't very much. If you look at that black water, you'll see it rides like a tide. A blast threw us at this, which turned out to be a cavern, or we'd be dead right now. I lost control of your head there, really sorry, you hit a granite wall. I got thrown around violently and temporarily went unconscious.

This was the first time I was able to fight back, get my head up, and protected on my midriff. I pulled some weed out of your esophagus and your breathing restarted after you threw up half the Adriatic. You gargled something about bombs. Fell out again and I lost the battle with my conscious. I don't know how long. I saw the missile silo shaped tunnel above us, rough edges, tried to cry out, failed. Or didn't hear anything. Let's sit down and reconnoiter. No rifle shot nor knife attack has taken you as close to death as this black tide. I'm sick that I couldn't keep your head in my arms away from the wall."

Lance rasped, "I'm clear headed now, less headache, and we need to see how we can get back to civilization. Don't spend energy being sorry for me; think about the other skills you applied and kept me alive. The obvious thing to start is calling up that tube. Let's alternate, I with bass tones and you with high soprano. All right, listen for a while to see if someone heard us. We don't know how far the silo extends.

Lance breathes, "That wasn't very successful. What else is obvious? I heard an echo that may or may not be real. What else, straight up.?"

Vanna hurries, "Lance, no! I spent half my time in base camp dealing with the physics of this kind of climbing. I see the problem clearly, maybe you haven't experienced it. If we try to walk up the wall with our backs and feet extended, the abrupt angles will shrug us off and we'll fall either to our death or injury that will stop us from exploring anything else. Let's follow the echo idea for now. Focus our faces toward what may be a back wall, alternate tones again, and look for anomalies. Use "hello" as the word now.

Several "hello's and another ten minutes gave no response. Lance followed up," Vanna, I think I learned something. In the dark, it appears there is only one big wall back there. There were too many different responses of voice for only one reflecting surface. There must be another wall or another tunnel. Did either of our iPhones make it?"

Vanna rustles around, "They're both here. They were strapped inside the backpack. I have to go back to the overhead openings to see if they work. Ok, something is working, wait one! Dam, one speaker only crackles. The other is mashed. One mic is crushed. The other is "iffy". The light on one is fully charged. The other has maybe, half a charge. What do we do with that?"

"Vanna, there may be something we can do with light back there, look up. It will be dark in ten minutes, and I am bushed. I imagine you are. We've got to tuck in with the remains of the wet suits and sleep as much as we can tonight. Tomorrow, when the meager backup light reflects at the right angle, we can get further with iPhone lights.

"Vanna, this is the time; not the place, to hold you with thanks for another life."

"Accepted, easy on the holding of the bruised ribs."

CHAPTER TWO

TUNNEL DOG

With tears in his eyes, Marko, on Zoom, told Roberto the horrid news. Roberto brushed off any blather about him owning a resort on the other side of the world. He honed in on the exact methods and times of searching. He gathered details of the Adriatic there and the shape and treachery of the shorelines and beaches. He googled "Rab" and printed out a topographic map of the island.

Roberto hurries, "Marko, get the police back to work with me. Two will be sufficient. Our friends have been lost completely for two days, correct. Get ropes and stretchers and first aid equipment including hydrating IV's. I will check Lance's itinerary on the computer here, try to duplicate, and call you from the plane with ETA for pick-up. No delay, with immediate transport to the shoreline. Marko, there are too many unknowns to give up and call this off in only two days. The tandem of Vanna and Lance are daringly impressive. Birdcage, out!"

Pedro Jet put them down on Roaban as the TACA jet was beginning to warm up. It took Roberto and partner a full eighteen hours with irritable delays in Miami and weather in Munich. He called Marko to the airport. The other passenger had a sleeping injection to make the trip tolerable. When they woke him, he was so woozy they couldn't fire right out searching. Roberto was lagged so Bucky licked him down until he slept for two hours. Roberto believed Bucky could be the key to this mystery. It took the police that long to arrive with the requested equipment.

CHAPTER THREE

DAY THREE, DRIPPING WATER AND RUBBING PLANTS

As typical, Vanna caught the glimmer first. Not so typical, she immediately shook Lance back to the living. She checked and updated his symptoms. The headache was only a reminder occasionally. He was hungry and all the foodstuffs in the backpack had washed away. Vanna, with a leaf bridge, rewired the dripping water from the walls for immediate hydration. Now, an unpleasant reminder of "Seal Time." She searched among the plants and leaves on the silo walls bringing two handfuls of green edibles that really could have been improved with salt. Lance, who might have been tempted to grouse, didn't. She went back for a second handful of each. Deep draughts of now cleaner water, badly needed, filled them up.

Lance quickly exhaled. They needed to search before they lost the meager sunlight. They retrieved the iPhone. They went gingerly without batteries until they hit what darkness was a wall. It dissipated into black as they clung to the left. A short distance to the right, the lapping of water again could be heard. Reaching to the left, the wall ended; the lapping was closer below us. It hadn't ended but broke off to the left appearing in our dim light to form the edge of a huge box or some kind of ragged terrain. There was no catwalk or ridge. The only way to go further could be suicide.

The depth of water was too deep to register on any of our tree limbs dunked to check. There could be currents carrying us out to sea or back into never-ending darkness. No idea of implements or rocks or blockages.

Lance, trying to speak to get an echo got very little, one double repeat back where they had met the water. "The echo wasn't much. I did see a second wall beyond this one. No sign of shadow or anything. Rushing water to the right. Returning and looking for another track is our only option.

They moved more quickly back the path they had forged to no success. When they started to see slight shadows, they were at the point in the wall where they had turned left. Lance cranked up the fully charged iPhone and showed it ahead. Solid wall, indeed, it went off into a "Y" variation competing two ways into the distance. One was parallel to our first old friendly wall. Lance moved immediately with light into the wall angle veering to the left. He returned after five minutes with the light extinguished.

Vanna, "Well, did you see something?"

Lance," the general answer is "no."

" Is there some other specific answer?"

"Let me think for a minute." The forty seconds he pondered about drove Vanna wild. "So?"

"Here's what I can say. The walkway is smooth, and regular, with no holes nor jagged edges as far as I went. There were no crossed paths on any side. A single walkway. There were no other things that I judged helpful except for two unevenly gouged tracks up four feet on the right wall. There was only water below them. There is no light. I saw these scratches only with my phone; we'll have to go above them."

"Lance, any thoughts?"

"Vanna, you have been a better planner than me for years. I can only suggest some probabilities, I wish I could be certain of something. I'll start and you stop me when I miss something or anything. Our choices include venturing into the black surf and being saved or worse swept out to sea. Currents could take us beyond search parameters or against ragged shores and final concussions. We have 'O' hints of what might be there.

We could foolishly try to climb the silo which you have convinced me would be suicide. Trying to yell up some communication has gained nothing. This "Y" shaped wall is a major risk, and dangerous. The danger is at least obvious to us. Echoes have hinted little. Those only led to that last path leading us into unknown water. Over, under, around, and through, this "Y" path is the only thing that doesn't already predict our doom."

"I agree. I see nothing else. We need to go back and get our backpacks with whatever tools may remain in them, wetsuits for sleeping, and any rehydration inventions."

They gathered what they could, avoided using their phones as much as possible, and carefully felt their way into the unknown.

CHAPTER FOUR

CAININE LEADS

B ucky was first to recover. With a wash of his damp tongue on his cheek, Roberto leaped to his feet. The two policemen, monitoring everything, smiled and got to their feet. Roberto shook Marko and sent him to Anika to locate any clothes Vanna or Lance had worn. Roberto called Bucky over. Bucky stopped, smelled, and headed flying to the surf on the north end of the beach. He stopped, smelled, and whined. That was accurate because that is where Vanna and Lance had headed in and down to the wedding.

Roberto took Bucky up onto one of the craggy rock formations blocking the sea from the shore. He repeated the smell reminder to no attention from Bucky. Bucky ran in every direction navigable for three hours before he put his head down to rest.

Roberto had studied all the winds, currents, and caves already known and searched. He now looked for any evidence of explosives. He looked around the terrain and took the clothes and Bucky further from the shore. He let him free and he scampered for another two hours. It was sundown on what would be the fourth day. Roberto could not release Bucky and give up for today. He fed him and he voluntarily drank a lot of water.

Roberto didn't have to give anything to smell. He guided Bucky to scour in parallel lines to the increasing altitudes from the shore. Roberto hadn't learned only about motivating shrimp in his Marine Science Masters.

With maps in Guanaja, he was on the ground running when he saw similar landforms here. He also knew the ugly realities of time lost in oceanic environments. They continued into the night. Bucky always was the favorite of Lance, and knew who he was smelling for. He would search for two hours and eat and drink and rest for one-half.

CHAPTER FIVE

ALMOST PASSED IN THE NIGHT

The two lost lovers hurried in the dark for two hours without stopping. They carefully helped each other over the four feet raised blocks returning down to the original level. All continued to be dark. There were odd scrapings on the walls. They rested for fifteen minutes and dragged themselves to their feet. Another hour and they had to hydrate and rest, not sleep. Forty-five minutes later, they began to sense twilight. Adrenaline hit the arteries and they sped up. Fifteen minutes later, they came to another full wall stopping them in their tracks. Losing their drive, they collapsed and scoured the area. It was light, at least, and finally, they spotted the source.

Looking more closely, they again felt disappointment. It was a rusted metal door pounded into the bedrock. Around the edges, light was sleeping in. Searching around the edges, they could see a continuation of a walkway and wall for the fifteen feet they could see.

After a half hour of resting, hydrating, and wishing there were some disgusting plants to eat, Lance stirred and said, "The only way out of here is not back. We've got to get through this door as small as its opening is. You'll fit fine. I better practice holding my breath."

Vanna answers, "We don't have the door open."

"Ok, I'm not going to make any headway with my

knuckles. What tools survived the deluge, something in a backpack?"

"Wait one!" Vanna continues, "There's something; not much. A climbing chisel may be some help. I guess you may have had some plan to climb somewhere."

"I don't remember. Tiredly, Vanna adds, "There are the two cutting torches. One tank is definitely broken and empty. I'm not sure about the other. Try the chisel first."

Lance jimmied the chisel blade into the thin opening between the metal and wall. Nothing. He tried the three other openings and got an inch and a half with one. He sat to rest. Vanna's brute strength in many areas is unbelievable, but not here.

"Vanna, I'm weakening. On the other hand, I don't want to live another day without some success. I'll keep at this, and look for a weakness. See if you can do something with that torch."

Vanna de-connected, re-hooked, bled gas to see if there was some, and finally returned to Lance.

"Lance, I may have some moderately good news. I'm far from sure. Any more gain with the chisel?"

"Yeah, I got it open enough to put your foot through. I need a break. Let's see what happens with the torch. It's small. Backpack sized.

They fired up the torch, not a blast. He went back to the spot where he had foot room for Vanna and cut at the hinge. It broke and the door bent, crunching, back enough to get two shoes through. He went to the adjacent hinge, cut it in half, and the torch went out. He tried it over and over. The gas was depleted."

He crawled over to Vanna, equally disappointed, and

rested his cheek on her thigh. "Honey, I'm not giving up. I have no spirit to do anything now. I need to rest. I'll get up in the night and continue. I don't need the light for the chisel.

CHAPTER SIX

MAN, AND DOG RAPPEL

Roberto dozed and watched Bucky following parallel furrows, feeling guilty that he couldn't do more. It was beginning to lighten in the east over the nearest highlands. He got up to give what he expected would be the final feeding of the morning when Bucky began running in circles, first, then barking and whining. Marko and the police were asleep, and Roberto scaled the furrows like a needy goat. Stopping for a minute to orientate himself, he could see the surf off the breakwater in the distance and a huge hole at his feet. Two more steps and he would be the lost one. Bucky could knock him off the edge in excitement and sharp barks. With Bucky like this, there was no doubt in his mind.

Roberto yelled loud enough to wake the quick and the dead and the police. Marko stirred hopefully, the only bilingual person here, he struggled to his post-grad legs. He had drunk enough beers with Roberto, he knew well when to get serious. In the distance, squinting, he heard Roberto call for the searchlight, power battery, rope, and firehouse wooden ladders. He translated that to the police and they responded correctly. He tore hard to Roberto.

The situation was obvious. Roberto snarled, "Marko, do you know anything about this big hole? Did the searchers miss it, did you, do you know how deep it is, what it is?"

"Roberto, I played in most of these areas when I was a kid. I would surely have seen it. This has to be something drilled here sometime during the Croatian Separation War. If it's deep, we may find the explosive that started this nightmare."

Roberto taken aback, "Didn't the explosion go out into the Adriatic?"

"I think so but don't know. I just don't know. Paula jumped into me and I didn't register until I felt her and her obvious wounds. My focus was nowhere else. According to others injured, it would have been coming out of the North. Unless there was another blast, which I would have noted, it went quickly from the right of the beach spreading wildly in a whirlpool of damaging pressure. From the right, not the left. Not here from the left side. It was coming in this direction."

"Marko, I want you to get these guys aiming the searchlight down there right now. We're not waiting till daylight. If they will give a bit of twilight, we're going. Put out the ropes for rappelling. I'll buckle Bucky up in a harness. Let him down in tandem with me so if he hits a crag or other danger, I can steer him.

Bucky whined a little when he was lifted over the edge, quieted, and rolled up into a fetal position. Roberto kept a hand on him as often as possible. He watched for anything that might be an explosive; and met the wet floor without problem.

Bucky howled, barked and snorted to get his harness off. He went in circles smelling every corner and abandoned backpack. Roberto took him back to a leash, too dangerous to let him run into the black unknown. He soon lurched over to the wall tugging Roberto the forty yards. Roberto's small flashlight was enough to deduce from walls, angles, and tracks the probable path for the trapped runners. Bucky knew exactly where they ran.

With his small light, Roberto had seen plenty. Bucky only confirmed it. He dragged the fighting dog back to the opening to communicate above.

"Marko, we need more. The pattern of the blast here is not accidental even though it may not be the cause of the beach carnage. I don't see or smell anything. I think we need to buck up our defense while we run with the hunt. We need another man. We need to select cautiously. I can't have some Yugoslavian cop with war anger still simmering purposely denying knowledge of this silo. I can't have you because I need you to translate up there. You were here during the war and communicated your danger to me on Zoom. Have an "informal" talk with these guys and steer me away from more trouble.

CHAPTER SEVEN

RELUCTANT NATIONAL POLICE SUPPORT

Hurriedly, Marko separated the men and spoke quietly one at a time. The one guy wouldn't say a thing. The other guy, very cautiously, told him that the first guy had lost family in the fighting. From what that guy could find out, my family couldn't determine that my kin weren't involved. It was 90% confirmed that another tribe had been guilty. Firmly ordered by his lieutenant officers to bury the past, repressing the doubt, they had been backing each other up appropriately in their police roles.

Marko walked away. He returned to the communication, speaker-off with Roberto in the silo. He told Roberto what had been said.

"Marko, you're going to have to trust your instincts. Think about their hand gestures, voice tension, eye movement, nervousness, hesitations, or other things you might identify."

"Roberto, "We need to move. I'm going to rule out the first guy that wouldn't talk to me. They could both be innocent bystanders. I don't have time to pry it out of the police department because they were chosen. I'll keep watching for anything dangerous and either contact you or act myself if you are in danger."

"Ok, send #2 down; we need more rope. Put the searchlight on its rollers, ease it down making sure the battery is full. Have a medium size cutting torch and tank standing by. Somehow pack the guy with a dozen or more liter bottles of water. Call Anika to send up some canned meat and three loaves of bread. Send three packs of blankets, and get four revolvers from Anika whose late husband had several. If she has silencers, get those. Keep those out of sight in the packing. You do the packing. Marko, you keep one of those pistols. You don't need a silencer up there. If you have dog food, send a couple of cans. Bucky is too excited to eat. Don't leave your protective position. Have Anika or one of the scuba trainers bring the stuff. Send the light now, and hold on to the cutting torch. I have to get back there ASAP for whatever waits. Bucky indicates life. If I have any antenna access, I will contact you to send it. Granite cliffs may interrupt the signal. If not, listen for a click, or after an hour, send it even without my signal. I need the carbon arc light and battery now. If you send anything without my signal, you'll have to send the other cop with it, or better, if the scuba trainer is there, send him."

I had to fight Bucky tooth and nail until the searchlight arrived. He didn't need any light. There was water in the structure. Splashing him with some, I relented and headed out.

CHAPTER EIGHT

Mobility Around A Rusty Door

L ance woke up at midnight and hammered and twisted on the impacted rectangle of rust. "Sleep, Vanna. I'm afraid tomorrow will bring more stress. I'll sleep when I can't stand." He finally slept before the glimmer began to glow in the walled corners. The momentum he had gained showed more long hours ahead. Vanna saw him collapse and rose to see what the glimmer would expose. Drawing from deep inside, keeping her noise down, she lay on her back to see what parts of her might slip through. She could get her legs to her hips up against the panel. She stepped back and found the chisel, silver now from the scraping rust. She sat and used the chisel not to hammer, but to bend and bend again the panel to move it away from the impacted wall. She shifted her focus away from the granite hitting the metal on the rebound. She was afraid she would wake Lance, but couldn't sit here stymied when her angle of view began to show more room for hips. She would have to free his bigger hips and six-pack if she got to the other side, hips scraped or not.

CHAPTER NINE

STUCK, FOREVER?

Stumbling, keeping his balance against the wall, Roberto kept Bucky in sight as he tried to leap ahead. There was no sense of death in Bucky's gate nor responses. The opposite. He would sense better than humans what to expect in the black distance. Horses evinced that same sense. The path jutted left unexpectedly. Roberto fell against the wall, grabbing granite and scraping it in the palm of his hands.

Swearing, standing again, he hoped he was correctly reading Bucky's actions. Sooner than he had wished, he rammed the handle on the searchlight. The iPhone may be needed later. He forced Bucky to heel, and quickly as the floor' sloped up, moved forward in bright arc-lit passages. Another lunge from Bucky confirmed without a doubt, the right passage. The intense burn from the arc washed out any glow that might be reflected in the distance.

CHAPTER TEN

SERIOUSLY STUCK, DE-HYDRATED

Vanna had struggled, this time with noticeable success. She would wake Lance in enthusiasm and show him how cleverly she got through. She pushed her shoes grinding into the wall of metal, pushed them again further into the middle opening, again into the opening of an exit on the opposite side. She tolerated the scratches on her hips as she forced them over the rough floor toward the other exit. She manhandled her shoulders toward the exit, shrugged them, and growled in pain. She threw them backward and forward now scratching her breasts to bleeding. She halted and uttered the Seals most distinguished profanity repeatedly. Her shoulders were too wide to go through. Her hips had flowed painfully around the edges. There was no way she could strain her tendons, in agony, to thrust her shoulders through. She had to stop; the pain was too great. She was sure Lance would make fun of her; she HAD to CRY OUT.

That was not SOP for a Seal. Lance came flying against the granite until, in trauma, he saw the blood and heard the pain. He knew she was horrified to sound off so hard. He could never get more than his hands close to her.

"Vanna, are you holding your back up to avoid bleeding, or is that position ok for you for a while."

Lance, I'm so sorry. I should have had you with me. I'm ashamed, my shoulder and back are searing beyond my tolerance. My breasts are stinging and bleeding. I don't know, Oh.

"Vanna, hold your back up for a minute more. I'll get you."

Lance ran over in the dim glow, located the backpacks, and pulled out all the wetsuit material still usable. He ran back again, put his head and the one hand he could force in. With the wetsuit in it, raised her shoulder as high as it would stretch and folded the three-quarter-inch rubber suit into a four-ply pillow. He waited until she eased her way back into it, and heard her limited relief.

Vanna huffed, "There's more trouble here."

Lance, close to tears, said, "I see it. It will be much more difficult; I will solve it somehow. Can you move back this way, or sideways in any direction?"

Vanna, "Let me check." A painful pause. "Ok, I can wriggle back to the point where the width of my hips grinds into the rusted metal. My arms are free."

"Vanna, Here's our first move. I'm crying for the pain this may cause. I'll put my arm back in again, put my palm under the makeshift pillow, and raise you again. Not stretching you up as much as I did before, should leave an open space for you to move your hips left and right carefully. Move it only until the scratches react, then come back the same. Stop anytime you need to. I will have no trouble supporting you while you get a breath. You will have to do this until you get your hips, thighs, and legs facing me. The shoulders will have to wait. First, wiggle and press your hips until they slip out into the opening between the walls.

What you need to do now may fail; we must try. Get your hips on my side of you, that is, your hips and legs pointing in my direction from you're wrenched wall space.

Here's the rub: you need to roll over to your back and slide the wet suit under to soothe. Swing your hips until you can straighten your legs out toward me, toward the entrance you first used. Roll face-up again.

"Vanna, I am making a pillow of my cleaner shirt. When I can reach your head close to the metal here, raise and put the wet suit under your thighs to protect them while I put the pillow back under your head.

CHAPTER ELEVEN

WHAT THE HELL?

"Lance, can you give me five to try to straighten out wrinkled skin pinched around the suit and shirt?"

"I may need more than that to invent a method to get your shoulders back on this side and into less pain."

Lance turned back to ruffle through the backpacks when a brilliant glare, shocking eyes dilated in the dark, knocked him to his knees.

"What the hell?" he saw nothing in the glare.

A shadow stepped out beside the light, ghostly in form, moving quickly toward him, saying "And Dios Mio to you too", pulling him up and hugging him."

"Roberto?"

"Roberto, and Bucky"

Bucky gave him the full bath.

"This police guy came to do any heavy lifting. He's armed."

"What the hell are you doing here, where I don't even know where is?

"Lance, where's Vanna?"

"She's back here, stuck, and we need help. She tried to

do the Seal 'tough rush', alone and her shoulders are too wide."

Roberto now in shock, why, how?"

"Roberto, we can't explain now. Both of us need medical care and I don't know how to get out or where we'll be if we get out."

"But I just rappelled down that missile silo and Bucky found you."

Vanna croaked, "Roberto, no!"

Roberto started, astonished.

Lance quickly followed, "Roberto, Vanna has analyzed that egress and projects one dead and others injured to the point they can't be evacuated. She has some serious Seal experience and I agree with her. We have tried every black wall and corner. You may have seen the surf in the cave when you came down. That's where we were thrown in here with concussions. Although now she knows she shouldn't have tried it alone, Vanna is going the way we'll have to go."

Roberto assesses, "Let me look at Vanna and this metal frame you're describing. Stay still, I won't hurt you, Vanna, dulce.

"Well, Lance, you and Vanna are the main planners usually. I can see in your eye dilation that all is not well. I'll take a crack at it, as you gringos call it. I have blankets, more water and food for us and Bucky up above. There also should be a cutting torch arriving. We're getting some silenced pistols which Marko will hide in the blankets. This guy doesn't speak English so let's keep it down. The last war here was not long enough ago to now know who loves whom. Any bomb, while maybe not be related to the past, can't be ignored."

Lance adds, "Well, communication could be difficult, too. I did tell Marko, your old roommate, to lower these things down if I didn't call or ping somehow sooner. What have you got on your cell phone?"

"Everything! Don't forget I'm still in a running battle with the Cartel. The granite foundation here may be a problem. GPS may be a bit stronger. Does Marko have GPS?"

Vanna answers, "I believe he does; would you use my regular phone and try to raise him? If you can, get a click-through; he'll get busy. I need to close my eyes for a moment."

Vanna lay back and Roberto ruminated his next move. He turned off the phone but got no reception. He walked to all corners and back down the path: nothing strong enough for a sickly click. Vanna raised again, trying to avoid going to sleep. They had smiles for each other and she realized what he was doing.

The cop had sat down dozing against the wall near the searchlight.

"No luck, Roberto, she murmured?"

"Zip."

"I've been lying here staring up thinking there is some tiny spot above. I'm not to be moving much. I may be hallucinating. Before you brought the searchlight, I thought that spot might be where some of the glimmer comes from. Give me your phone and I'll see if my jail here isn't below some weaker or thinner layer of granite. She raised herself to take the phone.

"Marko, Marko, Vanna calling, come in, over"

There was no slight noise indicating anything.

Vanna, unsure said, "Let me move my shoulders back to the portal which I hope will be our exit." Roberto sat and waited.

She called again, no response for some time. Seconds crawled like hours.

She called again and as if no one had been home, she got static. She waited again and got extended static. Fogged mind, she considered the alternatives. Did he hear her on a normal connection and couldn't respond? Was he able to understand her? Were the batteries too depleted? She wouldn't accept any hopelessness. "She adjusted her phone, Roberto's, and called "Marko, Marko, this is Vanna. Add GPS to your calling app. respond, over". She got a firm click and a crackled "Marko". Then nothing. She heard static that every iPhone user would understand, the machine was being adjusted, or re-positioned.

A horrid feedback, Marko's hurried voice. "I've got you, Vanna, for now. Know I've already sent the torch and others. If I lose you...... signal back to GPS.

Lance, "She woke him up. Lance, I got Marko for three seconds on Roberto's phone. The granite above me in this case is thinner. He said some things were on the way with the other diver. I lost him and can't reconnect."

"Roberto?"

"I'm here Lance, I'm coming. I'm leaving the phone with Vanna."

"Roberto, listen if I conk out again. There is a gas-cutting torch coming. Other food and supplies. You or the diver need to unpack. There are three pistols in there. I want you to take one, conceal it, and give one to Vanna and me, also concealed. You can trust the diver with any of this, not the cop until we confirm his true colors. Marko was leery but only had the two to pick from before the diver arrived. Shine the light back down the entrance pathway to help them find us. It'll be a few minutes; I need to rest again."

Vanna, in the distance, "I heard that. Roberto, minimize his sleeping. Short intervals only."

CHAPTER TWELVE

FRAUD FLAGS PRESENTED AND SNUFFED

Huffing noises in the distance. Search-light refocused. Vanna, still trapped; moving to an angle that might reduce her pain. Cop stood up against the wall. Lance and Robert, shoulder to shoulder as they had so often been, moved back to shield the reflections. The cop heard a voice in the distance and stood, freezing in place. Vanna, relieved, looked over at the cop as the diver stepped into the light. The cop pulled his gun. Vanna screamed; Roberto's burly fist hammered the pistol to the floor. No delay, he had been on guard since the inception. The cop dived to retrieve it. The diver hammered his foot into the cop's hand, putting his other foot on his neck cutting off any vision.

Roberto, realizing he'd been late in getting these down here, stepped quickly to the bundled blanket pulling and handing a pistol to Lance, reached another to Vanna, checked the load of a third, and kept it in his hand.

Lance quickly to the diver," Berndt, I'll get some ropes or rather, Berndt do you have any metal wire in there?"

Responding and moving the foot off the hand, "There's some bonding the gas tank to the torch, if not somewhere else. I'll get it."

Lance charges, "No, Berndt, Roberto, get it. Keep your foot on that hand until we can search him."

They kept him down and found a lead slug, a knife, and a stun grenade. Tied up with wire, they stood him up to see three silenced pistols aimed at his head, Vanna on her elbow. Ornery, slapped himself back to the wall.

Taking a breath, they looked at each other. Berndt now saw the cop in the light and froze, anger and disgust on his face.

Berndt snarls, "Lance, this guy is sick with things that happened in the last war. How he got to be a cop beats me. I need to talk to him, and it will have to be in Croatian. If we ever get out of here, I will inform you. In the meantime, while we are mounting this escape, you need to cede all responsibility for him, all, to me: life or death."

{Translation: Berber, and don't doubt that a lot of people know you, you need to listen to me right now. If you refuse to listen and take heed, you will be back in jail or worse. A traitor cop will have a nightmare in jail time.

You are carrying human anger for people you knew who were killed or injured. There are lots of others who have lost, and hurt, but remain "Humane." I lost my brother, my closest friend and idol. I feel pain every day. You can and must repress this, struggle against that emptiness, and live a decent life. I have that pain, but have a diving job, a decent salary and benefits package, and can live a tolerable life. You are working with a partner who was on the other side. As an Emergency Sea Officer, I see your reports and professional activities. You have been able to tolerate him and give appropriate back-up when required. That is exactly what you are required to do. If friendship should develop, that would be a bonus. Your actions here may or may not cause a suspension or other punishment. That is not my decision to make. My decision here is to get these people to safety. You have three ways this can go:

1. Behave and support and hope for clemency since you didn't kill or hurt someone.

2. Try to escape and find my foot again on your neck deciding where to drive in the heel causing permanent disability.

3. Kill you on the spot if your actions endanger any of these people or me. (End translation.)

CHAPTER THIRTEEN

THE RIGHT TECHNOLOGY OR WE'RE DEAD

Trendt came back to English and we ascertained that Berber was incapacitated against damaging us or our plans.

Roberto entered the conversation, "If these bars are not titanium or worse, this torch should work slowly and accurately. Vanna, here are some dinner choices and a blanket. No candles; all but one of us will be joining you. One of us will always be with you. We'll start this cutting in the morning. At that point, you will need to move your limbs as far as possible from the cutting points. You can cover yourself with a blanket.

Before you sleep, I assume Lance will apply all the antibiotics and dressings. We brought everything along in the pistol blankets. Getting Marko into a signal access cell location will be the most critical event of our rescue.

Vanna, in the least comfortable body position, kept an eye on Berber in the night. Turning the arc light on in what his watch said morning, Roberto woke her. Lance was dozing into twilight and the cop would be weak from his lack of sleep-in wires, as was the plan.

"Vanna, move over in the corner as much away from me as possible. Keep your blanket away from the flames; shade your eyes. Try to get some sign from Marko above. Use GPS however it works. If you have to use Morse code, we'll hope he knows it.

Lance sat up and turned away as Roberto lit off the gas cutter. That stirred the cop who also was smart enough to turn away. The bars were not titanium, but steel that reacted to the welding gas. It went slow. Everyone was praying the gas would not run out before the cutting was done. A larger opening was needed in front of Roberto; then he had to enter the cell and cut a similar shoulder-wide hole in the opposite side. Vanna stayed inside the cell. That was the only place they had raised Marko the night before. She kept the blanket up and her head away.

Lance prepared all the food and tools to be divided between backpacks. He loaded himself and the hunky diver with the most Despite the fact they had to maneuver the arc light into the dark of the other side. Forever, was 45 minutes, and Roberto finished openings on both sides. Now he had to guide the cutter ahead in case of other metal obstructions. Vanna brought the blanket and called repeatedly to Marko.

Marko undoubtedly had been sleeping. Her constant noise prodding brought a squawk. She took a shot at questioning "Morse". No response for minutes to hours of the length of ten minutes. In Morse, 'diver knows'. The other driver had raced from the dock across the island with other supplies, not usable now, maybe later.

Lance recommends, "Vanna, go ahead, your Morse is better than mine and you know what and where as well as any of us."

"Got it. Get everybody and everything through the holes. Roberto, do you have a compass?"

"Sorry, my cell is for eluding cartel animals."

CHAPTER FOURTEEN

DEADLY CLIFFSIDE

Vanna urges, "All right, we'll use Seal 'dead reckoning.' Comments are welcome. Let me bring you into my thinking. We walked from the surf west to the double wall where we turned north. We didn't change direction noticeably and ran into this elbow. West again now through the bars. Everybody minimizes cell use and moves west. I will code, "Moving, watch west".

The cop was dragging the speed down until Trendt took him by the neck. The eyes bulged and he sped up.

Vanna, Morse code, "West see, use GPS. Moving as fast as we can will make it more noticeable to them."

The layer of rock was thinning. No voice was heard either way. The path turned into a harrowing walkway next to a 30-foot fall into ragged granite.

The searchlight was critical and unwieldy. Lance joined Trendt in jockeying it around what became a 50-yard breathless traipse. Roberto handled the torch and tank himself. Vanna kept a hand against the wall, stopping to try the connection again and again.

It was forty yards past the tightrope before a crackle. Everyone including the cop was running with sweat. Vanna sent another cryptic burst. This time a complete sentence returned. "Burdan here, are you receiving? Lance turned to Trendt, "Yes that's our other diver. Vanna, try voice."

"This is Vanna. Do you need Morse code or do you hear me?" A crackle everyone could hear growled through, Burdan said four words, and the burst took him out again. Vanna impatiently paused, and quickly asked, "Are we on GPS?" Response, "GPS yes, voice intermittent."

Vanna again, "Are we heading west?"

Burdan crackles, "I only heard 'heading', assume direction, yes west."

Vanna to Lance, "Anything else you want, anybody."

Trendt responded, circling the light. "Look, thirty meters ahead, I see an opening, only darkness within.

Vanna back, "Burdan, proceeding west, can you confirm you are right above us?"

Burdan, "According to GPS, within a radius of 7 meters."

CHAPTER SIXTEEN

FOLLOW THE DOG

Bucky had stopped arguing the path when they finally went where he whined. When they got to the elbow, he watched every move the cop made. He was comfortable only with Lance, Vanna, and Roberto. Trendt didn't get any welcome. A completely unknown human.

When Roberto slammed the Berber's pistol, Bucky spurted to Lance's side with a glance toward Vanna. He easily vaulted the holes in the metal trap Roberto had opened and took the lead which he first smelled and trotted west.

The thirty meters melted away and at the option, Bucky smelled both north and West on the trails. He moved to lead West, and everybody stopped. He growled, yellow-orange eyes in the arc light. They just stood there.

Vanna, "Burdan, have you recovered our trail?"

"Still within seven yards."

"Burdan, we've come to a branch tunnel. Look at elevations; should we continue West or turn north? The dog is whining to go west."

Burdan, "I'm not knowledgeable of this area nor is anybody else. North of here either stays level or goes further into the mountain. Elevation as a guide, I'd follow the dog."

On into the arc-lighted path, orange eyes flickering and returning. If we didn't know exactly who was blinking those eyes, we'd feel like we were in a monster movie. We passed other three-quarters of a mile in darkness. Bucky howled, returning to try to egg us on. He saw it before we did, of course, and some soft dim rays soon surrounded us.

Breathless, Roberto gasped, "I hope we aren't approaching another missile silo."

Lance answered, turning the arc down, "Chances are Bucky has already been down there. We have no dog/human language for that."

Vanna sped to contact. "Burdan, do you still have us. Do you see a wash-out in the hill, if it is a hill?"

Burdan, "Vanna, we are still within 7 meters of you. There is some kind of landform, not exactly a hill, a rise coming toward us. Our communication has cleared. Either the ground layer is thinner here or we've lost the granite. Hang on!"

The dependability of communication raised spirits. All but one.

"Burdan, this is Trendt. You've got to order a bus immediately. We've got an attempted murder the court will have to sort out. Don't share this near the other cop if he is there. If so, keep an eye on him."

"Will do, hang on"

Marko called out excitedly, "Bucky's here. Burdan, tell Vanna he's here. Come on, follow him."

They ran the last thirty yards. Bucky was running circles around the lip of a rock. It was narrow, and thin, the shape of an open snake's mouth, or maybe a salamander.

You could imagine a slimy pointed tongue flipping out of it. Bucky kept barking leery of going in there again.

Marko got down and tried to slide to whatever cavern was below. He had a knapsack on and couldn't wiggle through. His loosened small rocks and gravel; got an "S O B" from below. Trendt. He hurried back to Burdan and asked him to inform Vanna.

Roberto said, "I'll take this, Lance, you still have eyes that beg rest. Marko, we're sending Vanna up to see if she fits. Be there for her.

Vanna dumped her blanket and gave the radio and a kiss to Lance. She tightened her clothes wishing she had some Vaseline or sun cream to make a smoother glide for her chest. It took her ten painful minutes to get to where Marko could pull her gently out.

She called back down, "Gentlemen, there is a chance. If you can't squeeze tight enough, we'll have to get a CAT to open the hole. There is no way you can get the arc light or torch equipment out.

Roberto replies. "I'm not gonna stay in here until a CAT comes from who knows where no matter what width of skin I wear off. Marko, please."

"Right here, Roberto."

"Do you have the pistol?"

"Yes"

"Check that it is loaded and functioning. We're sending Berber up next. His ankles will remain wired; he will need to use his arms. Don't wait a minute to re-wire his wrists even while he is being pulled out the last few feet. Trendt will be up next to take him into custody. Trendt, I think you'll have to go immediately behind to push him up until

Marko can get a hold of him. Watch out for his feet."

It took fifteen minutes of grueling wrestling with rocks and dirt to get the two up. Trendt slipped out as the "bus" arrived, rounded up the other cop, and along with two other armed officers on the bus escorted Berber to be booked.

Time for the last two. Roberto firmly decided he would go last, joking not to act like a captain of a ship, but because Lance with his big lungs and rippling back muscles would open more clearance for him to get through.

CHAPTER SIXTEEN

HOSPITAL DOG UNDER THE BED

On top of their concussions, Vanna and Lance had lost skin. Anika loaded them up with hydrates and lost no time to the hospital. Lance commanded Bucky to go with Marko. Whining he complied.

The emergency room staff lofted them quickly onto rolling beds, looking into eyes and starting saline hydration.

The injured duo had to stay in the hospital for two weeks of tests and strict bed rest. Still feeling guilty for their pain, Marko stopped in intermittently to visit. Roberto didn't leave their side; slept in a cot from war years. Bucky, back at camp was inconsolable. People had trouble sleeping over his whining. Finally, when Lance could sit up enough to look out the window, they brought Bucky over to be waved at. That helped.

Marko brought Bucky over when he was picking Petra up to take her home. Fast as a slash of lightning, Marko embracing Petra, Bucky jumped up the fire steps and sliding unerringly under Lance's bed, with Vanna laughing on. It took some serious coaxing to get him out of the hospital and home. At that point, he sensed they were alright. They were released three days later. Upon arrival, they got a full tongue washing on every point of skin Bucky could access.

CHAPTER SEVENTEEN

WILL IT BE PARASAILING?

The hospital had been very conservative, watching them carefully till the day they were released. They were told they could dive only to one atmosphere for two weeks. After that one week limited to 45 feet thereafter returning to regular depths. No lifting of tanks out of the water until after four weeks.

Two days after return, Vanna started her inescapable seduction. Lance said, I'm not ready. I'm afraid I'll hurt you.

Lay beside me. I'm not injured more than you, and I'm fine. You know how to caress me with no weight. Hope you didn't forget. Devil in her eyes. He slipped to 45 degrees from her body. It came unusually slow, then a final huge wrestle of her upper body put the proof to it. It had been well past enough. The bungalow slats vibrated with her joy.

The next night, "If you're still worried about the scratches on my breasts, which are only pink traces, get over and behind me. The following morning, all concerns had been addressed.

CHAPTER EIGHTEEN

ECUADORIC PARASAILING?

In their breathless bubbles after love, they had been discussing Lance's long-time dream of Ecuador and parasailing. After two weeks day and night with little to do in the hospital, they had formulated some plans. Many articles were out showing expats from several countries retiring there. If they were Americans, they could get bonfire residence and remain exempt from funding the dregs of Trumpian once-allied government-bashing.

They discussed their plans with Anika and the guys still manning a lot of the wreck diving. They had plans for opening a parasailing club off Guayaquil and settling, or if not, setting up a joint operation with the guys a kilometer or more up into a protected outcropping of Croatia, Rab. Complicated financial auditioning provided fair division pending what was decided. A secondary backup plan offered a closer jointly shared parasailing operation sharing client's coupons between resorts according to the use of scuba and parachutes.

CHAPTER NINETEEN

NOT ONLY THE CLIMATE IS HOT IN GUAYAQUIL

They planned a visit to Cuenca, the expat place, as well as Guayaquil, a possible new parasailing option for tourists. There were only three along the whole coast. There were surprisingly small scuba operations. Usually, those two sports are related in tandem. Maybe there was a market.

With medical capabilities becoming more important in their lives, they were given intense tours of three hospitals and senior living facilities. They met with many people older than them and a few younger. Some had had careers around seas and oceans.

They settled into a moderate size hotel for the Guayaquil visit. They wanted to see the life they might join there, see if there were any hidden, uncomfortable surprises. The food was delicious in the hotel, right on the ocean for seafood. They wandered further afar and after dinner stopped at a bar with a sea view, moon and all. There had been some Germans in the woodpile because the beer was excellent. There was a lot of activity and jostling as the evening drew on. We moved on towards our hotel to another street full of people passing, dancing; jostling by. In the hotel, we stopped at the bar to have an aquavit and sweet dreams. As most bars plan, there was no clock in the bar. Lance looked at his watch for the time, and it wasn't there. Sickness hit the pit of his stomach. He had been pickpocketed. Where, he had no idea. He hurried to talk to the bar tender whose English was out of a drinks menu. He was directed to the night manager who was fluent.

The story has been told a thousand times. There was nothing the hotel could do. You could try the police. You were in the crowd out there. The only slim glimmer of hope was going to the thieves market tomorrow and seeing if it was there. You could buy it back. Lance tossed and grumbled all night.

He slugged his breakfast down and we headed via taxi, who knew exactly who we were, to the one block area with four crossing side streets and bundles, piles and boxes of everything. The watch was not a new pristine Patel, or anything valuable. He was seething. I held his arm as we scoured every corner. We finally saw it, looked up at the crook who said 30 dollars. Lance wound up to flatten him. My purse was yanked out from under my arm. A knife cut the strap. I shouted, Lance! He hadn't landed the blow, grabbed my assailant, his head toward me, and I knocked him to stumbles. I took my purse and the knife. There were too many angry eyes around us. We beat it out of there post haste.

Lance was still steaming as we went into the hotel lobby and sat. The manager came over seeing the anger that was bubbling over. I stopped him and asked him to come back after we had a drink. One drink for Lance would never solve an issue like this. I comforted him with every feminine wile that can be applied in public.

Eventually, he settled and the manager returned. The conversation settled to "civil." The guy apologized over and over for what he had no control. He continued with his troubles which were dovetailed right back into thievery. Inadvertently he painted a damning picture of what life in this city was like.

We went back up to the room, I poured him a triple and put us au natural under a sheet which we didn't need at the Equator. This was for him and I didn't let him go until he was too tired to please. Secretly I was disappointed that as a Seal I hadn't handled that situation with more broken bones and faces.

We awoke together and I asked him if he needed more stress medicine. Happily, for me, the devil was back in his eye and everyone overdosed.

We limited ourselves to the hotel restaurant, avoiding the jostling bar. An old guy who had seen our "hurting" the night before slid over next to our bar stools. Native English speaker, his frame, sophistication, and presence led Lance to ask if he was British and/or, had been a diver. We divers can smell each other out.

"Yes, I have been, and have been around the world. I haven't been to Rab. People say it's mostly good for wreck dives. I like healthy, lovely reefs with an abundance of fish. Unfortunately, I settled here and have dived only twice in ten years.

Both our ears pricked up at that. Vanna, soothingly asked why that was. Alfonse was his name, "Alfi". He continued, "I had no idea when I came here how unbelievable an underwater habitat could be.

Lance gently prodded, "And?"

"Ever hear of El Nino?"

Lance carefully, "Of course. Does it come near shore here?"

Alfi guffawed, "It comes all the f...king way up the beach here. It's an underwater steam roller. Mind you, it doesn't come every year. Sometimes once a year sometimes two, sometimes remnants even three.

Lance isn't coy anymore, "What problems does it cause? Flooding, landslides, washouts? How would that affect diving?"

"Lance, my boy, if I may, flooding, landslides, or washouts, from my point of view are minor. The damage is not directly on land, it is a destroyer of the bottom and the reef. It rampages over reefs leaving brush. It doesn't come for two or three years. Thin traces begin to grow, some fish re-appear, and wham, year three. Only crusty rock bottoms.

It takes thousands of years to grow a reef. It is so unpredictable that few divers risk their monies on what may not only be sparse, but completely razed by the time they get here. Your ideas of parasailing also suffer. Scuba and parasailing have an interconnected existence. One enhances the other. You will see only three parasailing businesses within forty miles north and south of the city.

CHAPTER TWENTY

FALLBACK

Alfi wasn't drunk. We waited another day and went carefully down to the seafood restaurants whose pilings were deep in the structure of the beach. No jewelry, watches, or purses in view. Bouncers, no crooks. Money only on me in places Lance finds interesting. Watching for other people with diverse appearances; sipping a few aqua-vits. The experiences that confirm Alfi's sad story came sometimes with wet eyes.

CHAPTER TWENTY-ONE

BACK-UP, THANK GOODNESS

Until we had several drinks on the three flights, plane changes and layovers, we were quiet.

With a deep sigh, Lance comes conscious, "Lucky we did our homework with fallbacks. The pick-pockets were enough in themselves to drive me out. What a secret El Nino has hidden.

Vanna agrees, "If I lived there for six months, I would probably kill three thieves per month. Our backup on Rab is pleasant with friends and growing ties. Greg and Cheryl, a nice bonus. Neither of us is so decimated that we can't teach scuba from the pier and with an assistant, run a full parasailing adventure.

CHAPTER TWENTY-TWO

A DRAGON LIVES FOREVER, NOT SO LITTLE BOYS

The ideas studied before the uncomfortable journey to Guayaquil included options. There was a small bay just a few hundred meters from the resort dock we had used for years. Some structures had been renovated into homes. Three of the five structures were near the surf. Two that could be houses were abandoned. The third was right on the beach and could serve as a warehouse for tanks and parasail equipment, including the now-arrived security boat from Guanaja. The other three structures were higher up the side hill, maybe fifty feet. They were twins in construction. The third was fifty feet higher set above and between the twins. A few yards above the upper house were a tramway that had in its time provided a pathway for every can of paint, plank, or bag of groceries. It had remained serviceable and without that cable car, living in the upper house, our choice would have been untenable.

We chose that and carved out the working relationship with the two boys, now men, handling Bearn's original scuba resort, which we had owned until anticipated retirement. In the transfer, we stipulated twenty percent of yearly profits. Money was not an issue. We had hundreds of thousands from the sale of the Guanaja property to Roberto. We still received a check bi-annually for ten percent of the net profits there.

We also agreed that we, to keep busy, would run, in our bay, a beginner scuba class. Members who met safety standards would be seconded back to Bearn's for advanced training. We also kept the security boat for parasailing. A useful partnership blossomed.

CHAPTER TWENTY-THREE

REALITIES

Marko and Petra gave forth a little boy for whom we shouldered the pleasure of grandparents, once removed. Petra had healed and was able to dive again so we saw her frequently with little Petar pegged to her thighs. She made an exerted effort to bring us close to her family, especially Petar, whom she hoped to leave with us as babysitters while she dived, sometimes for a day or two.

Peter started with us before he was able to swim and by age 12 was fully trained in scuba. We also sweetened the deal by taking him parasailing. We spent many days and open-fire nights with him while Petra was gone and Marko working. We took him up to Munich to meet Greg and Cheryl. He was old enough to enjoy the folk-dance show in the Hofbrau house.

He would come from school every day, even raining, and spend time with us before going home to do homework. He worked on every element of the resort that didn't need a professional tech. He went over to Bearn's resort for advanced training. He cajoled his mother to take him to where he could see some real reef. We went along.

He helped us with renovation on the upper house noting the increase in invasion of the surf into the bay. We were glad we chose the upper house with global warming in mind.

Eventually, Petra and Marko decided to send him to 11th and 12th grade boarding school. Marko remembered his challenges in moving into a dorm in a U.S. university. He thought boarding school would allay that.

Vanna and I were only honorary grandparents so kept to ourselves. We knew what a huge hole that would put in our lives. The boarding school regimen started and he called us occasionally on zoom. We conversed back and for with Petra and Marko keeping everyone parent-wise in the loop.

When the first two-week break started, he spent the first night with his parents and most of the entire time with us in the anti-surf rooms. Immersed in the water borne life with scuba and parasailing he was enthralled. The break ended, and for the first time the good-bye was punctuated with deep hugs.

Vanna and Lance lived on keeping each other very warm in and around the bedroom. They ventured into the town and met a few friends that 'stuck'. Some cards. Some chess, Uber for beers. A few visited them in the above surf house. As time went by, expectedly Petar would visit or contact them less and less.

CHAPTER TWENTY-FOUR

SENSING THE IMPENDING TOO LATE.

Looking at the strength of the surf on a daily basis showed little change. Comparing after a year, and then two, something appeared to be concerned about. The one country doing the greedy-most to carbon gas the atmosphere was the U.S. led still by Republicans profiting from the lobbyists from the fossil fuel industry and interfering with monies for investments in renewable energy. Sick! We voted absentee but couldn't "donate" enough money to buy congressmen. We would suffer the destruction.

CHAPTER TWENTY-FIVE

ANTICIPATED IMPACTS

One day at sundown, we looked out at the waves in the bay and continued down the tram to the house. Not aware of what was happening with the surf, we were surprised when we got a dousing of salt water. We scurried up to the top floor and the wash no longer pelted. Worried about what could happen if we went out and tried to send up the tram, we stayed. Rogue waves more than fifty feet high crashing every object in their way. We hugged and heard the generator come on right next to us at the top vent outside. Waterproof lighting on the dock came on giving a hurried look at the wild water. Watching carefully and defensively, we saw the waning intensity. Surf receded, not to where it had been. We found a trunk of dry blankets and fitfully slept the rest of the night in the attic. One floor down sleep would be inundated.

At daybreak, they looked out and saw the mess. They started re-organizing the interior and ....in charge Petar. He headed to them for once-forgotten hugs.

He huffed, "I thought you might be swept away or under the water, or something. What do you need? I can arrange to return to class a few days later considering the circumstances."

Lance answers," You can begin by helping Vanna. I need to talk to your parents about the protocol for missing school. Cell phone towers are inland enough to be functioning. I should be able to get them. I doubt the wave would have affected them that far inland. You know that and slept there last night, didn't you?"

"Gramps, I didn't. My bus was delayed and all I heard on the radio placed you directly in the wall of water. My knapsack is upstairs outside the door." Lance, "OK, you can stay for a while. I want your folks to know you are all right."

"Petra, he is with us. His bus was late and he heard the news and guessed correctly that we were in the middle of the destruction. His help would be critical considering the damage here. God, I forgot Bearn's marina. I've got to get over there right now. I need to take Petar and Vanna with me and we'll plan accordingly later. Sorry to be so short! Bye.

Lance, "Come on you two, up the tram. The pick-up is there and will be faster. Watch carefully and tell me of any possible rescues needed from us or danger to us."

CHAPTER TWENTY-SIX

NEIGHBORS TOGETHER

The two men and apprentice were on their feet outside the house, glory be. They provided us some coffee and we quickly tried to set some priorities for the two properties. Their main residence was significantly further from the surf line than ours. We would have to concentrate quickly on the boat supply house, the sports equipment, the dock, and boats now lapping ten meters from the dock. With six of us, we quickly put those things back together. They would have to look at their house soon. The late Anika's house was built well above the water line at the time of planning and no rooms were flooded. It was becoming very clear about the judgment and territorial knowledge of Bearn and the sea. I asked them to come help at our house until the heavy lifting was done.

CHAPTER TWENTY-SEVEN

THE EVIL LOBBY GRINDS ON, MORE WILL COME

The contribution of the Republicans and their well-healed lobbyists floated on. Other countries with little foresight damaged the earth daily. The surf which had been moving up the beach under the dock was now hitting the sand shore a foot higher. It never returned to its previous levels.

The scuba training began again and parasailing increased by fits and starts. We moved back into the upper house. There were some high surfs occasionally doing no damage. Then reality hit!

The higher surfs made no impact on the main wreck-diving resort. It was located hundreds of yards down outside the bay. The shape of the bay shoveled huge washes of surf into a deluge into Lance and Vanna's operation squeezing and gaining deadly force. They jockeyed equipment around to stay safe. They were not contentedly in town playing when the next rogue hit, and hard. As they ran up to their front porch, angry water lapped at their ankles. It rose like a snake and pulled any loose materials down to break on the rocks. Lance grabbed an axe and her arm. They scrambled upstairs to the main living floor. Hoping this would be the extent of the disaster, they stopped in the living room to catch their breaths. The water surged up the stairs and around the stairwell forcing them up into the attic. Water reached their ankles again.

Lance growled, "I am not going to spend a lifetime in the sea to drown in a dam attic." Sinewy shoulders threw the axe hard into the roof. Water continued to rise. Getting the purchase of the axe out of the water caused him to slip and lose balance. Vanna was there holding him and suddenly shrieked, "Lance, stop. It's reached its peak here. Watch, its draining."

It was up to their waists and Lance was making little headway into the tarred roof. He stopped and they both stared heartbeats thumping.

In baseball, three strikes and you're out. They had had their two strikes. Friends and scuba leaders hauled their belongings into the house that Bearn built.

CHAPTER TWENTY-EIGHT

A PIVOT: Thanks, Ron J. We're out of our careers and you want to defund Social Security

Lance and I now lived full-time in Anika's indestructible house. Our operation in the bay was closed and what remained of the houses was fenced off from unwary wanderers. The frequency and thunder of water coming into the nature-made gorge couldn't be nailed down. We awkwardly attempted to help the boys, now men in the Starr2 resort.

"Lance holds Vanna in the thick German Bedcover and they enter their post-loving bubble. "Honey, I'm sure you agree we are spinning our wheels here. I'm getting embarrassed that we are living in what really belongs to the resort. We're getting our percentage but are interfering with whatever expansion they might be hoping to build. I have some ideas of how we might be able to support the resort, not from here. Let's go up to Munich and see what Cheryl and Greg might advise."

We tucked ourselves in with them for a week and hammered out a clean new career for us. Beer and wine for stimulating the right brain, getting sober completed intense pros and cons of the left. Cheryl was excited to live closer to us near the Hirsh-garten. Gruffly Greg signed onto the idea which was important for Lance, now friends and partners in Mercedes for decades. The usual parting shot from his reverie: "We don't want too much noise around here" drew our warm smile. He shuddered back into his lost world of untested inventions.

CHAPTER TWENTY-NINE

CAREER-TOPPING WANING YEARS

I guided Vanna to Marienstrasse, remembering the experience with the undressed model years before my old friend. Before I met Vanna, the model did entice marketing for Guanaja. I wisely held the memory and spoke with the realtor selecting a shop with a window on the major thoroughfare. It was the ideal location and our finances covered it easily. We named it LaVanna Packaged Gear, Inc. featuring gear and snorkeling of the Croatian Coast. We got out of underfoot of the diving camp with the purchase of an antique German-style house across from an entrance to the Hirsch-Garten.

CHAPTER THIRTY

A NEW CAREER START

A somewhat more liberal group around Marienstrasse thought it quite cute to have a couple of Americans interested in planting a new business in such a competitive area. Upon further review of what the business was, they wondered more.

The environment began with quality decorators guided by Vanna. We hired a model to double her eye candy. With some pieces of scuba wear, she showed a fanciful idea of what the purchaser might look like. Plaster models are sometimes substituted for gorgeous live women with not much more than scuba gear attached. Presentation racks followed the undersea colors of wetsuit wear. Changing rooms and utilities in the back with large boxes of a variety of sizes and shapes, usually requested by well-endowed women. A large aquarium with underwater creatures brought from the reef south of the Starr resort caught all passers-by's imagination. It was a splendid, sophisticated atmosphere. The neighbors couldn't fault that. The marketing study pointed toward sophisticated clientele and the highest quality name-brand merchandise.

The sales bloomed when we advertised a 'custom-made' diving dress and adaptable under-sea equipment. Dress and equipment. Found to market research, there were no similar sales and services in any nearby area. The key service was the custom-made trade. Marketing research had not overlooked the 'size' of the population. We could re-size for small people if they came our way. Mainly, those who came our way, sometimes shyly, needed sizing very much the opposite. Their nature was not of the middle class. They would pay handsomely for dresses that enhanced their positive attributes and reduced the noticeability of the negative.

Both Vanna and I had dealt with that desire mostly with clients who came on scuba resort stays.

At first contact, Vanna stepped forward. She had more languages with more fluency than I, not to mention poise and femininity. Comfort came to our major customer, the tens of clients who were women. They saw Vanna or our living model and decided what they were, she could do for them. Vanna became immediately a confidant as well, skilled in sizing whatever bulge or valley that needed hiding. Some might consider Vanna's shape and charm a form of false advertising. These were wealthy people who would consider any notable improvement a confidence-raising attraction. All had fallen prey to German food and drink. Stylish enlargement of wetsuit stock was immediately used and large sizes were put on order. There were more bumps and valleys to develop.

Suddenly the shop was a draw for large numbers of wealthy women who shopped on whims in entrenched nearby liberal businesses. Originally, owners had been distantly welcoming; and had had doubts about our chance of success. We had hit a niche!

Vanna smiles, "There was no doubt now and we were welcomed across the street in Gasthaus Pferd Und Flanke where new customers, good draft, and friends were frequent. Lance became the jolly, interesting American with adventures to share.

We visited the Starr2 less frequently as the years went by. With Lance's German notably fluent, we had social lives that bloomed. We learned much about the city and traveled to taste different brews in scores of different dorfs.

Slowly we began to inhabit more the Pferd, and chapters of our life escaped to friends over the bar. All around were friends and immediately I saw an opportunity for many nights of entertainment by their adopted Americans. I drank Lager and Vanna Weisbeer. We were welcomed to the Stamtisch and another chapter was born. Our eyes met and of like mind, we made our excuses and caught a taxi back to the Hirsch-garten.

With new friends and excitement sparking them, the thick German comforters spent most of the time on the floor. Intense loving was still alive. Vanna was beginning to move into the pretzel from the bubble when Lance whispered, "Vanna, this was a spectacular night for me. I need to enter myself into the bar scene with some caution. Going there every night or even every other night I think is too much. Obviously, you know the many stories I can recount or enhance. You know them because they are us. I want you there or I won't go. Perhaps we could start with a limit of three nights per week."

Vanna smiles a Jim Neighbor's smile and responds. "Lance, this is sincerely not corny. When I see you having such a good time, and at the same time hear the trials and secrets of our life together, my heart fills with joy."

"Ok, we'll try Tuesday, Friday, and Saturday starting not before seven p.m. ending promptly at ten. After that hour, I have other pressing business." His eyes now the devil, anticipate carefully the flash in Vanna's.

Their routine worked out in many ways. Keeping to it kept them physically and emotionally grounded. In a few years with some repeated stories they became an attraction in their burrow. Beer became free. They moderated it. Love only bloomed, never aged.

One Tuesday, neither of them came. No-one knew what to think and just waited hopefully for Friday. On Friday, only Lance appeared. He maintained his joviality at his best. Didn't drink any beer. On Friday he came alone again. Those who knew him for years noticed the difference in his eyes. He drank no beer and only made it through two short stories. One was the intimacy of the dive after Vanna's first kiss under his wetsuit. The other the explosion of her jealousy over Zulinda's non-clothing arrival at the planning of a response to cartel encroachment of Roberto's shrimp business.

CHAPTER THIRTY-ONE

BEARN'S PROPHESY

On Saturday he came no more. There were pictures of him and Vanna in the office behind the bar. Some made efforts to locate them or him. No sign whatsoever. Ulrich, the gasthof owner lost good friends and the GUMEIKLIKEIT they enthused..

Bear's Prophesy Realized :

After the initial screening for Starr2, Bearn and Anika sat closely behind the curtain at their kitchen table. They watched the two newly tested owners of Starr2 resort look slyly around and share a kiss worthy of merit. Looking carefully again, they walked bonded like matching puzzle pieces up the misty hill melding into one person.

Bearn's eyes glossed over long enough for Anika to note. He returned from his reverie, not smiling. Anika knew his looks after 45 years. This was new territory. "Bearn, what? This is not you. Why?"

He took her hand tightly. "Those two people are in an emotional bond of incomparable strength. The frivolity we see is far thinner than what is lurking below. Whatever their future may bring, within six weeks of the passing of one, the other will disappear never to be found." Anika snickers, "Oh Bearn, you old brute, with me you already have too many witches." Bearn's prophecy did not die with him.

Eventually on a Saturday, you would enter the Pferd through the main entrance and on the wall above the end of the bar, a picture. It was embossed and framed. It said:

"In life, a man as caring as Lance Starr could find no richer prize than Vanna Richards to share a protective, enduring adventure. TOGETHER, THEY WERE AS ONE.

--Roberto F.

Owner, Starr Resort1
Guanaja, Bay Islands

End of Book Three, Guanaja Defense, The Last Resort